TExES 117

English Language Arts and Reading 4-8

Teacher Certification Exam

Sharon A. Wynne, M.S.

XAMonline, Inc.

Boston

MW00489515

To obtain permission(s) to use the material from this work for any purpose including workshops or seminars, please submit a written request to:

XAMonline, Inc.
21 Orient Avenue
Melrose, MA 02176
Toll Free 1-800-301-4647
Email: info@xamonline.com
Web www.xamonline.com

Library of Congress Cataloging-in-Publication Data
Wynne, Sharon A.

   TExES English Language Arts and Reading 4-8 (117): Teacher Certification/Sharon A. Wynne.
   ISBN 978-1-60787-670-0

1. English Language Arts and Reading 4-8   2. Study Guides.   3. TExES
4. Teachers' Certification & Licensure.   5. Careers

Disclaimer:
The opinions expressed in this publication are the sole works of XAMonline and were created independently from the National Education Association, Educational Testing Service, or any State Department of Education, National Evaluation Systems or other testing affiliates.

Between the time of publication and printing, state specific standards as well as testing formats and website information may change that is not included in part or in whole within this product. XAMonline developed the sample test questions and the questions reflect similar content as on real tests; however, they are not former tests. XAMonline assembles content that aligns with state standards but makes no claims nor guarantees teacher candidates a passing score. Numerical scores are determined by testing companies such as NES or ETS and then are compared with individual state standards. A passing score varies from state to state.

Printed in the United States of America
TExES: English Language Arts and Reading 4-8 (117)
ISBN: 978-1-60787-670-0

About The Test

Test Name	English Language Arts and Reading 4-8
Test Code	117
Time Allowed	5 hours
Number of Questions	100 multiple-choice questions
Format Used	CAT (computer administered test)

The TExES Language Arts and Reading 4-8 (code 117) test will assess a test takers knowledge base and competency level that entry-level educators in this field of study, in Texas public schools, must possess as a basic requisite to employment and licensure. Each of the 100 multiple-choice questions are based on typical 117 English Language Arts and Reading 4-8 framework form the actual test. Questions on this test are a random mixture from grades 4-8. There may be questions that will not count toward the overall score. However, the number of questions do not vary; but the number of questions that are not scored MAY vary on the actual TExES 117 test. As in the real exam, your final score is only based on scored questions.

The Domains

Domain	Domain Title	Approx. Percentage of Test	Standards Assessed
I.	Language Arts, Part I: Oral Language, Early Literacy Development, Word Identification Skills and Reading Fluency	33%	English Lanugage Arts and Reading 4-8 I-III, VIII
II.	Language Arts, Part II: Reading Comprehension and Assessment, Reading Applications, Written Language, Viewing and Representing and Study and Inquiry Skills	67%	English Language Arts and Reading 4-8 IV-VIII

The Standards:

English Language Arts and Reading 4-8 Standard I:
Oral Language: Teachers of students in grades 4-8 understand the importance of oral language, know the development processes of oral language and provide ad variety of instructional opportunities for students to develop listening and speaking skills.

English Language Arts and Reading 4-8 Standard II:
Foundations of Reading: Teachers of students in grades 4-8 understand the foundation of reading and early literacy development

English Language Arts and Reading 4-8 Standard III:
Word Analysis Skills and Reading Fluency: Teachers understand the importance of word analysis skills (including decoding, blending, structural analysis, sight word vocabulary) and reading fluency and provide many opportunities for students to practice and improve their word analysis skills and reading fluency.

English Language Arts and Reading 4-8 Standard IV:
Reading Comprehension: Teachers understand the importance of reading for understanding, know the components of comprehension and teach students strategies for improving their comprehension.

English Language Arts and Reading 4-8 Standard V:
Written Language: Teachers understand that writing is a developmental process and provide instruction that helps students develop competence in written communication.

English Language Arts and Reading 4-8 Standard VI:
Study and Inquiry Skills: Teachers understand the importance of study and inquiry skills as tools for learning and promote students' development in applying study and inquiry skills.

English Language Arts and Reading 4-8 Standard VII:
Viewing and Representing: Teachers understand how to interpret, analyze, evaluate and produce visual images and messages in various media to provide students with opportunities to develop skills in this area.

English Language Arts and Reading 4-8 Standard VIII:
Assessment of Developing Literacy: Teachers understand the basic principles of assessment and use a variety of literary assessment practices to plan and implement instruction.

Domains and Competencies

The content covered by this test is organized into broad areas of content called **domains.** Each domain covers one or more of the educator standards for this field. Within each domain, the content is further defined by a set of **competencies.** Each competency is composed of two major parts:

- The **competency statement**, which broadly defines what an entry-level educator in this field in Texas public schools should know and be able to do.
- The **descriptive statements**, which describe in greater detail the knowledge and skills eligible for testing.

Table of Contents

DOMAIN I. **LANGUAGE ARTS, PART I: ORAL LANGUAGE, EARLY LITERACY DEVELOPMENT, WORD IDENTIFICATION, AND READING FLUENCY**

COMPETENCY 001 **ORAL LANGUAGE** 1

Skill A Knows basic linguistic concepts and developmental stages in acquiring oral language, including stages in phonology, semantics, syntax, and pragmatics, and recognizes that individual variations occur 1

Skill B Knows characteristics and uses of informal and formal oral language assessments and uses multiple, ongoing assessments to monitor and evaluate students' oral language competencies 4

Skill C Provides language instruction that acknowledges students' current oral language competencies and that builds on these competencies to increase students' oral language proficiency 6

Skill D Plans, implements, and adapts instruction that is based on informal and formal assessment of students' progress in oral language development and that addresses the needs, strengths, and interests of individual students, including English Language Learners 6

Skill E Recognizes when oral language delays or differences warrant in-depth evaluation and additional help or intervention 8

Skill F Knows how to provide explicit, systematic oral language instruction and supports students' learning and use of oral language through meaningful and purposeful activities implemented one-to-one and in a group. 10

Skill G Selects and uses instructional materials and strategies that promote students' oral language development; respond to students' individual strengths, needs and interests; reflect cultural diversity; and build on students' cultural, linguistic, and home backgrounds to enhance their oral language development 11

Skill H Understands relationships between the development of oral language and the development of reading and provides instruction that interrelates oral and written language to promote students' reading proficiency and learning 14

Skill I   Knows similarities and differences between oral and written language and how to promote students' awareness of these similarities and differences. 15

Skill J   Selects and uses instructional strategies, materials, activities, and models to strengthen students' oral vocabulary and narrative competencies in spoken language and teaches students to connect spoken and printed language. 17

Skill K   Selects and uses instructional strategies, materials, activities, and models to teach students competencies for speaking to different audiences for various purposes and for adapting spoken language for various audiences, purposes, and occasions. 19

Skill L   Selects and uses instructional strategies, materials, and models to teach students listening competencies for various purposes and provides students with opportunities to engage in active, purposeful listening in a variety of contexts...21

Skill M   Selects and uses instructional strategies, materials, activities, and models to teach students to evaluate the content and effectiveness of their own spoken messages and the messages of others. 22

Skill N   Knows how to promote students' development of oral communication competencies through the use of technology. 23

COMPETENCY 002   EARLY LITERACY DEVELOPMENT.........................25

Skill A   Understands the signification of phonological and phonemic awareness for reading and typical patterns in the development of phonological and phonemic awareness and recognizes that individual variations occur. 25

Skill B   Understands elements of the alphabetic principle and typical patterns of students' alphabetic competencies development and recognizes that individual variations occur. 28

Skill C   Understands that comprehension is an integral part of early literacy. 29

Skill D   Understands that not all written languages are alphabetic; that many alphabetic languages are more phonetically regular than English; and knows the significance of this for students' literacy development in English. 29

Skill E   Understands that literacy acquisition generally develops in a predictable pattern from pre-reading (emergent literacy) to conventional literacy and recognizes that individual variations occur..29

Skill F   Understands that literacy development occurs in multiple contexts through reading, writing, and the use of oral language......................31

Skill G   Knows characteristics of informal and formal literacy assessments. 31

Skill H   Knows how to select, administer, and use results from informal and formal assessments of literary acquisition. 36

Skill I   Knows how to use ongoing assessment to determine when a student needs additional help or intervention to bring the student's performance to grade level, based on state content and performance standards for reading in the Texas Essential Knowledge and Competencies (TEKS). 36

Skill J   Analyzes students' errors in reading and responds to individual students' needs by providing focused instruction to promote literacy acquisition. 38

Skill K   Selects and uses instructional materials that build on the current language competencies of individual students, including English Language Learners, to promote development from emergent literacy to conventional literacy...38

COMPETENCY 003   WORD IDENTIFICATION COMPETENCIES AND READING FLUENCY...41

Skill A   Understands that many students develop word analysis competencies and reading fluency in a predictable sequence and recognizes that individual variations occur. 41

Skill B   Understands differences in students' development of word identification competencies and reading fluency and knows instructional practices for meeting students' individual needs in these areas..42

Skill C   Understands the connection of word identification competencies and reading fluency to reading comprehension. 46

Skill D   Knows the continuum of word analysis competencies in the statewide curriculum and grade-level expectations for attainment of these competencies...48

Skill E   Knows how students develop fluency in oral and silent reading........48

Skill F   Understands that fluency involves rate, accuracy, and intonation and knows the norms for reading fluency that have been established in the Texas Essential Knowledge and skills (TEKS) for various age and grade levels...49

Skill G   Knows factors affecting students' word identification competencies and reading fluency. 51

Skill H   Understands important phonetic elements and conventions of the English language. 54

Skill I   Knows a variety of informal and formal procedures for assessing students' word identification competencies and reading fluency on an ongoing basis and uses appropriate assessments to monitor students' performance in these areas and to plan instruction for individual students, including English Language Learners. 54

Skill J   Analyzes students' errors in word analysis and uses the results of this analysis to inform future instruction..56

Skill K   Applies norms and expectations for word identification competencies and reading fluency, as specified in the Texas Essential Knowledge and Competencies (TEKS), to evaluate students' reading performance. 57

Skill L   Knows how to use ongoing assessment of word identification competencies and reading fluency to determine when a student needs additional help or intervention to bring the student's performance to grade level, based on state content and performance standards for reading in the Texas Essential Knowledge and Competencies (TEKS). 57

Skill M   Knows strategies for decoding increasingly complex words, including using the alphabetic principle, structural cues, and syllables, and for using syntax and semantics to support word identification and confirm word meaning. 57

Skill N   Selects and uses instructional strategies, materials, activities, and models to teach students to recognize high-frequency irregular words, to promote students' ability to decode increasingly complex words, and to enhance word identification competencies for students reading at different levels. 58

Skill O   Selects and uses appropriate instructional strategies, materials, activities, and models to improve reading fluency for students reading at different levels. 61

DOMAIN II.   **LANGUAGE ARTS, PART II: READING COMPREHENSION, WRITTEN LANGUAGE, STUDY AND INQUIRY, AND VIEWING AND REPRESENTING**

COMPETENCY 004   **READING COMPREHENSION AND ASSESSMENT** **62**

Skill A   Understands reading comprehension as an active process of constructing meaning. 62

Skill B   Understand the continuum of reading comprehension competencies in the statewide curriculum and grade-level expectations for these competencies. 64

Skill C   Understands factors affecting students' reading comprehension 67

Skill D   Knows characteristics of informal and formal reading comprehension assessments. 68

Skill E   Selects and uses appropriate informal and formal assessments to monitor and evaluate students' reading comprehension. 69

Skill F   Analyzes student errors and provides focused instruction in reading comprehension based on the strengths and needs of individual students, including English Language Learners. 71

Skill G   Knows how to use ongoing assessment to determine when a student needs additional help or intervention to bring the student's performance to grade level, based on state content and performance standards for reading in the Texas Essential Knowledge and Competencies (TEKS). 71

Skill H   Understands metacognitive competencies, including self-evaluation and self-monitoring competencies, and teaches students to use these competencies to enhance their own reading comprehension. 71

Skill I	Knows how to determine students' independent, instructional, and frustration reading levels and uses this information to select and adapt reading materials for individual students, as well as to guide their selection of independent reading materials.	72
Skill J	Uses various instructional strategies to enhance students' reading comprehension.	73
Skill K	Knows how to provide students with direct, explicit instruction in the use of strategies to improve their reading comprehension.	74
Skill L	Uses various communication modes to promote students' reading comprehension.	75
Skill M	Understands levels of reading comprehension and how to model and teach literal, inferential, and evaluative comprehension competencies.	76
Skill N	Knows how to provide instruction to help students increase their reading vocabulary.	80
Skill O	Understands reading comprehension issues for students with different needs and knows effective reading strategies for those students.	81
Skill P	Knows the difference between guided and independent practice in reading and provides students with frequent opportunities for both.	81
Skill Q	Knows how to promote students' development of an extensive reading and writing vocabulary by providing them with many opportunities to read and write.	81
COMPETENCY 005	**READING APPLICATIONS**	**84**
Skill A	Understands competencies and strategies for understanding, interpreting, and evaluating different types of written materials, including narratives, expository texts, technical writing, and content-area textbooks.	84
Skill B	Understands different purposes for reading and related reading strategies.	88
Skill C	Knows and teaches strategies to facilitate comprehension of different types of text before, during, and after reading.	89

Skill D   Provides instruction in comprehension competencies that support students' transition from "learning to read" to "reading to learn." 90

Skill E   Understands the importance of reading as a competency in all content areas. 91

Skill F   Understands the value of using dictionaries, glossaries, and other sources to determine the meanings, pronunciations, and derivation of unfamiliar words and teaches students to use these sources. 92

Skill G   Knows how to teach students to interpret information presented in various formats and how to locate, retrieve, and retain information from a range of texts and technologies. 94

Skill H   Knows how to help students comprehend abstract content and ideas in written materials. 98

Skill I   Knows literary genres and their characteristics. 98

Skill J   Recognizes a wide range of literature and other texts appropriate for students. 101

Skill K   Provides multiple opportunities for students to listen and respond to a wide variety of children's and young people's literature, both fiction and nonfiction, and to recognize characteristics of various types of narrative and expository texts. 103

Skill L   Understands and promotes students' development of literary response and analysis, including teaching students elements of literary analysis and providing students with opportunities to apply comprehension competencies to literature. 105

Skill M   Selects and uses a variety of materials to teach students about authors and about different purposes for writing. 108

Skill N   Provides students with opportunities to engage in silent reading and extended reading of a wide range of materials, including expository texts and various literary genres. 109

Skill O   Engages students in varied reading experiences and encourages students to interact with others about their reading. 109

Skill P   Uses strategies to encourage reading for pleasure and lifelong learning. 111

Skill Q   Knows how to teach students strategies for selecting their own books for independent reading. 112

Skill R   Uses technology to promote students' literacy and teaches students to use technology to access a wide range of appropriate narrative and expository texts.. 113

COMPTENCY 6.0   WRITTEN LANGUAGE—WRITING CONVENTIONS **115**

Skill A   Knows predictable stages in the development of writing conventions and recognizes that individual variations occur. 115

Skill B   Knows and applies appropriate instructional strategies and sequences to teach writing conventions and their applications to all students, including English Language Learners. 117

Skill C   Knows informal and formal procedures for assessing students' use of writing conventions and uses multiple, ongoing assessments to monitor and evaluate students' development in this area................... 125

Skill D   Uses ongoing assessment of writing conventions to determine when a student needs additional help or intervention to bring the student's performance to grade level, based on state content and performance standards for writing in the Texas Essential Knowledge and Competencies (TEKS). 126

Skill E   Analyzes students' errors in applying writing conventions and uses the results of this analysis as a basis for future instruction................ 126

Skill F   Knows writing conventions and appropriate grammar and usage and provides students with direct instruction and guided practice in these areas.. 126

Skill G   Understands the contribution of conventional spelling toward success in reading and writing. 127

Skill H   Understands stages of spelling development and how and when to support students' development from one stage to the next. 128

Skill I   Provides systematic spelling instruction and gives students opportunities to use and develop spelling competencies in the context of meaningful written expression.. 129

COMPETENCY 007   WRITTEN LANGUAGE—COMPOSITION **132**

Skill A   Knows predictable stages in the development of written language and recognizes that individual variations occur. 132

Skill B   Promotes student recognition of the practical uses of writing, creates an environment in which students are motivated to express ideas in writing, and models writing as an enjoyable activity and a tool for lifelong learning. 133

Skill C   Knows and applies appropriate instructional strategies and sequences to develop students' writing competencies. 134

Skill D   Knows characteristics and uses of informal and formal written language assessments, and uses multiple, ongoing assessments to monitor and evaluate students' writing development. 138

Skill E   Uses assessment results to plan focused instruction to address the writing strengths, needs and interests of all individuals and groups, including English-language learners...138

Skill F   Uses ongoing assessment of written language to determine when a student needs additional help or intervention to bring the student's performance to grade level, based on state content and performance standards for writing in the Texas Essential Knowledge and Competencies (TEKS) 139

Skill G   Understands the use of self-assessment in writing and provides opportunities for students to self-assess their writings (e.g., for clarity, interest to audience, comprehensiveness) and their development as writers..141

Skill H   Understands differences between first-draft writing and writing for publication and provides instruction in various stages of writing, including pre-writing, drafting, editing, and revising 143

Skill I   Understands the development of writing in relation to the other language arts and uses instructions strategies that connect these various aspects of language...149

Skill J   Understands similarities and differences between language (e.g., syntax, vocabulary) used in spoken and written English and helps students use knowledge of these similarities and differences to enhance their own writing...150

Skill K   Understands writing for a variety of audiences, purposes, and settings and provides students with opportunities to write for various audience, purposes, and settings 151

Skill L   Knows how to write using voices and styles appropriate for different audiences and purposes, and provides students with opportunities to write using various voices and styles 154

Skill M   Understands the benefits of technology for teaching writing, and writing for publication and provides instruction in the use of technology to facilitate written communication 155

COMPETENCY 008   **VIEWING AND REPRESENTING.............................. 158**

Skill A   Knows grade-level expectations in the Texas Essential Knowledge and Competencies (TEKS) and procedures for assessing students' competencies in interpreting, analyzing, evaluating, and producing visual images, messages, and meanings. 158

Skill B   Uses ongoing assessment and knowledge of grade-level expectations in the Texas Essential Knowledge and Competencies (TEKS) to identify students' needs regarding the interpretation, analysis, evaluation, and production of visual images, messages, and meanings and to plan instruction. 160

Skill C   Understands characteristics and functions of different types of media and knows how different types of media influence and inform. 160

Skill D   Compares and contrasts print, visual, and electronic media. 162

Skill E   Evaluates how visual image makers represent messages and meanings and provides students with varied opportunities to interpret and evaluate visual images in various media. 163

Skill F   Knows how to teach students to analyze visual image makers' choices and evaluate how these choices help to represent or extend meaning. 164

Skill G   Provides students with opportunities to interpret events and ideas based on information from maps, charts, graphics, video segments, and technology presentations and to use media to compare ideas and points of view. 164

Skill H   Knows steps and procedures for producing visual images, messages, and meaning to communicate with others. 166

Skill I   Teaches students how to select, organize, and produce visuals to complement and extend meanings. 167

Skill J   Provides students with opportunities to use technology to produce various types of communications and helps students analyze how language, medium, and presentation contribute to the message. 169

COMPETENCY 009   STUDY AND INQUIRY COMPETENCIES................... 170

Skill A   Understands study and inquiry competencies and knows the significance of these competencies for student learning and achievement. 170

Skill B   Knows grade-level expectations for study and inquiry Competencies in the Texas Essential Knowledge and Competencies (TEKS) and procedures for assessing students' development and use of these competencies. 174

Skill C   Knows and applies instructional practices that promote the acquisition and use of study and inquiry competencies across the curriculum by all students, including English Language Learners. 175

Skill D   Knows how to provide students with varied and meaningful opportunities to learn and apply study and inquiry competencies to enhance their achievement across the curriculum. 177

Skill E   Uses ongoing assessment and knowledge of grade-level expectations in the Texas Essential Knowledge and Competencies (TEKS) to identify students' needs regarding study and inquiry competencies, to determine when a student requires additional help of intervention, and to plan instruction. 179

Skill F   Responds to students' needs by providing direct, explicit instruction to promote the acquisition and use of study and inquiry competencies 179

Sample Test... 182

Answer Key 213

Explanation of Rigor and Rigor Table... 214

Answers with Rationales... 215

Great Study and Testing Tips!

What to study in order to prepare for the subject assessments is the focus of this study guide but, equally important, is *how* you study.

You can increase your chances of truly mastering the information by taking some simple, but effective, steps.

Study Tips:

1. **Some foods aid the learning process.** Foods such as milk, nuts, seeds, rice, and oats help your study efforts by releasing natural memory enhancers called CCKs (*cholecystokinin*) composed of *tryptopha*n, *choline*, and *phenylalanine*. All of these chemicals enhance the neurotransmitters associated with memory. Before studying, try a light, protein-rich meal of eggs, turkey, and fish. All of these foods release the memory enhancing chemicals. The better the connections, the more you comprehend.

Likewise, before you take a test, stick to a light snack of energy boosting and relaxing foods. A glass of milk, a piece of fruit, or some peanuts all release various memory-boosting chemicals and help you to relax and focus on the subject at hand.

2. **Learn to take great notes.** A by-product of our modern culture is that we have grown accustomed to getting our information in short doses (i.e., TV news, sound bites, or *USA Today*-style newspaper articles.)

Consequently, we've subconsciously trained ourselves to assimilate information better in neat little packages. If your notes are scrawled all over the paper, it fragments the flow of the information. Strive for clarity. Newspapers use a standard format to achieve clarity. Your notes can be much clearer through use of proper formatting. A very effective format is called the *"Cornell Method."*

> Take a sheet of loose-leaf lined notebook paper and draw a line all the way down the paper about 1-2" from the left-hand edge.
>
> Draw another line across the width of the paper about 1-2" up from the bottom. Repeat this process on the reverse side of the page.

Look at the highly effective result. You have ample room for notes, a left hand margin for special emphasis items or inserting supplementary data from the textbook, a large area at the bottom for a brief summary, and a little rectangular space for just about anything you want.

3. Get the concept then the details. Too often, we focus on the details and don't acquire an understanding of the concept. However, if you simply memorize only dates, places, or names, you may well miss the whole point of the subject.

A key way to understand things is to put them in your own words. If you are working from a textbook, automatically summarize each paragraph in your mind. If you are outlining text, don't simply copy the author's words.

Rephrase them in your own words. You remember your own thoughts and words much better than someone else's, and you will subconsciously tend to associate the important details with the core concepts.

4. Ask Why? Pull apart written material paragraph by paragraph and don't forget the captions under the illustrations.

Example: If the heading is "Stream Erosion," flip it around to read "Why do streams erode?" Then answer the questions.

If you train your mind to think in a series of questions and answers, not only will you learn more, but it will also help to lessen the test anxiety because you are used to answering questions.

5. Read for reinforcement and future needs. Even if you only have ten minutes, put your notes or a book in your hand. Your mind is similar to a computer; you have to input data in order to have it processed. *By reading, you are creating the neural connections for future retrieval.* The more times you read something, the more you reinforce the learning of ideas.

Even if you don't fully understand something on the first pass, *your mind stores much of the material for later recall.*

6. Relax to learn - so go into exile. Our bodies respond to an inner clock called biorhythms. Burning the midnight oil works well for some people but not everyone.

If possible, set aside a particular place to study that is free of distractions. Shut off the television, cell phone, and pager and exile your friends and family during your study period.

If you really are bothered by silence, try background music. Light classical music at a low volume has been shown to aid in concentration over other types. Music that evokes pleasant emotions without lyrics is highly suggested. Try just about anything by Mozart. It relaxes you.

7. <u>Use arrows, not highlighters</u>. At best, it's difficult to read a page full of yellow, pink, blue, and green streaks. Try staring at a neon sign for a while, and you'll soon see that the horde of colors obscures the message.

A quick note, a brief dash of color, an underline, and an arrow pointing to a particular passage is much clearer than a horde of highlighted words.

8. <u>Budget your study time</u>. Although you shouldn't ignore any of the material, *allocate your available study time in the same ratio that topics may appear on the test.*

Testing Tips:

1. <u>Get smart, play dumb</u>. Don't read anything into the question. Don't assume that the test writer is looking for something else than what is asked. Stick to the question.

2. <u>Read the question and all the choices</u> *twice* <u>before answering the question</u>. You may miss something by not carefully reading and then re-reading both the question and the answers.

If you don't have a clue as to the right answer, leave it blank on the first time through. Go on to the other questions, as they may provide a clue as to how to answer the skipped questions.

If later, you still can't answer the skipped ones . . . *Guess.* The only penalty for guessing is that you *might* get it wrong. Only one thing is certain; if you don't put anything down, you will get it wrong!

3. <u>Turn the question into a statement</u>. Look at the way the questions are worded. The syntax of the question usually provides a clue. Does it seem more familiar as a statement rather than as a question? Does it sound strange?

By turning a question into a statement, you may be able to spot if an answer sounds right, and it may also trigger memories of material you have read.

4. <u>Look for hidden clues</u>. It's very difficult to compose multiple-foil (choice) questions without giving away part of the answer in the options presented.

In most multiple-choice questions, you can often readily eliminate one or two of the potential answers. This leaves you with only two real possibilities and, automatically, your odds go to fifty-fifty for very little work.

5. <u>Trust your instincts</u>. For every fact that you have read, you subconsciously retain something of that knowledge. On questions that you aren't certain about, go with your basic instincts. **Your first impression on how to answer a question is usually correct.**

6. <u>Mark your answers directly on the test booklet</u>. Don't bother trying to fill in the optical scan sheet on the first pass through the test. *Just be very careful not to miss-mark your answers when you eventually transcribe them to the scan sheet.*

7. <u>Watch the clock</u>! You have a set amount of time to answer the questions. Don't get bogged down trying to answer a single question at the expense of ten questions you can more readily answer.

DOMAIN I.	LANGUAGE ARTS, PART I: ORAL LANGUAGE, EARLY LITERACY DEVELOPMENT, WORD IDENTIFICATION, AND READING FLUENCY

COMPETENCY 001   ORAL LANGUAGE

SKILL A: Knows basic linguistic concepts and developmental stages in acquiring oral language, including stages in phonology, semantics, syntax, and pragmatics, and recognizes that individual variations occur

See Competency 2.A for information on phonological and phonemic awareness.

See Competency 3.B for information on syntax, semantics, morphology and pragmatics.

Theories of Language Acquisition

Learning Approach

Early theories of language development were formulated from learning theory research. The assumption was that language development evolved from learning the rules of language structures and applying them through imitation and reinforcement. This approach also assumed that language, cognitive, and social developments were independent of each other. Thus, children were expected to learn language from patterning after adults who spoke and wrote Standard English. No allowance was made for communication through child jargon, idiomatic expressions, or grammatical and mechanical errors resulting from too strict adherence to the rules of inflection (*childs* instead of *children*) or conjugation (*runned* instead of *ran*). No association was made between physical and operational development and language mastery.

Linguistic Approach

Studies spearheaded by Noam Chomsky in the 1950s formulated the theory that language ability is innate and develops through natural human maturation as environmental stimuli trigger acquisition of syntactical structures appropriate to each exposure level. The assumption of a hierarchy of syntax downplayed the significance of semantics. Because of the complexity of syntax and the relative speed with which children acquire language, linguists attributed language development to biological rather than cognitive or social influences.

Cognitive Approach

Researchers in the 1970s proposed that language knowledge derives from both syntactic and semantic structures. Drawing on the studies of Piaget and other cognitive learning theorists, supporters of the cognitive approach maintained that children acquire knowledge of linguistic structures after they have acquired the cognitive structures necessary to process language. For example, joining words for specific meaning necessitates sensory-motor intelligence. The child must be able to coordinate movement and recognize objects before she can identify words to name the objects or word groups to describe the actions performed with those objects.

Adolescents must have developed the mental abilities for organizing concepts as well as concrete operations, predicting outcomes, and theorizing before they can assimilate and verbalize complex sentence structures, choose vocabulary for particular nuances of meaning, and examine semantic structures for tone and manipulative effect.

Socio-cognitive Approach

Other theorists in the 1970s proposed that language development results from sociolinguistic competence. Language, cognitive, and social knowledge are interactive elements of total human development. Emphasis on verbal communication as the medium for language expression resulted in the inclusion of speech activities in most language arts curricula.

Unlike previous approaches, the socio-cognitive approach asserted that determining the appropriateness of language in given situations for specific listeners is as important as understanding semantic and syntactic structures. By engaging in conversation, children at all stages of development have opportunities to test their language competencies, receive feedback, and make modifications. As a social activity, conversation is as structured by social order as grammar is structured by the rules of syntax. Conversation satisfies the learner's need to be heard and understood and to influence others. Thus, his choices of vocabulary, tone, and content are dictated by his ability to assess the language knowledge of his listeners. He is constantly applying his cognitive competencies to using language in a social interaction. If the capacity to acquire language is inborn without an environment in which to practice language, a child would not pass beyond grunts and gestures as did primitive man.

Of course, the varying degrees of environmental stimuli to which children are exposed at all age levels creates a slower or faster development of language. Some children are prepared to articulate concepts and recognize symbolism by the time they enter fifth grade because they have been exposed to challenging reading and conversations with well-spoken adults at home or in their social groups. Others are still trying to master the sight recognition competencies and are not yet ready to combine words in complex patterns.

Stages of Language Acquisition

There is wide agreement that there are generally five stages of second language development. The first stage is "pre-production." While students may actually understand what someone says to them (for the most part), they have a much harder time responding in the target language.

Teachers must realize that if a student cannot "produce" the target language, it does not mean that they aren't learning. Most likely, they are. They are taking it in, and their brains are trying to figure out what to do with all the new language.

The second phase is "early production." This is where the student can start to produce the target language. It is quite limited, and teachers most likely should not expect students to produce eloquent speeches during this time.

The third phase is "emergent speech" or "speech emergence." Longer, more complex sentences are used, particularly in speech, as well as in social situations. But students aren't fully fluent in this stage, and they cannot handle complex academic language tasks.

The fourth phase is "intermediate fluency." This is where more complex language is produced. Grammatical errors are common.

The fifth stage is "advanced fluency." While students may appear to be completely fluent, they will still need academic and language support from teachers.

Many people say that there are prescribed periods of time in which students should reach each stage. However, teachers must keep in mind that it depends on the level at which students are exposed to the language. For example, students who get opportunities to practice with the target language outside of school may have greater ease in reaching the fifth stage. In general, though, it does take years to reach the fifth stage, and students should never be expected to have complete mastery within one school year.

Factors that Affect Oral Language Development

The development of speaking and listening competencies requires an intensive attention to make sure that children acquire a good stock of words, learn to listen attentively, and speak clearly and confidently. In many instances, however, students with speech and listening disabilities will experience speaking and listening difficulties.

Some of the most common factors that affect oral language development are:

- **Blindness:** Learners who are blind will not be able to see who is speaking nor will they be able to use facial expression and body language as an additional means of interpreting what other people are saying.
- **Hearing Impairments/Deafness:** A young child's inability to hear properly can affect his or her ability to learn and develop language. Before they even reach school, children undergo hearing tests which can help determine a child's ability to hear. Hearing can be impaired for many reasons. They could have been born with a hearing deficiency, exposed to dangerously high decibel noise, or suffered a sickness.

For example, some children who have experienced recurring ear infections have been found to have delays in language development due to chronically having their ears "clogged" with fluid which inhibits clear hearing. Deaf learners who use sign language will only be able to follow a discussion by looking at their sign language interpreter. This will inevitably slow down the speed with which they can receive inputs, and it also means that they cannot always focus on the facial expressions of the speaker.

- **Autistic Disorders:** Some learners with autistic disorders may find it very hard to communicate directly with other people. Their disability makes aspects of social communication (e.g., eye contact) particularly difficult.

For more information on delays in oral language development, see Competency 1.E.

Strategies for Addressing Oral Language Needs

See Competency 1.G.

SKILL B: **Knows characteristics and uses of informal and formal oral language assessments and uses multiple, ongoing assessments to monitor and evaluate students' oral language competencies**

Formal Assessments

Formal assessment is summative in nature. It refers to tests given to students at the end of a unit, term, or course of study. The results of formal assessment usually translate into a mark or grade that the students receive to determine the percentage of achieved course objectives. The teacher or tester controls the testing environment for formal assessment, and all students perform the same assessment. Diagnostic assessment given at the end of a grade level is a formal assessment as well where the results are compared to that of a control group.

For assessing oral language, formal assessment can take the form of:

- Presentations that students have to prepare for and deliver to a group
- Debates
- Scheduled interviews between the teacher and student in which the student has to prepare answers to questions

Informal Assessments

Informal assessments pave the way for formal assessment. These assessments take place throughout the course of study and help prepare the student to succeed. The teacher uses informal assessments to determine where the student needs help or where the instruction needs to change to meet the needs of the student.

Ways in which teachers can use informal assessment for oral language include:

- Running records of students' reading
- Checklists of student behavior and needs while giving informal presentations
- Student questions and answers in class discussion
- Student discussion in Literature Circles
- Overall conversation in the class
- Interviews between student and teacher, such as in discussing the books students are reading and questioning on comprehension
- Anecdotal records of student performance, needs, and improvement

Some general language competencies to evaluate during informal assessments include determining that the students:

- Converse easily
- Continue to extend oral vocabulary
- Can talk at length with few pauses and fill time with speech
- Can call up appropriate things to say in many contexts
- Increase the size and range of their vocabulary and syntax competencies
- Display coherence of their sentences and the ability to speak in reasoned and semantically dense sentences
- Possess knowledge of the various forms of interaction and conversation for various situations
- Possess knowledge of the standard rules of conversation and appropriate sentence structure
- Can be creative and imaginative with language and express themselves in original ways
- Can invent, entertain, and take risks in linguistic expression

See Competencies 2.G and 2.I.

SKILL C: **Provides language instruction that acknowledges students' current oral language competencies and that builds on these competencies to increase students' oral language proficiency**

Through instruction of the conventions of the English language and practice in writing and speaking, students develop knowledge of how to use these conventions in their oral language. Students often don't realize that speaking in conversations with their friends and speaking for different purposes require different oral language competencies.

The use of the proper conventions of verb usage and subject-verb agreement is just as important in oral language as it is in written language. Development of student vocabulary is important to help them expand on their knowledge of words and their synonyms. Dialects often play a part in the difficulties students experience with oral language.

Teachers must take care when correcting students' use of words and help them develop more proper ways of communicating orally.

See Competencies 1.D, 1.E, 1.F, and "Considering Individuality" in 1.G.

SKILL D: **Plans, implements, and adapts instruction that is based on informal and formal assessment of students' progress in oral language development and that addresses the needs, strengths, and interests of individual students, including English Language Learners**

Oral language competencies are an important component of the Language Arts curriculum for middle school. Teachers need to take the objectives for each grade and plan experiences related to the reading material students are using in the class to find opportunities for oral language experiences for the students in which to engage. By making notes about specific observations, teachers can tailor instruction in subsequent classes to demonstrate how to use vocabulary and the proper conventions of language in all speaking experiences. These can take the form of mini-lessons for the whole class or small groups of students that need this instruction.

Evaluating Messages

Class presentations and speeches can be impromptu for students to learn how to speak in front of a group. These would not need to be assessed formally as the teacher can use them to determine the needs of the students and plan appropriate instruction.

Students need time to write their speeches and presentations, and they need time to practice. During the practice sessions, teachers can instruct the students on the proper way to project their voices, add expression, and provide constructive criticism on the content of the material. The writing can also take place within the context of a writing workshop where the teacher can conference with individual students, and the students can engage in peer editing.

As part of the process of planning and implementing instruction in oral language, students should be exposed to guest speakers in the classroom, or the teacher can use videotapes of speakers and ask students to critique the performance. Teachers can also videotape the students giving a presentation and ask the students to critique their own performances.

Analyzing the speech of others is a very good technique for helping students improve their own public speaking abilities. In most circumstances, students cannot view themselves as they give speeches and presentations, so when they get the opportunity to critique, question, and analyze others' speeches, they begin to learn what works and what doesn't work in effective public speaking.

However, a very important word of warning: DO NOT have students critique each other's' public speaking competencies. It could be very damaging to a student to have his or her peers point out what did not work in a speech. Instead, video is a great tool teachers can use. Any appropriate source of public speaking can be used in the classroom for students to analyze and critique.

Students should always know the assessment criteria for oral language so that they know what the teacher is looking for in a formal assessment. Exemplars demonstrating good, fair, and poor performances should be part of the instruction so students know what they should and should not do.

Some of the things students can pay attention to include the following:

- Volume: A speaker should use an appropriate volume—not too loud to be annoying but not too soft to be inaudible
- Pace: The rate at which words are spoken should be appropriate—not too fast to make the speech incomprehensible but not too slow so as to put listeners to sleep
- Pronunciation: A speaker should make sure words are spoken clearly. Listeners do not have a text to go back and re-read things they didn't catch
- Body language: While animated body language can help a speech, too much of it can be distracting. Body language should help convey the message, not detract from it
- Word choice: The words speakers choose should be consistent with their intended purpose and the audience
- Visual aids: Visual aids, like body language, should enhance a message. Many visual aids can be distracting, and that detracts from the message.

Overall, instead of telling students to keep these above factors in mind when presenting information orally, having them view speakers who do these things well and poorly will help them know and remember the next time they give a speech.

Second Language Learners

Students who are raised in homes where English is not the first language and/or where Standard English is not spoken may have difficulty with hearing the difference between similar sounding words like "send" and "sent." Any student who is not in an environment where English phonology is practiced may have difficulty perceiving and demonstrating the differences between English language phonemes.

If students cannot hear the difference between words that "sound the same" like "grow" and "glow," they will be confused when these words appear in a print context. This confusion will, of course, sadly impact their comprehension.

Teachers should not use the same assessment criteria for assessing students learning English as they would for those who are native English speakers. This also applies to the instructional techniques the teacher uses as the second language learners may not understand all the instruction.

Research recommends that ELL students learn to read initially in their first language. It has been found that a priority for ELL should be learning to speak English before being taught to read English. Research supports oral language development since it lays the foundation for phonological awareness.

SKILL E: **Recognizes when oral language delays or differences warrant in-depth evaluation and additional help or intervention**

Delays in Oral Communication

Speech or language delays in children can be cause for concern or intervention. Understanding the development of language in young children can provide information on delays or differences. The efficiency of language for children develops in a pragmatic manner from the caregivers and social environment that children are exposed to during this crucial time of language acquisition. The focus during this period of development should not be on perceived problems such as a child's ability to pronounce certain vowels or consonants (for example, a child's pronunciation of /r/ that sounds like /w/ making the word "right" sound like "white."

Without immediate, consistent, and appropriate intervention, children who begin their formal education with cultural/language differences or delays in literacy development quickly fall behind and, typically, they do not "catch up." By the time they reach middle school, these students may have already repeated several grades and/or have been assigned to numerous transition classes.

Speech intelligibility guidelines provide a tracking of a child's oral speech development. General researchers have shown that the following guidelines are recognizable age/language acquisitions:

- Children at 2 years old should have speech patterns that are about 70% intelligible.
- Children at 3 years old should have an increased 10% speech pattern that is about 80% intelligible.
- Children at 4 years old should have a 20% speech pattern that is about 90% intelligible.
- Children at 5 years old should have a speech pattern that is 100% intelligible.
- Children >5 years old will develop speech patterns that continue at 100% intelligibility with increased vocabulary databases.

Given the speech intelligibility guidelines, parents, adult caregivers, and teachers can track what is normal development versus language developmental delays or differences. If a child is not developing intelligible and recognizable speech patterns at age appropriate development levels, intervention and additional in-depth evaluations will provide the proper tools to address and correct language delays that could have long range impacts on a child's final development of speech pattern intelligibility.

By the time students are in middle school, they are expected to use reading as a primary method of learning and to be able to communicate effectively orally and in writing. Students who have fallen behind in the early grades fail to meet these expectations and are forced to develop coping strategies to compensate for their perceived failures. These coping strategies, which often include inappropriate, problematic, and disruptive behavior, serve to further isolate and remove these students from the mainstream educational process and from effective interventional efforts.

Middle school students with delays in literacy development can be identified in a number of ways: they avoid reading as much as possible; when reading out loud, they read everything at a slow or inhibited rate; they do not read outside of school; they demonstrate a limited vocabulary; they rely on teachers or classmates for information; they resist participation in classroom discussions; they have limited attention spans; they demonstrate a lack of comprehension of material they have read; they are unfamiliar with and do not exhibit reading strategies; they are poor listeners; their writing is unstructured and contains a high rate of misspellings and grammatical and mechanical errors; they "give up" quickly when given a reading or writing task; they do not ask relevant questions;

they do not know what to do when they encounter material they do not understand; and they read and write without a sense of purpose.

In addition to students with delayed literacy development, non-English-speaking students may also need in-depth evaluation and intervention. Because command of the spoken language serves as a basis for understanding and learning alphabetic principles, as well as the structure and content of the language, oral proficiency precedes proficiency in reading and writing. Thus, children without strong oral competencies need special consideration—assisting them in gaining oral proficiency must become the primary task.

There are trade books teachers can use with struggling students that are of interest to the age group yet do not have the higher level of vocabulary as books geared toward the middle grades. This allows these students to increase their reading competencies and develop their vocabulary. The use of graphic organizers also helps struggling students as it helps them organize the material they read and helps prepare them for writing.

Teachers can make accommodations to the requirements for struggling students to allow them to experience success. The accommodations must not change the objectives of the course for the students so that they still achieve the outcomes of the grade or course.

Teachers and parents who have concerns about a child's language development should be proactive in addressing language delays. Contacting speech pathologists, auditory specialists to test for hearing disorders, pediatricians to test for motor functioning delays, as well as utilizing other assessment resources for evaluation are effective steps for those concerned about a child's language delays or differences. Early intervention is the key to addressing children's language delays or differences.

SKILL F: **Knows how to provide explicit, systematic oral language instruction and supports students' learning and use of oral language through meaningful and purposeful activities implemented one-to-one and in a group**

Explicit instruction and teacher modeling is essential for teaching oral language competencies in the middle school setting. Quite often students at these grade levels use grammatically incorrect speech and, therefore, the teacher must provide the instruction necessary for the students to be able to recognize and correct the mistakes they make.

The teacher must model the proper conventions of the English language when speaking to the students. Reading aloud to the class presents an opportunity to provide explicit instruction by stopping at places in the reading to point out mistakes in speech and asking the students what the correct speech would be.

By showing videotapes to students of different speakers and pointing out where improvements can be made, the teacher offers explicit instruction. Students can prepare charts individually or as a group about the qualities of good speakers. A class chart should be posted in the classroom where it is visible to all students.

When preparing students to critique presentations, the teacher should provide them with a checklist or what to look for in the presentation. This allows students to recognize mistakes and helps them prepare for speaking themselves. As a modeling exercise, the teacher should go through a presentation using the checklist and demonstrating how students can use it.

As a teacher of middle school students, the presentations the teacher uses to model conventions of oral language should never be those of students in the class. The presentations should be by people that the students do not know. This will prevent any student being held up to ridicule for the rest of the class.

Direct instruction in the conventions of language helps students in both their writing and speaking. Teachers need to determine the needs of the students and provide this instruction to the whole group (if there is a need for it) or to small groups of struggling students. Even one-on-one work with a struggling student is warranted if the situation demands.

Through informal assessment, teachers can find the mistakes students make and where each student needs intervention or instruction. It often becomes difficult for teachers to demonstrate for students the need for changing their language to suit the situation. Role-playing in the classroom is one way of providing instruction. One example of this could be having students use their normal language when interviewing for a job. Then the same students, or different ones, can role-play the same situation using conventional oral language that suits the situation. Group discussion can then help demonstrate the difference between the two and which role-play situation was more effective for the purpose. Explicit instruction in oral language competencies also helps to reinforce the students' listening competencies.

SKILL G: **Selects and uses instructional materials and strategies that promote students' oral language development; respond to students' individual strengths, needs and interests; reflect cultural diversity; and build on students' cultural, linguistic, and home backgrounds to enhance their oral language development**

Strategies for Addressing Oral Language Needs

Oral Language involves both expressive (speaking) and receptive (hearing) language competencies. Some students with language impairments will request to have directions repeated, while others may not be self-monitoring enough to recognize their own lack of comprehension. Students with severe oral language disabilities will require extensive support services. However, the following strategies may also be utilized with students:

- Demonstrate or model what you want the student to do, talking through the task while performing it
- Provide plenty of time for verbal responses to questions
- Have the student sit close to the teacher or in front of the classroom
- Have the student orally describe visual materials such as a picture or poster
- Increase oral fluency by having the student say as many words in a category as he or she can think of within a minute time period
- Use the student's interests and nonacademic and academic strengths as conversational topics

Teachers can support the development of listening and speaking competencies in several ways by:

- Modeling how language is used to communicate – Children understand the meanings conveyed through facial expressions, body gestures, and voice tomes. They can then learn how to pronounce specific words, make sense of standard of rules of grammar, and enlarge their vocabularies.
- **Talking with children** - Children should be encouraged to express their needs, feelings, ideas, stories, and imaginations. Children learn how to be conversation partners by taking turns, staying on the topic, and waiting until the speaker is finished
- **Reading to children** - This allows children to enjoy spending time with a favorite adult and associate reading with these positive feelings. Children also can begin to make discoveries about the connections between spoken and written words

Activities for Promoting Oral Language

The most basic activity is to let the children practice their oral language competencies, so it's ok if your classroom is noisy at times. There are many activities that encourage the development of oral language. Activities can include the following:

- Using finger puppets for retellings of stories
- Utilizing computer games for stimulating language development
- Writing new verses to existing poems and then reading them aloud
- Singing songs and chants that are fun to say
- Engaging in "word play" activities in which children change beginning, middle, or ending letters of related words, thus changing the words they decode and spell
- Having discussions that focus on a variety of topics including problem solving
- Practicing rhyming word families

Considering Individuality

Students have individual strengths and weaknesses in oral language development. Teachers must take these individual differences into consideration. The goal is to take the students from where they are to the next level.

For students who are already well-developed in their oral language, teachers should praise them and allow them to experiment with other forms of the language. They should also provide students with many opportunities for speaking. Many students who have well-developed speaking competencies may also be shy and, therefore, it is the job of the teacher to help them with their self-confidence issues.

For students who are experiencing difficulty, the teacher needs to take the family and cultural situations into consideration. Since these students may not recognize the mistakes they make, the teacher can point them out by conferencing one-on-one with the students. Another way of doing this is to provide mini-lessons to a small group of students who have similar needs.

Considering Culture

See "Second Language Learners" in Competency 1.D and Competency 4.C.

Teachers can encourage the development of a child's oral language competencies by providing classroom environments filled with language development opportunities. Teachers should understand that each child's language or dialect is worthy of respect as a valid system for communication. It reflects the identities, values, and experiences of the child's family and community. Allowing children to discuss their culture shows them that their culture is respected. Teachers should also encourage positive interaction among children within their classroom. Peer learning is an important part of language development, especially in mixed-age groups. Activities involving a wide range of materials should promote talk, such as dramatic play, block-building, book-sharing, or carpentry.

Teaching students who are learning English as a second language poses some unique challenges, particularly in a standards-based environment. The key is realizing that no matter how little English a student knows, the teacher should teach with the student's developmental level in mind. This means that instruction should not be "dumbed-down" for ESOL (English for Speakers of Other Languages) students. Different approaches should be used, however, to ensure that these students get multiple opportunities to learn and practice English while still learning content.

Many ESOL approaches are based on social learning methods. By being placed in mixed level groups or by being paired with a student of another ability level, students will get a chance to practice English in a natural, non-threatening environment. Students should not be pushed in these groups to use complex language or to experiment with words that are too difficult. They should simply get a chance to practice with simple words and phrases.

In teacher-directed instructional situations, visual aids (such as pictures, objects, and video) are particularly effective at helping students make connections between words and items with which they are already familiar.

ESOL students may need additional accommodations with assessments, assignments, and projects. For example, teachers may find that written tests provide little or no information about a student's understanding of the content. Therefore, an oral test may be better suited for ESOL students. When students are somewhat comfortable and capable with written tests, a shortened test may actually be preferable. Take note that they will need extra time to translate.

SKILL H: **Understands relationships between the development of oral language and the development of reading and provides instruction that interrelates oral and written language to promote students' reading proficiency and learning**

Literacy competencies, speaking, listening, reading, and writing, develop concurrently (together) rather than sequentially (one after the other). They are social competencies that develop because the child wants to interact and communicate with others. Development of these competencies occurs during meaningful interactions, experiences, and activities, as well as during explicit instruction from observant and sensitive adults.

Reading and writing Competency development basically follows two strands – language comprehension and decoding. These strands are complex, involving all the aspects of literacy development. Language comprehension has two major strands under its umbrella – background knowledge and linguistic knowledge. Linguistic knowledge encompasses phonology, syntactic, and semantic proficiency. Decoding involves both cipher knowledge (based on letter/sound) and lexical knowledge (based on recognition by sight, not sound). This requires proficiency in letter knowledge, phoneme awareness, and the alphabetic principle.

Comprehension of language, and subsequently reading comprehension, is based on both being able to use the language and being able to understand the substance of what is communicated. For example, having a schema for shopping in a store enables a child to first communicate orally and then later in writing about that event. Reading about that event will "make sense" because the student has a schema for it.

Encourage sharing of information
By encouraging each student to share information about an idea, the student can vocalize words and thoughts in a logical sequence.

Other Strategies:

- Engage the students in discussions about writing and sharing responses to texts.
- Literature Circles require the students to discuss books they are reading.
- Encourage the students to take part in poetry readings, short skits, and role-playing in the classroom.
- Have students listen to recordings, such as songs and presentations, to find the inherent message. This will start a discussion on the different student interpretations.
- Present oral instructions for student projects, such as how to draw an illustration or create a piece of art.
- Have students listen to presentations, such as excerpts from a television show, and ask them to listen for evidence of bias.

See Competencies 1.C, 1.I, and 4.A.

SKILL K: **Selects and uses instructional strategies, materials, activities, and models to teach students competencies for speaking to different audiences for various purposes and for adapting spoken language for various audiences, purposes, and occasions**

It's important to take the characteristics of the audience into account when organizing a presentation. If the audience can be counted on to have a high level of interest in what is being presented, little would need to be done in the way of organizing and presenting to hold interest. On the other hand, if many of those in the audience are there because they have to be, or if the level of interest can be counted on not to be very high, a visual presentation such as PowerPoint can be very helpful. Both the lead-in and introduction need to be structured not only to be entertaining and interest-grabbing but should also create an interest in the topic. For example, if the audience members are fellow middle school students, it's important to keep the presentation upbeat and to be careful not to "speak down" to them.

No speaker should stand up to make a presentation if the purpose has not been carefully determined ahead of time. If the speaker is not focused on the purpose, the audience will quickly lose interest. To best organize for a particular purpose, some of the decisions to be made are where the statement of the purpose will occur in the presentation—beginning, middle, or end—and whether displaying the purpose on a chart, PowerPoint, or banner will enhance the presentation.

The purpose might be the lead-in for a presentation if it can be counted on to grab the interest of the listeners, in which case, the organization will be deductive. If it seems better to save the purpose until the end, the organization, of course, will be inductive.

Have students break into groups and ask them to prepare a plan for how to best communicate to their audience (the other members of their group). Tell them to keep these guidelines in mind:

- **Values**- What is important to this group of people? What is their background, and how will that affect their perception of your speech?
- **Needs**- Find out in advance what the audience's needs are. Why are they listening to you? Find a way to satisfy their needs.
- **Constraints**- What might hold the audience back from being fully engaged in what you are saying, agreeing with your point of view, or processing what you are trying to say?
- **Demographic Information**- Take the audience's size into account, as well as the location of the presentation.

Speaking for Various Purposes

One of the most important things in helping children learn to speak is to have frequent, friendly conversations with them. Treat children as if they are conversationalists. Children learn at a very early age about how conversations work, for example: taking turns, asking questions, looking attentively, using facial expressions, etc.

In public speaking, not all speeches deserve the same type of speaking style. For example, when providing a humorous speech, it is important to utilize body language in order to accent humorous moments. However, when giving instructions, it is extremely important to speak clearly and slowly, carefully noting the mood of the audience so that if there is general confusion on peoples' faces, the speaker can go back and review.

In group discussions, it is important for speakers to ensure that they are listening to other speakers carefully and tailoring their messages so that the messages fit into the general mood and location of the discussion at hand. When giving an oral presentation, the mood should be both serious and friendly. The speaker should focus on ensuring that the content is covered while also relating to audience members as much as possible.

See Competency 1.G.

SKILL L: **Selects and uses instructional strategies, materials, and models to teach students listening competencies for various purposes and provides students with opportunities to engage in active, purposeful listening in a variety of contexts**

Listening is not a Competency that is talked about much except when someone clearly does not listen. The truth is, though, that listening is a very specific Competency for very specific circumstances. There are two aspects to listening that warrant attention. The first is comprehension or understanding what someone says, the purposes behind the message, and the contexts in which it is said. The second aspect is purpose. While someone may completely understand a message, what is the listener supposed to do with it—just nod and smile or go out and take action?

While listening, comprehension is indeed a significant competency in itself that deserves a lot of focus in the classroom (much in the same way that reading comprehension does), we will focus on purpose here. Often, when we understand the purpose of listening in various contexts, comprehension will be much easier. Furthermore, when we know the purpose of listening, we can better adjust our comprehension strategies.

Listening is often done for the purpose of enjoyment, and schools must teach students *how* to listen and enjoy such work. Teachers can accomplish this by making it fun and giving many possibilities and alternatives to capture the wide array of interests in each classroom.

Students like to listen to stories, poetry, and radio dramas and theater. Listening to literature can also be a great pleasure. In the classrooms of exceptional teachers, we will often find that students are captivated by the reading-aloud of good literature.

Strategies for Active Listening

Oral speech can be very difficult to follow. When complex or new information is provided to us orally, we must analyze and interpret that information. Often, making sense of this information can be tough when presented orally because students have no place to go back and review material already stated.

Students must have opportunities to listen in large and small group conversation. The difference here is that conversation requires more than just listening. It involves feedback and active involvement. This can be particularly challenging, as in our culture, we are trained to move conversations along, to discourage silence in a conversation, and to always get the last word in. This poses significant problems for the art of listening. In a discussion, for example, when we are instead preparing our next response—rather than listening to what others are saying—we do a large disservice to the entire discussion.

Students need to learn how listening carefully to others in discussions actually promotes better responses on the part of subsequent speakers. One way teachers can encourage this, in both large and small group discussions, is to expect students to respond *directly* to the previous student's comments before moving ahead with their new comments. This will encourage them to pose their new comments in light of the comments that came just before them.

Students must also be able to listen for transitions between ideas. Sometimes, in oral speech, this is pretty simple when voice tone or body language changes. Of course, we don't have the luxury of looking at paragraphs in oral language, but we do have the animation that comes along with live speech. Human beings would have to try very hard to be completely non-expressive in their speech. Listeners should take advantage of this and notice how the speaker changes character and voice in order to signal a transition of ideas. Also, simply looking to see expression on the face of a speaker can do more to signal irony, for example, than trying to extract irony from actual words.

One good way to follow oral speech is to take notes and outline major points. Because oral speech can be more circular (as opposed to linear) than written text, it can be of great assistance to keep track of an author's message. Other classroom methods can help students learn good listening competencies. For example, teachers can have students practice following complex directions. They can also have students orally retell stories—or retell (in writing or in oral speech) oral presentations of stories or other materials. These activities give students direct practice in the very important competencies of listening. They provide students with outlets in which they can slowly improve their abilities to comprehend oral language and take decisive action based on oral speech.

SKILL M: **Selects and uses instructional strategies, materials, activities, and models to teach students to evaluate the content and effectiveness of their own spoken messages and the messages of others**

Different from the basic writing forms of discourse is the art of debating, discussion, and conversation. The ability to use language and logic to convince the audience to accept your reasoning and to side with you is an art. This form of writing/speaking is extremely confined and structured, and it is logically sequenced with supporting reasons and evidence. At its best, it is the highest form of propaganda. A position statement, evidence, reason, evaluation, and refutation are integral parts of this writing schema.

Interviewing provides opportunities for students to apply expository and informative communication. It teaches them how to structure questions to evoke fact-filled responses. Compiling the information from an interview into a biographical essay or speech helps students to list, sort, and arrange details in an orderly fashion.

Speeches that encourage them to describe persons, places, or events in their own lives or oral interpretations of literature help them sense the creativity and effort used by professional writers.

Students also need to be able to evaluate speeches to determine the message of the speech and the techniques the speaker used. This is an important aspect of teaching students how to deliver their own speeches.

A checklist is a useful tool for students to use when evaluating speeches. In this way, they know what to listen for in the presentation. The teacher should limit the number of items on the checklist when teaching students how to use this tool. Having too many things for them to listen for will be confusing for the students.

Some items that a teacher could use for helping students evaluate a speech include:

- What is the message the speaker is trying to get across?
- Does the speaker use effective supports in the speech?
- Is the speech appropriate for the occasion and the audience?
- Does each part of the speech flow smoothly into the next so that there is no loss of information on the part of the listener?

Teachers can engage the students in preparing their own speeches and delivering them to the class or a small group of their peers who will then offer suggestions and ask questions for clarification.

For more information on evaluating speech, see "Evaluating Messages" in Competency 1.G

Useful resources

> Price, Bren T.. *Basic Composition Activities Kit*. The Center for Applied Research in Education, Inc. This resource provides practical suggestions and student guide sheets for use in the development of student writing.

> Simmons, John S., R.E. Shafer, and Gail B. West. (1976). *Decisions About The Teaching of English - "Advertising, or Buy It, You'll Like It."* Allyn & Bacon.

SKILL N: **Knows how to promote students' development of oral communication competencies through the use of technology**

Instructors are obligated to become familiar with and competent in the use of available technologies (computer, Internet, video cameras, tape recorders, digital cameras, etc.). Such technologies can serve to greatly enhance the development of students' oral communication competencies. Whether it is encouraging and assisting students in preparing a PowerPoint presentation for their oral presentations or videotaping an interpretive reading, the use of technology can serve to increase the students' interest and participation in developing these critical competencies. For example, video-taped presentations can be saved so students can view, for themselves, the progress they are making in utilizing facial expressions, hand gestures, and tone in conveying their messages.

As proficiency in spoken English is enhanced, so is a student's personal confidence and self-image. In addition, increased proficiency in oral communication competencies often translates to an increased proficiency in reading and writing.

Through the use of technology, students can research topics to help them develop the content of presentations and speeches. They can also use technology to help them acquire graphics, such as posters and graphs, which they can use as visual aids for the audience to provide further support for the content of the speech.

Students can also use technology to help them find the correct conventions of the English language so that they can write their messages and speeches correctly and, therefore, deliver them using the proper oral language. There are also numerous opportunities for students to read stories, speeches and other written communications online. They can use these examples for ideas for their topics and get useful tips they can use in their own speaking opportunities.

Students who use email know that there are various ways of communicating with others using language that doesn't work effectively in their oral language experiences. Abbreviations, for example, used in emails are not used in speaking. However, through technology, students can learn the various ways of communicating the same message.

Through technology, students can develop different multimedia to aid them in speaking, such as in developing Power Point Presentations.

COMPETENCY 002 EARLY LITERACY DEVELOPMENT

SKILL A: **Understands the signification of phonological and phonemic awareness for reading and typical patterns in the development of phonological and phonemic awareness and recognizes that individual variations occur**

Phonemic Awareness

Phonemic awareness is the understanding that words are comprised of sounds. When phonemically aware, students possess the ability to break down and hear separate and/or different sounds, as well as the ability to distinguish between the sounds one hears. The majority of phonemic awareness tasks, activities, and exercises are ORAL. Phonemic awareness is required to begin studying phonics where students will require the ability to break down words into the smalls units of sound, or phonemes, to later identify syllables, blends, and patterns.

Phonemes are the smallest sounds in a spoken word. Thus, changing a phoneme can change the meaning of the word. For example, the first sound or phoneme in "hat" is /h/. Change the sound /h/ to the phoneme /p/, and you change "hat" to "pat."

Since the ability to distinguish between phonemes within words is a prerequisite to association of sounds with letters and manipulating sounds to blend words (a fancy way of saying "reading"), the teaching of phonemic awareness is crucial to emergent literacy. Children need a strong background in phonemic awareness in order for phonics instruction (sound-spelling relationship-printed materials) to be effective.

Instructional methods that may be effective for teaching phonemic awareness can include:

- Clapping syllables in words
- Distinguishing between a word and a sound
- Using visual cues and movements to help children understand when the speaker goes from one sound to another
- Incorporating oral segmentation activities which focus on easily distinguished syllables rather than sounds
- Singing familiar songs (e.g., Happy Birthday) and replacing key words in it with words with a different ending or middle sound (oral segmentation)
- Dealing children a deck of picture cards and having them sound out the words for the pictures on their cards or calling for a picture by asking for its first and second sound

Phonological Awareness

Phonological awareness is the ability of the reader to recognize the sounds of spoken language. This recognition includes how these sounds can be blended together, segmented (divided up), and manipulated (switched around). This awareness then leads to phonics, a method for teaching children to read. It helps them "sound out" words.

Children learn phonological awareness when taught about the sounds made by the letters, the sounds made by various combinations of letters, and how to recognize individual sounds in words. Development of phonological competencies may begin during preschool years. Indeed, by the age of five, a child who has been exposed to rhyme can recognize a rhyme. Such a child can demonstrate phonological awareness by filling in the missing rhyming word in a familiar rhyme or rhymed picture book.

Phonological awareness competencies include:

- Rhyming and syllabification
- Blending sounds into words—such as pic-tur-bo-k
- Identifying the beginning or starting sounds of words and the ending or closing sounds of words
- Breaking words down into sounds ("segmenting" words)
- Recognizing other smaller words in the big word

A Phonics Program

Phonics is a widely-used method for teaching students to read. This method includes studying the rules and patterns found in language. By age five or six, children can typically begin to use phonics to begin to understand the connections between letters, their patterns, vowel sounds (i.e., short vowels, long vowels) and the collective sounds they all make.

As opposed to phonemic awareness, the study of phonics must be done with the eyes open. It's the connection between the sounds and letters on a page. In other words, students learning phonics might see the word "bad" and sound each letter out slowly until they recognize that they just said the word.

Phonics is a method of teaching that focuses on the letter-sound relationships. Rules of spelling are included in good phonics instruction. For example, a child must be taught about "silent E" and that when two vowels are next to each other in a word, the first one determines the pronunciation. Spelling rules in English can be complex, since most letters can produce more than one sound. For this reason, children need to learn to sight read words as well as read and spell them using phonics.

Patterns of Development

Most phonemic and phonological awareness occurs at the primary level. Listed below are the approximate ages at which certain developmental patterns of reading tend to occur.

Preschool
- Basic level of phonological awareness (rhyming)
- Knowledge of several letter names and sounds
- Some basic print concepts

Kindergarten/First Grade
- Understands all of the individual letter names and sounds (K)
- Identifies spoken words with the same initial sound (K)
- Recognizes the more advanced basic print concepts (K)
- Blends individual phonemes to form a one-syllable word) (Gr. 1)
- Can segment one-syllable words into individual phonemes (Gr. 1)
- Has knowledge of sounds for letter patterns, such as "sh," "ch," "th" (Gr. 1)
- Decodes a wide range of one-syllable words such as: walk, stop, book (Gr. 1)

Second/Third Grade
- Has a growing knowledge of sounds for ordinary letter patterns (Gr. 2)
- Increases ability in decoding two-syllable and multi-syllable words (Gr. 2)
- Gains knowledge of sounds of common prefixes such as: in-, re-, un-, and suffixes such as: -tion, -ment, -ness) (Gr. 2–3)
- Applies knowledge of root words and morphemes to read multi-syllable words (Gr. 3)
- Possesses the competencies for decoding most words accurately and quickly, including multi-syllable words (Gr. 3)

By the end of first grade, children should be reading at least 40 words correctly per minute. By the end of second grade, students should be able to read at least 90 words correctly per minute. By the end of third grade, students should be reading 110 words correctly per minute.

Teachers should be aware that each student will be developing at various rates of learning. Therefore, do not expect each student to achieve these competencies in the order in which they are presented.

Assessing Phonological and Phonemic Awareness

See Competency 3.I.

SKILL B: **Understands elements of the alphabetic principle and typical patterns of students' alphabetic competencies development and recognizes that individual variations occur**

The alphabetic principle can be defined as the use of letters to represent sounds (i.e., speech can be turned into print, and print can be turned into speech). Typically, there are four stages or levels in the development of students' alphabetic competencies:

1. **Pre-alphabetic**—At this level, students become aware of the relationship between sounds and letters. That is, they are developing phonemic awareness. Recognizing initial and final phonemes in words and matching them with their alphabetic representatives (graphemes, i.e., the letter "h" represents the sound /h/) and playing rhyming games ("/p/ig" to "/b/ig" to "/f/ig") are examples of activities at this level.

2. **Early Alphabetic Reading**—Students at this level begin blending single sounds into words. Most programs begin with printed words that have a limited set of sounds (i.e., a few consonants and one or two vowels). Decoding strategies are implemented. Students may finger-point and sound out the words becoming more and more fluent as they read.

3. **Mature Alphabetic Level**—Now students should know and be able to decipher simple words. As they progress, students readily recognize often repeated initial letter groupings (ch, th, sh, sl, gr) and word endings (-ing, -ed, and -est).

4. **Orthographic Stage**—Students continue to practice reading and are becoming familiar with larger and more complex words and sentence structures. They move from sounding out words, letter by letter, to learning new words by their analogy to known words.

Students who do not come from a print-rich environment, are not familiar with the alphabet, and have not fully mastered oral competencies will need additional opportunities and encouragement to develop awareness of this sound-to-letter relationship.

Individual variations will occur in students' developmental patterns of learning the alphabetic principle. Student may develop various difficulties of understanding and using the alphabetic principle due to the inability to understand the idea that letters methodically represent spoken words. In order to learn English, the early reader must learn the connections between the approximately 44 phonemes and the 26 letters of the alphabet. Some students often need more time in which to develop their comprehension competencies in order to gain meaning from the text. Another learning variation may occur if a young reader is incapable of or delayed in developing the comprehension competencies to connect speaking competencies to reading the text.

See Competency 3.M.

SKILL C: **Understands that comprehension is an integral part of early literacy**

See Competencies 4.A and 4.B.

SKILL D: **Understands that not all written languages are alphabetic; that many alphabetic languages are more phonetically regular than English; and knows the significance of this for students' literacy development in English**

The English language utilizes a Roman alphabetic script which has letters that represent individual sounds (phonemes). Groupings of these letters then form words, and decoding these groupings is the basis of reading. Other languages that employ a Roman alphabetic script include French, German, and Spanish. Speakers of these languages will be familiar with the relationship between the letter(s) and the sounds of words, and they will find many similarities between the sound-symbols in both languages.

However, not all languages employ a Roman alphabetic script. Examples of such non-Roman alphabetic languages are Arabic, Greek, Russian, and Thai. Although these languages employ alphabets, the symbols for their letters are different, as may be the directionality of the writing (for example, Arabic is written from right to left). These students will need extra time in practicing writing, and they may have difficulty in immediately correlating sounds with the alphabetic symbols.

Finally, some languages, such as Chinese or Japanese, have non-alphabetic scripts. These languages, when written, have symbols that represent entire words rather than separate sounds. These students will need to establish an "alphabetic strategy" to be able to learn to read and write in English.

For students with a primary alphabetic language, studies have shown that reading and teaching phonemic awareness tend to reinforce each other. At the same time, research shows that for students with a non-alphabetic background, there is still a strong correlation between reading ability and phonological awareness, making the phonological principle in reading independent of the writing system employed.

SKILL E: **Understands that literacy acquisition generally develops in a predictable pattern from pre-reading (emergent literacy) to conventional literacy and recognizes that individual variations occur**

The process of moving from emergent literacy to conventional literacy is influenced by many things: a child's physical and mental capabilities and/or handicaps; primary language differences; home environment; involvement, commitment, and capabilities of primary caregivers; and the classroom teachers and school administrators.

There are several facets that may cause variations in the method or time frame in which a young child develops reading literacy. Young readers may develop literacy acquisition at uneven times due to experiencing difficulties linking speech sounds to letters. This is a fair indicator that their decoding competencies are labored and weak, resulting in very slow reading. This awkward reading tends to make comprehension quite challenging.

Social and cultural factors also may contribute to a variation in a child's literacy development. Research has proven that parents or caregivers who provide opportunities in which a child can enjoy print are increasing that child's chances of a higher level of literacy acquisition. Skilled reading depends upon the development of automaticity and fluency which factors in with a child also learning to write in a timely manner. If a student presents a lack of motivation, this may also affect the timeliness of their language acquisition.

While understanding that deficits in one or more of the areas listed above can hinder and delay literacy development, by the time children enter kindergarten, and begin formal literacy instruction, they have reached the stage of emergent literacy. To be successful at this stage, children should already have strong oral competencies and be familiar with books, often imitating reading by telling stories from pictures. The tone of voice they use when "reading" from their favorite books is similar to that of adult readers, and the vocabulary employed by emergent readers is taken from the stories and materials that they have repeatedly heard.

Children at this level also continue their experimentation with writing, which typically begins between the ages of three and four. While their earliest attempts involved squiggles and curvy lines in imitation of script, students at the emergent level will now add strings of letters to their scribbles, regardless of the sounds associated with the letters. As they advance, they employ invented or phonetic spellings thus bringing their writing efforts closer and closer to that which they are imitating.

Between first and third grade, most students move from emergent to conventional literacy. This is a gradual process with no set time limit on arriving at the conventional literacy level. During this transitional stage, students become more and more adept at identifying and remembering words in print, at decoding words, and using known words to decipher new words. Their spelling becomes more recognizable as they are now able to apply spelling rules and are remembering the correct spelling of frequently used and seen words. At the conventional literacy level, students are spending less and less time decoding printed words as they are reading for meaning.

That final point is critical for understanding middle school literacy problems. Most middle school age students have reached the conventional level of literacy and are ready to read for meaning. Unfortunately, students who have fallen behind in the early grades are often lumped together in single-purpose remedial classrooms where not enough attention is paid to developing advanced strategies for enhancing the comprehension capabilities of the students.

SKILL F: **Understands that literacy development occurs in multiple contexts through reading, writing, and the use of oral language**

See Competencies 5.E and 6.N.

SKILL G: **Knows characteristics of informal and formal literacy assessments**

Assessment is observing an event and making a judgment about its status of success. There are seven purposes of assessment:

- To assist student learning
- To identify students' strengths and weaknesses
- To assess the effectiveness of a particular instructional strategy
- To assess and improve the effectiveness of curriculum programs
- To assess and improve teaching effectiveness
- To provide data that assists in decision making
- To communicate with and involve parents

The purpose of informal assessment is to help our learners learn better. This form of assessment helps the teacher to understand how well the learners are learning and progressing. Informal assessment can be applied to homework assignments, field journals, and daily class work – all good indicators of student progress and comprehension.

Formal assessment, on the other hand, is highly structured, keeping the learner in mind. It must be done at regular intervals, and if the progress is not satisfactory, parent involvement is absolutely essential. A test or exam is a good example of formal assessment. A science project is also a formal assessment. The types of assessment discussed below represent many of the more common types of assessment, but the list is not comprehensive.

Anecdotal Records

These are notes recorded by the teacher concerning an area of interest or concern with a particular student. These records should focus on observable behaviors and should be descriptive in nature. They should not include assumptions or speculations regarding effective areas such as motivation or interest. These records are usually compiled over a period of several days to several weeks.

Rating Scales & Checklists

These assessments are generally self-appraisal instruments completed by the students or observations-based instruments completed by the teacher. The focus of these is frequently on behavior or effective areas such as interest and motivation.

Informal Reading Inventories

The setting in which you administer the informal reading inventory (IRI) should be as quiet and isolated as possible. Speak in a relaxed tone and reassure the student that this is not for a "grade." An informal reading inventory can be used to estimate a student's reading level and to assess a student's ability to use word identification strategies. Specifically, an IRI will help you assess a student's strengths and needs in these areas:

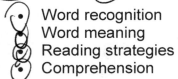

- Word recognition
- Word meaning
- Reading strategies
- Comprehension

IRIs can assist a teacher in determining reading fluency as well as strengths and weaknesses in the progress of reading comprehension. The inventory provides graded word lists and graded passages that assess oral reading, silent reading, and listening comprehension. Some IRIs provide narrative and expository passages with longer passage options. After reading a passage, the student answers questions or retells the passage. IRIs record students' errors while they are reading to the teacher, and they provide information about a student's word recognition, oral reading fluency, and listening comprehension. Analyzing a student's reading abilities includes: phonological awareness, letter identification, sound-letter correspondence knowledge, and recognizing sight-words.

Fluency Checks

Fluency is a student's ability to read a text accurately and quickly. They can make connections among the ideas in the text and their background knowledge. In other words, fluent readers recognize words and comprehend at the same time. Fluent readers read aloud effortlessly and with expression. Readers who have not yet developed fluency read slowly, word by word. Their oral reading is choppy and plodding.

To complete a fluency check, teachers should have a student read independently during a teacher-student conference. The teacher will select a passage from the student's independent reading book. The student will then read the passage while the teacher times him/her and takes a running record of the student's oral reading. The student will be assessed using the fluency standard expectations for that grade level. The number of words read correctly per minute is an indicator of a student's progress in all aspects of reading – decoding, fluency, and comprehension.

Minimum Fluency Rates

An expected quantitative level of 60 WPM (words per minute) for first grade and 90 WPM for second grade is to be met by the end of the year. The expected quantitative level of 110 WPM is required for the third grade and 118 WPM is required for the fourth grade. To put these rates into perspective, fluent adults read about 200 wpm during oral passage reading.

Think Alouds

Poor readers are often delayed at the basic level of comprehension as they concentrate on decoding words and sentences. They often don't see how various parts of a whole text relate to each other and work together to create a larger meaning. Struggling readers often cannot draw on background knowledge as they read, nor can they make predictions as they read. They frequently cannot visualize the events of a text as they are reading. These students often experience trouble thinking about the text while they are reading it.

The use of think-alouds can be used to improve reading comprehension by getting students to reflect on the process of thinking aloud as they read. Teachers can encourage them to recognize the difference between reading the words and comprehending the text by implementing coached practice.

Have students read a short passage to you. Tell students to continually pause and ask themselves the question, "Does this make sense to me?" Remind the students that you will be stopping occasionally to ask them what they are thinking about as they are reading. When a student shares his thoughts and the connection to the text is not clear, encourage the student to explain himself.

Rubrics

Subjective tests put the student in the driver's seat. These types of assessments usually consist of short answer, longer essays, or problem solving that involves critical thinking competencies requiring definitive proof from the short reading passages to support answers. Sometimes teachers provide rubrics that include assessment criteria for high scoring answers and projects. Sometimes, the rubric is as simple as a checklist and, other times, a maximum point value is awarded for each item on the rubric. Either way, rubrics provide a guideline of the teacher's expectations for the specifics of the assignment. The teacher usually discusses and/or models what is expected to fulfill each guideline, as well as provides a detailed outline of these expectations for reference.

For example, students being asked to write a research paper might be provided with a rubric. An elementary school teacher may assign a total of 50 points for the entire paper. The rubric may award ten points for note taking quality, ten points for research competencies, twenty points for content covered, five points for creative elements, and five points for organization and presentation. Then a certain number of points will be awarded in accordance with the students' performance. Rubrics allow students to score in multiple areas, rather than simply on a final product.

Another type of rubric can be used for holistic scoring. Holistic scoring involves assessing a child's ability to construct meaning through writing. It uses a scale which ranges from 0 until 4 –

O- In this rubric would be for a piece which cannot be scored. It does not respond to the topic asked or is illegible.

1- Would be a response which does respond to the topic but does not cover it accurately.

2- Would be a response which addresses the questions but lacks sufficient details to convey the purpose and to accomplish the writing task requested.

3- Would be a response which, in general, fulfills the purpose of the writing assignment and demonstrates that the reader correctly constructed meaning. The reader also will have showed that he or she understands the writer's purpose and message.

4- This response has the most details, the best organization, and presents a well-expressed reaction to the original writer's piece.

Running Records

Running Records permit teachers to determine students' reading strengths, weaknesses, readability levels, and fluency. Running records can be given on a book that has never been seen by the reader or one that has been read only once or twice. This often will give a more accurate measure of a child's ability to handle text at the assessed level. The Running Record, for example, requires that each child read 100 words of text out loud to the teacher. The teacher notes the time it takes the child to read the passage and the accuracy with which the child reads the passage.

Errors are tallied during the reading whenever a child does any of the following:

- Substitutes another word
- Omits a word
- Inserts an erroneous word
- Must be told a word by the person administering the running record

Teachers can administer this type of assessment multiple times during the year to note progress in fluency as well as accuracy in reading. Running records should be administered with greater frequency at the earlier stages of reading.

Story Re-Telling

After the student has read the target book and the teacher has recorded a running record, have the child do an oral retelling of the story. Ask the student to close the book and then tell you about the story in as much detail as she or he can remember. If the child has difficulty retelling parts of the story or remembering certain details, the teacher can use prompts such as "Tell me more about (character x)" or "What happened after...."

Retelling Checklist

- Can the child tell you what happened in the story or what the factual book was about in his or her own words?
- Does the child include details about the characters in the retelling? Can s/he explain the relationships between the characters?
- Can the child describe the setting? How detailed is the description?
- Can the child recall the events of the story, and can he or she place them in the correct sequence?

Portfolio Assessment

The use of student portfolios for some aspects of assessment has become quite common. The purpose, nature, and policies of portfolio assessment vary greatly from one setting to another. In general, though, a student's portfolio contains samples of work collected over an extended period. The nature of the subject, age of the student, and scope of the portfolio all contribute to the specific mechanics of analyzing, synthesizing and, otherwise, evaluating the portfolio contents.

In most cases, the student and teacher make joint decisions as to which work samples go into the student's portfolios. A collection of work compiled over an extended time period allows teachers, students, and parents to view progress from a unique perspective. Qualitative changes over time can be readily apparent from work samples. Such changes are difficult to establish with strictly quantitative records typical of the scores recorded in the teacher's grade book.

Questioning

One of the most frequently occurring forms of assessment in the classroom is oral questioning by the teacher. As the teacher questions the students, a great deal of information can be collected about the degree of student learning and potential sources of confusion for the students. While questioning is often viewed as a component of instructional methodology, it is also a powerful assessment tool.

Tests

Tests and similar direct-assessment methods represent the most easily identified types of assessment. Thorndike (1997) identifies three types of assessment instruments:

1. Standardized achievement tests
2. Assessment material packaged with curricular materials
3. Teacher-made assessment instruments
   Pencil and paper tests
   Oral tests
   Product evaluations
   Performance tests
   Effective measures (p.199)

SKILL H: **Knows how to select, administer, and use results from informal and formal assessments of literary acquisition**

See Competencies 2.G and 2.I.

SKILL I: **Knows how to use ongoing assessment to determine when a student needs additional help or intervention to bring the student's performance to grade level, based on state content and performance standards for reading in the Texas Essential Knowledge and Competencies (TEKS)**

Ongoing assessment is assessment for learning. As teachers assess students before, during, and after a lesson or unit of study, they can easily see what the students have learned during the instruction and ensuing activities. Thus, the grade a student earns is not based on just one test or activity, but it also shows progress over time. A student who does poorly on a test or activity and then demonstrates understanding with a better grade later on should not have the lesser grade included in the overall mark. In ongoing assessment, averaging the marks takes on a new meaning. Some marks may be crossed out altogether. This provides students with a greater chance of experiencing success and being rewarded for their efforts.

How can a teacher provide good feedback so that students will learn from their assessments? First, language should be helpful and constructive. Critical language does not necessarily help students learn. They may become defensive or hurt and, therefore, they may be more focused on the perceptions than the content. Language that is constructive and helpful will guide students to specific actions and recommendations that would help them improve in the future.

When teachers provide timely feedback, they increase the chance that students will reflect on their thought-processes as they originally produced the work. When feedback comes weeks after the production of an assignment, the student may not remember what it was that caused him or her to respond in a particular way.

Specific feedback is particularly important. Comments such as, "This should be clearer." and "Your grammar needs to be worked on." provide information that students may already know. They may already know they have a problem with clarity. What they can benefit from is commentary that provides very specific actions students can take to improve their grammar.

Tips for Assessment

- Assess students at the beginning of each year to determine grouping for instruction
- Judge whether a student recognizes when a word does not make sense
- Monitor whether the student corrects him/herself as well as if they know when to ignore and read on or when to reread a sentence
- Look for competencies such as recognizing cause and effect, finding main ideas, and using comparison and contrast techniques
- Use oral reading to assess reading competencies. Pay attention to word recognition competencies rather than the reader's ability to communicate the author's message. Strong oral reading sounds like natural speech, utilizes phrasing and pace that match the meaning of the text, and uses pitch and tone to interpret the text
- Keep dated records to follow individual progress. Focus on a few students each day. Grade them on a scale of 1-5 according to how well they perform certain reading abilities (e.g., logically predicts coming events). Also include informal observations such as "Ed was able to determine the meaning of the word 'immigrant' by examining the other words in the sentence."
- Remember that evaluation is important, but enjoyment of reading is the most important thing to emphasize. Keep reading as a pressure-free, fun activity so students do not become intimidated by reading. Even if the student is not meeting excellent standards, if they continue to want to read each day, that is a success

Monitoring Reading Development

Teachers need to continually monitor students' reading development throughout the school year. Aside from formal state and classroom assessments, teachers can gather information about students' reading progress in informal ways, too.

Some of these ways include:

- Reader's workshop portfolios
- Literature circles
- Running records
- Portfolio assessment
- Journal writing
- Assignments scored with rubrics
- Application of writing to other subject areas and projects

Together with formal assessments, these methods can help teachers and parents watch students' writing develop throughout the year.

See Competency 2.G.

SKILL J: **Analyzes students' errors in reading and responds to individual students' needs by providing focused instruction to promote literacy acquisition**

See Informal Reading Inventories in Competency 2.G.

Providing timely feedback to students has been proven to a highly effective tool which a teacher can use to improve student achievement. Feedback is best when it is corrective in nature. Help students see their errors and learn how to correct them by providing explicit and informative feedback when returning student work. Requiring students to re-work an assignment or continue working on a task until it is completed and accurate improves student achievement.

See Competency 2.I.

SKILL K: **Selects and uses instructional materials that build on the current language competencies of individual students, including English Language Learners, to promote development from emergent literacy to conventional literacy**

Academic literacy, which encompasses ways of knowing particular content and refers to strategies for understanding, discussing, organizing, and producing texts, is key to success in school. To be literate in an academic sense, one should be able to understand and articulate conceptual relationships within, between, and among disciplines. Academic literacy also encompasses critical literacy, that is, the ability to evaluate the credibility and validity of informational sources. I n a practical sense, when a student is academically literate, s/he should be able to read and understand interdisciplinary texts, articulate comprehension through expository written pieces, and further knowledge through sustained and focused research.

Children need rich materials to support their literacy development. For preschoolers, teachers can provide simple art materials such as crayons, markers, or papers for them to explore and manipulate. Teachers can also introduce emergent literacy competencies by allowing students to create menus for a restaurant, writing grocery lists, or making invitations to the classroom. Teachers can read nursery rhymes, books with photographs, or display drawings of animals, people, and brightly colored objects. Through these activities, children learn to focus their attention on words and pictures. Finger plays, songs, poems, games, chants, listening to oral readings, and discussion all help children pick up new vocabularies which helps them understand the similarities and differences in language and develop phonemic awareness. As students develop conventional literacy, teachers may incorporate audiotapes, electronic games, videotapes, and computer-based instruction.

See Competency 2.E.

Working with ESL Readers

Students who are using English as a second language may need special consideration. If they are not able to comprehend at a passing level in your class, they should be referred to an ESL or ELL class. Special classes, guidance counselors, speech pathologists, and school psychologist are available in most schools.

Developing academic literacy is especially difficult for ESL students who are struggling to acquire and improve the language and critical thinking competencies they need to become full members of the English academic mainstream community. The needs of these ESL students may be met through the creation of a functional language learning environment that engages them in meaningful and authentic language processing through planned, purposeful, and academically-based activities. This teaches them how to extract, question, and evaluate the central points and methodology of a range of materials and construct responses using the conventions of academic/expository writing.

Sustained content area study is more effectively carried out when an extensive body of instructional and informational resources, such as that which is found on the Internet, is available. Through its extensive collection of reading materials and numerous contexts for meaningful written communication and analysis of issues, the Internet creates a highly motivating learning environment that encourages ESL students to interact with language in new and varied ways. Used as a resource for focus discipline research, the Internet is highly effective in helping these students develop and refine the academic literacy so necessary for a successful educational experience.

Used as a tool for sustained content study, the Internet is a powerful resource that offers easier, wider, and more rapid access to interdisciplinary information than do traditional libraries. Using the Internet allows ESL students to control the direction of their reading and research, teaches them to think creatively, and increases motivation for learning as students work individually or collaboratively to gather information. By allowing easy access to cross-referenced documents and screens, Internet hypertext encourages students to read widely on interdisciplinary topics. This type of reading presents cognitively demanding language in a wide range of linguistic forms and enables ESL students to build a wider range of schemata and a broader base of knowledge, which may help them grasp future texts. Additionally, hypermedia provides the benefit of immediate visual reinforcement through pictures and/or slideshows, facilitating comprehension of the often-abstract concepts presented in academic readings.

Academic research competencies are often underdeveloped in the ESL student population making research reports especially frightening and enormously challenging. Instruction that targets the development of research competencies teaches ESL students the rhetorical conventions of term papers, which subsequently leads to better writing and improved performance in class. Moreover, the research competencies acquired through sustained content study and research enable students to manage information more effectively which serves them throughout their academic years and upon entering the workforce.

COMPETENCY 003   **WORD IDENTIFICATION COMPETENCIES AND READING FLUENCY**

SKILL A: **Understands that many students develop word analysis competencies and reading fluency in a predictable sequence and recognizes that individual variations occur**

Structural Word Analysis

Word analysis (a.k.a. phonics or decoding) is the process readers use to decode unfamiliar words based on written patterns Word recognition is the process of automatically determining the pronunciation and some degree of the meaning of an unknown word. In other words, fluent readers recognize most written words easily and correctly without consciously decoding or breaking them down.

To decode means to change communication signals into messages. Reading comprehension requires that the reader learn the code within which a message is written and can decode it to get the message. Encoding involves changing a message into symbols. For example, a student can encode oral language into writing (spelling), encode an idea into words (writing), or encode a mathematical or physical idea into appropriate mathematical symbols (mathematics/computations).

Although effective reading comprehension requires identifying words automatically, children do not have to be able to identify every single word or know the exact meaning of every word in a text to understand it. Indeed, Nagy (1988) says that children can read a book with a high level of comprehension even if they do not fully know as many as 15 percent of the words within a given text.

Teachers should know students will develop word analysis competencies that include the learning of phonetically regular words in a simple-to-complex progression (i.e., phonemes, blending onsets, short vowels, consonant blends, consonant patterns, and syllables). Since students develop word analysis competencies in a predictable sequence, the development of reading fluency occurs because the word meanings learned earlier are prerequisites to understanding word meanings that are taught later.

However, teachers need to be aware that individual variations may occur due to various influencing factors. Students who have had a rich vocabulary exposure in the home environment tend to have parents who read to them, exposing them to language experiences that promote early literacy by actively explain word meanings during conversation, story reading, etc.

Young readers may develop literacy acquisition at uneven times due to experiencing difficulties linking speech sounds to letters which is a fair indicator that their word analysis competencies are weak resulting in very slow reading. This awkward reading almost always makes reading fluency very difficult.

For more information on decoding, see Competencies 3.M and 3.N.

See Competencies 1.A, 2.A, 2.C, and 2.E.

SKILL B: **Understands differences in students' development of word identification competencies and reading fluency and knows instructional practices for meeting students' individual needs in these areas**

Word identification competencies help individuals recognize unknown words accurately and rapidly. These competencies include phonetic, structural, and contextual analysis. Word identification competencies are important for secondary struggling readers in content-area classes. Here, students are required to read large amounts of text that often contain multisyllabic words the students may not know. Students need word identification competencies to tackle these unknown words. The ability to decode unknown words rapidly and accurately is necessary for effective and efficient comprehension.

When students do not recognize words with automaticity, they spend time on decoding that could be devoted to comprehending text. The goal of word identification instruction for secondary students is to help students develop and apply strategies for tackling unfamiliar or difficult words accurately, effortlessly, and rapidly.

Instructional Guidelines for Teaching Word Identification Competencies

Explicit, systematic instruction is an effective procedure for teaching word identification competencies and strategies.

- Words should be taken from the content-area materials that students have difficulty reading in the context of their classes
- Students should possess basic word identification competencies which include the following: sound-symbol correspondence, recognition of phonetically regular consonant-vowel-consonant words, and recognition of some sight or high frequency words
- Word identification competencies include phonetic analysis, structural analysis, and contextual analysis to read multisyllabic words

Some research-based interventions for teaching word identification competencies to secondary struggling readers can include the following:

Word Identification Strategy: Students learn how to break words into parts to facilitate decoding. It is helpful if students know prefixes and suffixes and have a working knowledge of phonics.

Overt Word Parts Strategy: Student circle word parts at the beginning and end of the word and underline letters representing the vowel sounds in the remaining part of the word. Students pronounce the parts to say the word.

Making Words: Students use their knowledge of sound-letter correspondences, orthographic patterns, structural analysis, and content-specific vocabulary to form words.

Strategies for English-language learners can include teaching words with vowel combinations because these words may be difficult for English language learners. Also, correct differences in speech sounds judiciously because some speech sounds in English may be different from those of the students' first language. Various materials can be used to develop word identification competencies which may include: syllable puzzles, letters to form words, lists of words from content-area texts, and lists of prefixes and suffixes. Curriculum Associates, Good Apple, and Sopris West are some examples of publishers that offer age-appropriate materials for word identification competencies.

How Words Are Built

Knowledge of how words are built can help students with basic and more advanced decoding.

Morphology

Morphology is the study of word structure. When readers develop morphemic competencies, they are developing an understanding of patterns they see in words. For example, English speakers realize that cat, cats, and caterpillar share some similarities in structure. This understanding helps readers recognize words at a faster and easier rate, since each word doesn't need individual decoding.

A *root word* is the primary base of a word. A *prefix* is the affix (a morpheme that attaches to a base word) that is placed at the start of a root word but can't make a word on its own. Examples of prefixes include re-, pre-, and un-. A *suffix* follows the root word to which it attaches and appears at the end of the word. Examples of suffixes include –s, -es, -ed, -ly, and –tion. In the word unlikely, "un" is the prefix, "like" is the root word, and "ly" is the suffix.

Contractions are shortened forms of two words in which a letter or letters have been deleted. These deleted letters have been replaced by an apostrophe.

Compound words occur when two or more base words are connected to form a new word. The meaning of the new word is, in some way, connected with that of the base word.

Syntax and Semantics

Syntax refers to the rules or patterned relationships that correctly create phrases and sentences from words. When readers develop an understanding of syntax, they begin to understand the structure of how sentences are built and, eventually, the beginning of grammar.

Example: "I am going to the movies."
This statement is syntactically and grammatically correct

Example: "They am going to the movies."
This statement is syntactically correct since all the words are in their correct place, but it is grammatically incorrect with the use of the word "They" rather than "I."

Semantics refers to the meaning expressed when words are arranged in a specific way. This is where connotation and denotation of words eventually will have a role with readers. These Competency sets are important to eventually developing effective word recognition competencies which help emerging readers develop fluency.

Pragmatics

Pragmatics is concerned with the difference between the writer's meaning and the sentence meaning (the literal meaning of the sentence) based on social context. When someone is competent in pragmatics, he or she can understand the writer's intended meaning of what the writer is trying to convey. In a simpler sense, pragmatics can be considered the social rules of language.

For example, a child sitting beside her mother at a fancy restaurant after her great-grandmother's funeral looks over at the table next to them. She sees a very elderly woman eating her dessert. "Mom?" she asks, patiently waiting for a response. When her mother addresses her, she states loudly, "That woman is old like Grandma. Is she going away soon, too?" Of course, embarrassed, the mother hushes her child. However, this is a simple example of immature pragmatics. The child has the vocabulary, the patience to wait her turn, and some knowledge of conversational rules; however, she is not aware that certain topics are socially inappropriate and, therefore, adapts her language to the situation.

Contextual Redefinition

This strategy helps students use context more effectively by presenting them with sufficient context BEFORE they begin reading. It models the use of contextual clues to make informed guesses about word meanings.

To apply this strategy, first select unfamiliar words for teaching. No more than two or three words should be selected for direct teaching. Present the words only on the experiential chart or as letter cards. The children should pronounce the words. As they pronounce them, they should be challenged to come up with a definition for each word. After more than one definition is offered, they should decide, as a whole group, what the definition is. The children can then write down their agreed upon definition with no comment as to its true meaning.

Then the children should be given a sentence in which there are sufficient clues supplied for them to successfully figure out the meaning. Among the types of context clues that can be used are: compare/contrast, synonyms, and direct definition. The children should read the sentences aloud and come up with another definition for each word. They should justify their definitions by making specific references to the context clues in the sentences.

Then the children can discuss the differences between their guesses about the word when they saw only the word itself and their guesses about the word when they read it in context. Finally, the children can check their use of context competencies to correctly define the word by using a dictionary.

This type of direct teaching of word definitions is useful when the children have dictionary competencies and the teacher knows there are not sufficient clues about the words to help the students define them. In addition, struggling readers and students from ELL backgrounds may benefit tremendously from being walked through this process that highly proficient and successful readers apply automatically.

By using this strategy, the teacher can also "kid watch" and note the students' prior knowledge as they guess the word in isolation. The teacher can also actually witness and hear how various students use context competencies.

Through their involvement in this strategy, struggling readers gain a feeling of community as they experience the ways in which their struggles and guesses resonate in other peers' responses to the text. They are also getting a chance to be "walked through" this maze of meaning, and they are learning how to use context clues in order to navigate it themselves.

Using Pictures & Visualization

The use of books that include both text and pictorial scenes can further stimulate a child's ability to understand how pictures can be used to tell a story or provide a symbol for a word. For example, in a beginning reader book, the word "apple" can be written using letters on one page and a picture of an apple on the opposite page so that children see that a visual apple has a written equivalent.

Studies have shown that good readers form mental pictures as they read. Readers who use visualization techniques have better comprehension scores than those who do not visualize. Good teachers encourage their students to visualize the setting, characters, and/or events being read about.

Visualization can be taught explicitly; teaching strategies help the student form pictures in the mind. These strategies can include activities like reading descriptions and relating to prior knowledge of what something looks like or what something similar looks like. Cooperative learning groups can discuss what the mental pictures might be, sharing prior knowledge with each other and increasing the visual images for all. Helping students learn to use visualization in combination with other reading strategies will enhance reading comprehension.

SKILL C: Understands the connection of word identification competencies and reading fluency to reading comprehension

Word Analysis Competencies & Reading Comprehension

The explicit teaching of word analysis requires that the teacher pre-select words from a given text for vocabulary learning. These words should be chosen based on the storyline and main ideas of the text. Create a story map for a narrative text or develop a graphic organizer for an expository text. Once the story mapping and/or graphic organizing have been done, compile a list of words which relates to the storyline and/or main ideas. Next, decide which key words are already well defined in the text. Obviously, these will not need explicit class review.

Identify the words that the child can determine through use of prefixes, suffixes, or base words. Again, these words will not require direct teaching. Then reflect on the words in relation to the children's background, prior knowledge base, and language experiences (including native language/dialect words). Based on the above steps, decide which words need to be taught.

The number of words that require explicit teaching should only be two or three. If the number is higher than that, the children need guided reading, and the text needs to be broken down into smaller sections for teaching. When broken down into smaller sections, each text section should only have two to three words which need explicit teaching. Some researchers, including Tierney and Cunningham, believe that a few words should be taught as a means of improving comprehension. It is up to the teacher whether the vocabulary selected for teaching needs review before, during, or after reading.

Introduce vocabulary BEFORE READING if...

- Children are having difficulty constructing meaning on their own. Children, themselves, have previewed the text and indicated words they want to know
- The teacher has seen that there are words within the text which are keys necessary for reading comprehension
- The text, itself, in the judgment of the teacher, contains difficult concepts for the children to grasp

Introduce vocabulary DURING READING if . . .

- Children are already doing guided reading
- The text has words which are crucial to its comprehension, and the children will have trouble comprehending it if they are not helped with the text

Introduce vocabulary AFTER READING if. . .

- The children themselves have shared words which they found difficult or interesting
- The children need to expand their vocabulary
- The text itself is one that is particularly suited for vocabulary building.

Strategies which can be used to support word analysis and as a vehicle for enhancing and enriching reading comprehension include:

- Use of a graphic organizer such as a word map
- Semantic mapping
- Semantic feature analysis
- Hierarchical and linear arrays
- Preview in context
- Contextual redefinition
- Vocabulary self-collection

SKILL D: **Knows the continuum of word analysis competencies in the statewide curriculum and grade-level expectations for attainment of these competencies**

Per the Texas Essential Knowledge and Competencies (TEKS), expectations for word analysis competencies are as follows:

- The student is expected to rely on context to determine meanings of words and phrases such as figurative language, idioms, multiple-meaning words, and technical vocabulary
- Apply meanings of prefixes, roots, and suffixes to comprehend
- Use reference materials such as glossaries, dictionaries, thesauruses, and available technology to determine precise meanings and usage

SKILL E: **Knows how students develop fluency in oral and silent reading**

When children begin to learn to read, they bring to the task a set of well-developed oral language comprehension competencies. These competencies, developed in a remarkably short period of time, are relative and important to the task of learning to read. Learning to read is not only learning the language but also learning to decode *symbols* for the language they already know. A child's language competencies continue to develop as s/he grows, and learning to read plays a role in that development.

In reading, that is, in visually decoding the written words, aspects of the spoken word play a role including stress, intonation, and other prosodic features. Temporal characteristics of speech, such as pauses and changes in speed, often provide clues for the chunking of words into larger constituents. Also, pauses and breaths occur at the ends of sentences. Pauses at phrase and clause boundaries increase comprehension. We rely on stress in spoken language to communicate those boundaries and convey meaning.

Even so, written language does have some compensatory aspects. Paragraph demarcations, for example, are an organizational aid not available in oral language. Also, the ability to look back over passages that have been previously read and make corrections the second time around is only available in writing. A major strategy a student must develop is a method for using the permanence of text, for example, keeping some structure of the text in mind to facilitate looking back and checking a fact. In oral language, of course, the listener may just ask for clarification.

3. Reading materials are used that students would be unable to read independently

Experts recommend that a beginning reading program should incorporate partner reading, practice of reading difficult words prior to reading the text, timings for accuracy and rate, opportunities to hear books read, and opportunities to read to others.

Prosody

Prosody concerns versification of text and involves such matters as which syllable of a word is accented. With regards to fluency, it is that aspect which translates reading into the same experience as listening within the reader's mind. It involves intonation and rhythm through such devices as syllable accent and punctuation.

See Competency 2.G.

SKILL G: **Knows factors affecting students' word identification competencies and reading fluency**

Learning to Read

In 2000, the National Reading Panel released its now well-known report on teaching children to read. In a way, this report slightly put to rest the debate between phonics and whole-language. It argued, essentially, that word-letter recognition was important as well as understanding what the text means. The report's "big 5" critical areas of reading instruction are as follows:

- Phonemic Awareness: The acknowledgement of sounds and words. The key in phonemic awareness is that when you teach it to children, it can be taught with the students' eyes closed. In other words, it's all about sounds not about ascribing written letters to sounds.
- Phonics: As opposed to phonemic awareness, the study of phonics must be done with the eyes open. It's the connection between the sounds and letters on a page.
- Fluency: See Competency 3.F
- Comprehension: Comprehension simply means that the reader can ascribe meaning to text.
  Content area vocabulary: The specific vocabulary related to the concepts of various academic disciplines (social science, science, math, art, etc.).

Research on reading development has yielded information on the behaviors and habits of good readers vs. poor readers. Some of the characteristics of good readers are:

- They think about the information that they will read in the text, formulate questions that they predict will be answered, and confirm those predictions from the information they read

- When faced with unfamiliar words, they attempt to pronounce them using analogies to familiar words
- Before reading, good readers establish a purpose for reading, select possible text structure, choose a reading strategy, and make predictions about what will be in the reading
- As they read, good readers continually test and confirm their predictions, go back when something does not make sense, and make new predictions

Delays in Reading Development

While we can anticipate that certain competencies can be mastered by certain ages, all children are different. But when development is too far off the general target, then intervention may be necessary. By their third year, children have more advanced competencies in listening and speaking. Within the next few years, children are capable of using longer sentences, retelling parts of stories, counting, and "scribbling" messages. They are capable of learning the basics of phonemic awareness.

At about five years old, children are ready to start in on phonics. Many teachers mistake phonics as being just a step in the process toward comprehension when, in fact, children are fully capable of learning how to comprehend and make meaning at the same age. Phonics will, ideally, be mastered by second to third grade.

As young students enter and work through the emergent stage of literacy, some common difficulties may be noticed by the teacher. Some of these common problems include:

- Difficulty maintaining concentration
- Finding the appropriate text level
- Frustration with not being able to understand the text
- Limited vocabulary hindering comprehension

Strategies for Assisting with Reading Delays

For students experiencing problems with concentration, make sure their desks are away from distractions and that their overall learning environment is comfortable and well lit. Try to encourage the student to work for set amounts of time and then, as the student's concentration improves, increase the amount of time.

To help students select appropriate reading material, it is often helpful to organize your classroom library by level. For example, simpler texts may be labeled with a yellow dot, grade-level texts may be labeled with a red dot, and challenging texts may be labeled with a green dot. This helps students see which books may best suit their comfortable reading needs.

When students become frustrated and feel they do not understand the text, encourage students to break down the text into chunks. Then, after each chunk, encourage students to ask themselves questions about what they have read to improve understanding.

Limited vocabulary can often get in the way of a student's comprehension of a text. Have the students focus on the structure of words to help decode unfamiliar words. A helpful tip is for students to record new words in a notebook to create a personal glossary for each student. This way, students can refer to a dictionary with their list of words, when necessary, to help build their vocabulary.

Additional Strategies

Reading aloud to children helps them acquire information and competencies such as the meaning of words, how a book works, a variety of writing styles, information about their world, differences between conversations and written language, and the knowledge of printed letters and words along with the relationship between sound and print. Using different types of books assures that each child will find at least a few books that meet his or her interests and preferences.

Children's storybooks are traditional favorites for many young students. Some children prefer to see books that have informational text such as those about animals, nature, transportation, careers, or travel. Alphabet books, picture dictionaries, and books with diagrams and overlays (such as those about the human body) catch the interest of children as well. Some children particularly enjoy books containing poetry, children's songs and verses, or folktales. Offering different types of books also gives flexibility in choosing one or two languages in which to read a story.

Illustrations for young children should support the meaning of the text, and language patterns and predictable text structures should make these texts appealing to struggling readers. The teacher should model for the child how to reference an illustration for help in identifying a word in the text the child does not recognize.
Finally, children, particularly the emergent and beginning early readers, benefit from reading books with partners. The partners sit side by side, and each one takes turns reading the entire text.

Children with Special Needs

Introducing language and literacy experiences through concrete, multi-sensory approaches will provide many children with disabilities the support they need to build the foundation for decoding words and understanding meaning. Having access to early literacy activities as part of the curriculum is key to the educational success of all children, including children with mild to severe disabilities. Each child's unique learning needs should be considered in a comprehensive approach to early literacy.

SKILL H: **Understands important phonetic elements and conventions of the English language**

A phoneme is the smallest contrastive unit in a language system and the representation of a sound. The phoneme is said to have mental, physiological, and physical substance: our brains process the sounds; the sounds are produced by the human speech organs; and the sounds are physical entities that can be recorded and measured.

For more information on phonics and phonological awareness, see Competencies 2.A and 3.I.

Common English Conventions

See Competency 6.B.

SKILL I: **Knows a variety of informal and formal procedures for assessing students' word identification competencies and reading fluency on an ongoing basis and uses appropriate assessments to monitor students' performance in these areas and to plan instruction for individual students, including English Language Learners**

Informal assessments for children's word-analysis and decoding competencies include such things as:

- **Oral reading records -** In this procedure, the teacher has a copy of the text that the student reads. S/he marks the words the student reads correctly, whether the students does not know a word at all and has to be told what the word is, or whether the student makes a mistake and then self-corrects. When students self-correct, the teacher can make note of what the student does. This type of assessment is intended to monitor ongoing progress in reading, identify the particular competencies and strategies students are using, focus on the specific needs of individual students, group students with similar needs, and help students choose books that are at the appropriate reading levels
- **List of sight words** - There are many lists of grade level sight words that teachers can use as an informal assessment of what words students readily recognize. When teachers have individual students read a list of words, a record can be made of groups of sounds for which students need instruction

- **Guided reading** - Guided reading is one of the components of a balanced literacy framework in which the teacher works with a small group of students who need help with a particular reading strategy. The teacher focuses on one strategy in the lesson and then has the students practice that strategy in other tasks

Some of the different methods that teachers can employ to assess for learning involve both formative and summative evaluation. Since formative assessment consists of testing, these do play a part. However, teachers can make summative assessment part of their daily routine by using such measures as:

- Anecdotal records
- Portfolios
- Listening to children read
- Oral presentations
- Checklists
- Running records
- Samples of work
- Self-evaluation

- Information gathered from these sources provides the teacher with the needed material to determine how much help students require to become independent readers and to communicate to parents about how their children are doing.

Assessing Phonological and Phonemic Awareness

Assessing phonological and phonemic awareness is designed for two purposes: to screen for problems and to monitor progress during instruction. Further, some assessments identify components of phonological development in which the student is weakest, thus requiring more intense focus on that Competency.

Two major difficulties in assessing phonological and phonemic awareness can potentially negate the benefit of such assessment. The first is the tendency to assess broad domains of emergent competencies rather than discrete abilities. The second is the individual variations in oral prompts being presented. These can be avoided, first, by choosing assessments that include measurement of the individual components that make up phonological awareness and, second, by using computer programs that pronounce phonemes and words for the student being assessed. If this is not possible, the same person should be responsible for assessment during the school year.

There are several different competencies involved in phonological awareness.

Some of these competencies are:

1. Rhyme recognition
2. Rhyme application
3. Oddity tasks: Beginning sounds
4. Oddity tasks: Ending sounds
5. Oddity tasks: Middle sounds
6. Blending body-codas
7. Blending onset-rimes
8. Blending phonemes
9. Segmenting onset-rimes
10. Segmenting phonemes
11. Phoneme deletion
12. Phoneme Substitution: Beginning sounds
13. Phoneme Substitution: Ending sounds
14. Phoneme Substitution: Middle sounds

Children who have problems with phonics generally have not been exposed to or successfully acquired phonemic awareness activities usually fostered at home and in preschool-2nd grade.

SKILL J: Analyzes students' errors in word analysis and uses the results of this analysis to inform future instruction

Teachers may need to perform a close analysis of a child's spelling of each word to provide the key to the stage of spelling development attained to determine which spelling strategies need to be emphasized in the teaching program. Teachers may need to implement visual strategies such as teaching students to look for highly predictable patterns or letter sequences of English. Teachers may also need to teach morphemic strategies by encouraging students to learn meanings by what they represent and not the actual spelling of the word. Students need to learn how to develop sound symbol strategies recognizing that letter-sound correlation is different in different words.

Common Language Errors:

- Applying a general rule to all cases even when there are exceptions
- Trying to cut corners by using an incorrect word or syntactic form
- Avoiding use of precise vocabulary or idiomatic expressions
- Using incorrect verb tense

SKILL K: **Applies norms and expectations for word identification competencies and reading fluency, as specified in the Texas Essential Knowledge and Competencies (TEKS), to evaluate students' reading performance**

See Competencies 2.G, 3.D, and 3.M.

SKILL L: **Knows how to use ongoing assessment of word identification competencies and reading fluency to determine when a student needs additional help or intervention to bring the student's performance to grade level, based on state content and performance standards for reading in the Texas Essential Knowledge and Competencies (TEKS)**

See Competency 3.I.

SKILL M: **Knows strategies for decoding increasingly complex words, including using the alphabetic principle, structural cues, and syllables, and for using syntax and semantics to support word identification and confirm word meaning**

Alphabetic Principle

The Alphabetic Principle is sometimes called graphophonemic awareness. This multi-syllabic technical reading foundation term details the understanding that written words are composed of patterns of letters which represent the sounds of spoken words.

There are basically two parts to the alphabetic principle:

- An understanding that words are made up of letters and that each of these letters has a specific sound
- The correspondence between sounds and letters leads to phonological reading. This consists of reading regular and irregular words and doing advanced analysis of words

Since the English language is dependent on the alphabet, being able to recognize and sound out letters is the first step for beginning readers. Relying simply on memorization for recognition of words is just not feasible as a way for children to learn to recognize words. Therefore, decoding is essential. The most important goal of beginning reading teachers is to teach students to decode text so that they can read fluently and with understanding.

There are four basic features of the alphabetic principle:

1. Students need to be able to take spoken words apart and blend different sounds together to make new words
2. Students need to apply letter sounds to all their reading
3. Teachers need to use a systematic, effective program to teach children to read
4. The teaching of the alphabetic principle usually begins in Kindergarten

It is important to keep in mind that some children already know the letters and sounds before they come to school. Others may catch on to this quite quickly and, still others, need to have one-on-one instruction to learn to read.

Critical competencies that students need to learn are:

- Letter-sound correspondence
- How to sound out words
- How to decode text to make meaning

For information on context cues, syntax and semantics, see Competency 3.B.

SKILL N: **Selects and uses instructional strategies, materials, activities, and models to teach students to recognize high-frequency irregular words, to promote students' ability to decode increasingly complex words, and to enhance word identification competencies for students reading at different levels**

Decoding text is age appropriate for children who have existing knowledge of the reading material. When children decode words, they can read single words and understand meaning of single words as singular entities in a textual context. There is a foundational pattern to language acquisition that children must first develop before the complexity of decoding text can begin. Children must be able to learn individual alphabet sounds and understand that each letter has a sound. As students progress from alphabet sound, they can learn about how letters are put together to form words that produce different sounds and meanings. Children develop the ability to decode and recognize words automatically. They then can extend their ability to decode to multi-syllabic words.

Tasks for assessing word-analysis and decoding competencies can be grouped into three categories:

- comparing sounds
- blending phonemes into words
- segmenting words into phonemes

Procedures for assessing how students compare sounds are the easiest to use. Teachers can ask the student which words begin with the same sound or ask them to find words that rhyme. Teachers need to assess the students' general level of phonemic awareness in order to adjust the instructional time and effort in accordance with students' prior knowledge and needs.

Teachers can use a list of words and ask the students to read the words. When students have difficulty, the teacher should ask them to try to sound out the word and make note of the strategies used. Another informal assessment is to use cards with letters on them. Ask the students to make the sound of the letter. They can also use cards with nonsense words on them that contain various combinations of consonants and vowels. A checklist of various phonemes is also helpful in recording students' needs. These would include such items as:

- identify individual phonemes
- identify patterns of phonemes
- categorize phonemes
- blends
- segmenting words into phonemes
- adding phonemes
- substituting phonemes

The best way to assess students' reading needs is to use decodable texts for informal reading tests. Decodable texts help students develop decoding abilities. Beginning readers are encouraged to sound out words and rely on phonetic cues. Once the strategies are in place, these readers can read short texts easily and quickly.

Teachers should assess for learning early in the school year, preferably during the month of September. They can then make note of which strategies students use and which ones they need to be taught. The teacher can then plan the instruction based on these needs and assess at regular intervals.

Teachers can provide a multitude of opportunities for children to progress from sounding out words orally to decoding words silently. When a child decodes a text that is age appropriate, he or she can look at the spelling and pronunciation of specific words that are familiar. *The Cat in the Hat* series provides children with story scenarios that are rhythmic and patterned. Crucial to decoding is the child's knowledge of word meaning from prior knowledge and current word usage.

Classroom and social interactions that create child-centered opportunities to question, respond, and decode the world around them can create bridges of understanding in decoding simple and complex words, as well as language, into smaller understandable chunks of relevant information. Providing children with lessons and activities that require decoding to understand a context of meaning will provide practice for decoding mechanics. For example, children who are engaged in a dramatic play must understand the simple phrases that constitute meaning for the parts they portray. Having that incentive to use decoding competencies will promote the acquisition of language development.

Teaching New Vocabulary

Now, how do content area teachers teach vocabulary? First and foremost, teachers should help students learn strategies to figure out the meanings for difficult vocabulary when they encounter it on their own. Teachers can do this by teaching students how to identify the meanings of words in context (usually through activities where the word is taken out and the students must figure out a way to make sense of the sentence). In addition, dictionary competencies must be taught in all subject areas.

When teachers explicitly teach vocabulary, it is best when they connect new words to other words, ideas, and experiences with which students are already familiar. This will help to reduce the strangeness of the new words. Furthermore, the more concrete the examples are, the more likely students will know how to use the word in context.

When high frequency, irregular words are isolated from the contextual resources and presented to children as activities that require definition, pronunciation, application, and synthesis, children can master and internalize the words more thoroughly. Classroom and learning opportunities which include exposure to irregular words are beneficial for children seeking to increase reading, vocabulary, and communication competencies.

Language and oral development are contingent upon children being provided with a diversity of word applications for use in language development and oral communication. As more irregular words are constantly being added to the dictionary, a child's vocabulary list is becoming inclusive of irregular words that are now becoming today's regular words in communication and written application.

Finally, students need plenty of exposure to the new words. They need to be able to hear and use the new words in many naturally-produced sentences. A child's ability to recognize high-frequency, irregular words through a selection process of choosing words in regular children's books and reviewing difficult words frequently can provide a comprehensive vocabulary list. When children learn the decoding of regular words in children's books, the foundational learning of decoding strategies can help children recognize and provide phonetic pronunciation for new words.

SKILL O: **Selects and uses appropriate instructional strategies, materials, activities, and models to improve reading fluency for students reading at different levels**

Students who have not achieved fluency tend to read word-to-word or create unnatural groupings, and their reading is usually monotonous, reflecting their inability to transfer prosodic elements that occur naturally in speech onto written text.

A repeated-reading strategy has been demonstrated to be successful in developing fluency. If a student is reading a story with which s/he is familiar, attention can be given to developing fluency since it will not be necessary to concentrate on the content as much. The teacher can concentrate on teaching oral reading competencies more easily if the story is already known.

Echo-reading text twice, followed by the students' reading without the echo, has been demonstrated to promote fluency. A variation of genres is useful in these exercises because students need to learn to reflect in their oral reading phrasing, pitch, and emphasis, typical of fluent readers. Reading poetry in addition to prose has been shown to be advantageous in these exercises.

Differentiated Instruction

The effective teacher will seek to connect all students to the subject matter through multiple techniques with the goal that each student, through their own abilities, will relate to one or more techniques and excel in the learning process.

Differentiated instruction encompasses several areas:

- Content: What is the teacher going to teach? Or, perhaps better put, what does the teacher want the students to learn? Differentiating content means that students will have access to content that piques their interest about a topic, with a complexity that provides an appropriate challenge to their intellectual development
- Process: A classroom management technique where instructional organization and delivery is maximized for the diverse student group. These techniques should include dynamic, flexible grouping activities, where instruction and learning occurs both as whole-class, teacher-led activities, as well as peer learning and teaching (while the teacher observes and coaches) within small groups or pairs
- Product: The expectations and requirements placed on students to demonstrate their knowledge or understanding. The type of product expected from each student should reflect each student's own capabilities

DOMAIN II.

LANGUAGE ARTS, PART II: READING COMPREHENSION, WRITTEN LANGUAGE, STUDY AND INQUIRY, AND VIEWING AND REPRESENTING

COMPETENCY 004   READING COMPREHENSION AND ASSESSMENT

SKILL A: Understands reading comprehension as an active process of constructing meaning

All text contains a message. Even when a child cannot read the words and instead "play reads" text using pictures and memory, the child demonstrates an understanding of this concept. Comprehension is important to literacy because it is the reason and purpose behind reading (i.e., we learn to read, so we can read to learn).

The concept that print carries meaning is demonstrated every day in the elementary classroom as the teacher holds up a selected book to read it aloud to the class. The teacher should explicitly and deliberately think out loud about how to hold the book, how to focus the class on looking at its cover, where to start reading, and in what direction to begin. Even in writing the morning message on the board, the teacher provides a lesson on print concepts. The children see that the message is placed at the top of the board and then is followed by additional activities and a schedule for the rest of the day.

Children become curious about printed symbols once they recognize that print, like talk, conveys meaningful messages that direct, inform, or entertain people. By school age, many children are eager to continue their exploration of print.

The goal is to develop fluent and proficient readers who are knowledgeable about the reading process. Effective reading instruction should enable students to eventually become self-directed readers who can:

- Construct meaning from various types of print material
- Recognize that there are different kinds of reading materials and different purposes for reading
- Select strategies appropriate for different reading activities
- Develop a life-long interest and enjoyment in reading a variety of material for different purposes

To assist teachers in achieving these goals, apply the use of a wide variety of fiction and non-fiction resources including:

- environmental signs and labels
- rhymes, chants, and songs
- poetry
- wordless picture books

- predictable books
- cumulative stories
- maps
- charts
- novels
- print resources from all subject areas
- notes, messages, and letters
- folktales
- myths and legends
- writing by students and teachers
- newspapers, magazines, and pamphlets
- mysteries

The resources shared with students should stimulate their imaginations and kindle their curiosity. Familiarization with narrative and expository materials and frequent opportunities to write in all subject areas facilitate the reading process. By becoming authors themselves, students increase their awareness of the organization and structures of printed language.

To read for meaning, students must simultaneously utilize clues from all cueing systems. Readers bring knowledge and past experiences to the reading task to construct interpretations and to determine if the print makes sense to them. It is easier for readers to understand print when the content is relevant to their personal experiences.

Familiar content and topics convey meaning or clues through the semantic cueing system. When students are comfortable and familiar with the content of a passage, they can predict upcoming text and take greater risks in reading. Research has repeatedly shown that fluent readers risk more guesses when interacting with unfamiliar print than poorer readers. They derive more meaning from passages than readers who frequently stop to sound or decode words by individual phonemes or letters.

Reading experiences that focus on relevant and familiar content, vocabulary, and language patterns increase students' chances of constructing meaning and being successful readers. At the middle school level, successful reading experiences reaffirm students' confidence as language users and learners. The holistic approach to the reading process stresses the importance of presenting students with whole and meaningful reading passages. This approach is based on the principle that the readers' understanding of an entire sentence, passage, or story facilitates the reading and comprehension of individual words within those passages.

SKILL B: **Understand the continuum of reading comprehension competencies in the statewide curriculum and grade-level expectations for these competencies**

Students need to be aware of their comprehension, or lack of it, in particular texts. So, it is important to teach students what to do when the text suddenly stops making sense. For example, students can go back and re-read the description of a character. They could also go back to the table of contents or the first paragraph of a chapter to see where they are headed.

The point of comprehension instruction is not necessarily to focus just on the text(s) students are using at the very moment of instruction but, rather, to help them learn the strategies that they can use independently with any other text. Some of the most common methods of teaching comprehension are listed here.

Summarization

This is where, either in writing or verbally, students go over the main point of the text and strategically choose details that highlight the main point. This is not the same as paraphrasing, which is saying the same thing in different words. Teaching students how to summarize is very important, as it will help them look for the most critical areas in a text. For example, it will help them distinguish between main arguments and examples. In fiction, it helps students learn how to focus on the main characters and events and distinguish those from the lesser characters and events.

Question Answering

While this tends to be over-used in many classrooms, it is still a valid method of teaching students to comprehend. As the name implies, students answer questions regarding a text either out loud, in small groups, or individually on paper. The best questions are those that cause students to have to think about the text (rather than just find an answer within the text).

Question Generating

This is the opposite of question answering as students use the text to generate their own questions about what was read. Students can then be asked to answer their own questions or the questions of peer students. In general, teachers want students to constantly question texts as they read. This is important because it causes students to become more critical readers. To teach students to generate questions helps them to learn the types of questions they can ask. This gets them thinking about how best to be critical of texts.

Making Connections

Making connections involves three areas: text-to-self, text-to-text, and text-to-world. In text-to-self, the student connects what is being read to personal prior knowledge (something previously experienced or that the student is knowledgeable about). In text-to-text, the student connects what is being read to another reading passage. In text-to-world, the student connects what is being read to prior knowledge that involves the world.

Prompts that help a student make connections in reading are:

- **text-to-self**
  - That reminds me of…
  - That made me think of the time…
  - I can relate…

- **Text-to-Text Connection**
  - This part is just like…
  - That reminds me of…
  - I read another book where…
  - This is similar to…

- **Text-to-World Connections**
  - That reminds me of…
  - This is like…
  - I know about this… but I didn't know that

Making Predictions

With this strategy, students are asked to make their own predictions about what will happen in the text to come. Teachers encourage students at the end of a section or chapter to project possible scenarios about what they think will happen. It is helpful for students to write down these predictions and then, as they read, they can see if these predictions are confirmed or not. Making predictions keeps students actively engaged in what they are reading as they are required to stop and think about what was read to make their prediction about what may come.

Inferential Comprehension

One theory or approach to the teaching of reading that gained currency in the late sixties and the early seventies was the importance of asking inferential and critical thinking questions which would challenge and engage the children in the text. This approach to reading went beyond the literal level of what was stated in the text to an inferential level using text clues to make predictions and to a critical level involving the child in evaluating the text.

To draw inferences and make conclusions, a reader must use prior knowledge and apply it to the current situation. A conclusion or inference is never stated. You must rely on your common sense. An example of making inferences and drawing conclusions can be seen in the following sample question.

Read the following passage:

> The Smith family waited patiently around carousel number 7 for their luggage to arrive. They were exhausted after their 5-hour trip and were anxious to get to their hotel. After about an hour, they realized that they no longer recognized any of the other passengers' faces. Mrs. Smith asked the person who appeared to be in charge if they were at the right carousel. The man replied, "Yes, this is it, but we finished unloading that baggage almost half an hour ago."

From the man's response we can infer that:

(A) The Smiths were ready to go to their hotel.
(B) The Smith's luggage was lost.
(C) The man had their luggage.
(D) They were at the wrong carousel.

Since the Smiths were still waiting for their luggage, we know that they were not yet ready to go to their hotel. From the man's response, we know that they were not at the wrong carousel and that he did not have their luggage. Therefore, though not directly stated, it appears that their luggage was lost. Choice (B) is the correct answer.

See Competency 4.M.

5th & 6th Grade Reading Expectations

1. Determine the definition, various meanings, and structure of content-specific vocabulary by using syntax (parts of speech), context clues, and phonetics.
2. Demonstrate the ability to use glossaries, dictionaries, and indexes.
3. Distinguish between statements of fact and opinion.
4. Sequence events.
5. Follow a series of written directions in a text.
6. Determine the stated or implied main idea and supporting details in text.
7. Read for literal comprehension.
8. Paraphrase and summarize information from a variety of written works.
9. Identify cause and effect.
10. Interpret visual information (for example, maps, lists, flowcharts, graphs, tables, charts, diagrams, and timelines).
11. Identify literary elements such as character, plot, and setting.

7th Grade Reading Expectations

1. Identify conflict.

8th Grade Reading Expectations

1. Demonstrate the ability to use a thesaurus.
2. Identify point of view.
3. Identify literary devices (such as similes and metaphors).

SKILL C: **Understands factors affecting students' reading comprehension**

See Competency 3.G.

Environmental/Cultural Factors

Environmental factors affecting a child's literacy development include: (1) parents' attitudes and beliefs about early learning; (2) the nature and extent of parent-child interactions and other experiences that support the kinds of learning that schools tend to expect from children; and (3) social conventions that affect the ways in which knowledge and competencies pertinent to early learning are communicated among and used by family members. (The primary language used at home is also an important factor that affects children's adjustment to school)

Meaningful, age-appropriate reading experiences directly affect literacy development. Children benefit from environments that have high amounts of language and print-related experiences. Literacy development is also encouraged when children are asked for information with open-ended questions that challenge them to use reasoning competencies rather than simply to find the "right" answer. It is not the simple presence or absence of an activity, such as storybook reading, that most affects children's early learning. Rather, it is the language and social interaction that surround such activities that are associated with the early acquisition of literacy and numeracy competencies.

Cultural aspects of life influence children in both development and learning. Cultures may have belief systems which run counter to societal norms and, in these cases, both must be understood and respected. Sharing of information is the best strategy to ensure children's development and learning progress in appropriate manners.

In sharing aspects of various cultures, developmental patterns can be adjusted, if necessary, to ensure the child is meeting appropriate expectations for their culture. Additionally, within school systems, learning may be impacted due to language barriers or other cultural influences. It is important to respect, share, and communicate in an open manner with parents and school personnel to provide appropriate educational opportunities.

Impacts on children's literacy include expectations they bring to school about appropriate language use based on their experiences at home. Culturally-shaped conventions of conversation include wait time, the pace and call-response patterns that characterize conversations, and participation structures. The use of pauses in between questions and responses varies between differing cultures, as do accustomed ways of entering conversations and participating in group activities. The context in which children are most comfortable talking in groups also varies between cultures. In some cultures, parents engage in story-talk or co-narrating in conversation. In other cultures, an approach which involves each participant in talking exclusively for a period of time is the standard in conversation. These two extremes necessitate a different teaching approach to literacy.

See Competency "Considering Culture" in Competency 1.G.

Social & Family Factors

As children age and progress, peer influence can begin to take precedence to other factors. This is one example of how society can impact both the development and learning of students. Societal norms and attitudes can have significant impacts on the social development of children. Acceptable behavior is often at odds with children's curiosity and innate need to explore.

Additionally, children will constantly test the boundary and push the limits of social acceptability. Some children have difficulty balancing their own needs with the socially approved methods. For many students, social situations present significant problems which then impact learning.

Social interaction and conventions have significant effects on the ease and comfort with which children make the transition to school. Conversational rules and discourse patterns appear to vary widely. In some families, individuals who talk a lot are considered smart. Others families feel talking a lot is an indication of a lack of intelligence. This affects how much children will talk and how comfortable they are likely to be with demands to talk more or less. In some families, children are treated by adults as conversational partners. In others, children adopt the role of observer.

SKILL D: Knows characteristics of informal and formal reading comprehension assessments

See Competencies 2.G and 3.I for types of reading assessments.

Competencies to evaluate include the ability to:

- Understand what is happening in a story
- Use more than one example or piece of information when responding to the reading
- Ask questions regarding the reading to show analytical thinking
- Make predictions based on information from the story or from personal experiences that are similar to events in the story
- Make clear and understandable connections between the literature and personal experiences, as well as other literature the student has read

Additional Methods of Evaluation:

- Have students keep reading journals that document their reactions to the literature they are reading
- Assign free writing exercises in which students respond to any element of the story as well as prompt-driven responses in which students respond to a specified topic you assign. Make sure the prompts are created to get the students thinking deeply about the reading. An example might be, "Write about the main conflict in the story, tell why it is so important, and discuss how it is solved."
- Ask that students back up any assertions or assumptions they make with evidence from the text. This clearly demonstrates their mental comprehension processes

SKILL E: **Selects and uses appropriate informal and formal assessments to monitor and evaluate students' reading comprehension**

If students take turns reading aloud in your classroom, those who read word for word and haltingly have probably not developed reading fluency and could use some special help to improve their reading competencies. Readers who are not fluent must intentionally decode a majority of the words they encounter in a text. Fluent readers can read texts with expression or prosody (the combination that makes oral reading sound like spoken language).

If students don't read aloud in your classroom but have assignments that call for written reports, those reports will have clues to reading ability also. If sentences are poorly structured, if words are left out, and if the student is using a vocabulary s/he does not have control of, these are signs that the student's reading level is below par.

There are several reliable reading tests that can be administered to provide empirical data to assess your students' reading competencies. Some of these can be given at the beginning of the school year and at the end to let you know what impact your teaching is having.

For slow, immature readers, a special section with activities designed to improve reading may be in order. Some of the activities that might be useful are:

- Repeated readings: Using short passages, the group will read it several times, trying to improve with each reading.
- Echo reading: The teacher reads a sentence and students read after her. Once a story has been completed, use the same text and do the exercise one more time.
- Wide reading: The teacher reads a sentence and students read after her, but they move on to a new reading once the first one is finished.
- Choosing a story that the students like, such as a *Harry Potter* story, have each student read a page, going around the group, until the selection is completed.
- Discuss what the story is about, and then give an exam on the content of the reading. When the focus of an assignment is on meaning, students tend to make greater gains in comprehension than when the focus is on word analysis and accurate reading.
- Sometimes watching a dramatization of a story played on a television set or a screen will encourage an interest in reading a particular story and provide variety as well as an opportunity to think about language in spoken as well as written form.

Competencies to Evaluate:

- Ability to use syntactic cues when encountering an unknown word. A good reader will expect the word to fit the syntax with which s/he is familiar. A poor reader may substitute a word that does not fit the syntax, and will not self-correct
- Ability to use semantic cues to determine the meaning of an unknown word. A good reader will consider the meanings of all the known words in the sentence. A poor reader may read one word at a time with no regard for the other words
- Ability to use schematic cues to connect words read with prior knowledge. A good reader will incorporate what is known with what the text says or implies. A poor reader may think only of the word being read without associating it with prior knowledge
- Ability to use phonics cues to improve ease and efficiency in reading. A good reader will apply letter and sound associations almost subconsciously. A poor reader may have one of two kinds of problems: 1) underdeveloped phonics competencies and a tendency to use only an initial clue without analyzing vowel patterns before quickly guessing the word; or 2) use of phonics competencies in isolation becoming so absorbed in the word "noises" that the message of the text is ignored
- Ability to process information from text. A student should be able to get information from the text as well as store, retrieve, and integrate it for later use

- Ability to use interpretive thinking to make logical predictions and inferences
- Ability to use critical thinking to make decisions and insights about the text
- Ability to use appreciative thinking to respond to the text, whether emotionally, mentally, ideologically, etc.

See Competency 2.G for types of reading assessments.

See Competency 2.I for more information on assessing reading comprehension.

SKILL F: **Analyzes student errors and provides focused instruction in reading comprehension based on the strengths and needs of individual students, including English Language Learners**

See Competency 2.J.

SKILL G: **Knows how to use ongoing assessment to determine when a student needs additional help or intervention to bring the student's performance to grade level, based on state content and performance standards for reading in the Texas Essential Knowledge and Competencies (TEKS)**

See Competency 2.I.

SKILL H: **Understands metacognitive competencies, including self-evaluation and self-monitoring competencies, and teaches students to use these competencies to enhance their own reading comprehension**

Metacognition refers to the ability of students to be aware of and monitor their learning processes. In other words, it is the process of "thinking about thinking." Provide students with a mental checklist of factors to keep in mind while reading:

- Do I understanding what I am reading?
- Am I reading words by sounding them out?
- Am I paying attention to what I read?
- Am I reading fast enough to keep up?
- Does what I'm reading make sense?
- Am I constructing the meaning of words I don't know?

When teaching students to monitor their own comprehension, make sure students are aware of what they understand and of what they do not understand in their readings. Good readers are active, purposeful readers who use metacognition strategies. That is, they have a purpose in mind before they read.

Good readers also adjust their reading speed as the text becomes easier or more difficult; they clarify information they do not understand; they anticipate what they will read next; and they review what they have read and what they have learned from their readings.

SKILL I: **Knows how to determine students' independent, instructional, and frustration reading levels and uses this information to select and adapt reading materials for individual students, as well as to guide their selection of independent reading materials**

Books can be on one of three levels for each student: Easy, Just Right, or Challenging. Students should be encouraged to read mostly books that are a "just right" fit for them. Matching young children with "just right" books fosters their independent reading, no matter how young they are. The teacher needs to have an extensive classroom library of books. Books that emergent readers and early readers can be matched with should have large print, appropriate spacing so that the reader can easily see where word begins and ends, and few words on each page so that the young reader can focus on all important concerns of top-to-bottom, left-to-right, directionality, and the one-to-one match of oral to print.

Students should be permitted to read easy books occasionally but should also receive help in reading challenging books from time to time. In a reading log or journal, have students record titles of books they've read and the level. This way, teachers can monitor that a student is meeting their individual reading needs.

Students who have access to books and who read regularly learn to read more easily and more quickly, keep improving their reading competencies throughout their school years, perform better on language tests, are better writers, develop oral competencies and literacy in a second language more easily, have better levels of reading comprehension, have a higher vocabulary, and have better general knowledge.

So, how can we encourage reading and an enjoyment of reading? Remember, books won't work by themselves. As a teacher, you must make sure books are read by setting aside time regularly for reading. For example:

Have a DEAR period - Drop Everything and Read: Everyone can participate in a DEAR period and read for 15 minutes. This often works well right at the beginning of the school day, every day.

SSR period - Sustained silent reading: Have everyone choose a book and read without interruption for 20 to 30 minutes. Ideally, this should take place daily, but even twice a week will show results.

Independent reading sessions: Set aside one day a week for learners to select new books, read independently or in pairs, and have time to respond to the books they have read. This should take place weekly. Break time, after school and free periods are good opportunities to read.

Read with children: Taking books home is a very good option as learners can read to and with other family members. Even if children can read alone, they will still benefit from being read to.

Encourage reading of any suitable and relevant written material if books are not accessible. Try newspaper or magazine articles, street signs, food packaging labels, posters, etc. Anything can be used, provided it is at the correct level. Encourage readers to make their own material and/or bring additional material to school to read. Also, having books in a classroom is one of the easiest and most effective ways of increasing reading, linguistic and cognitive development. No other single variable can be shown to carry the same significance.

Once regular reading habits have been established, independent reading should be encouraged. Reading independently:

- Allows a learner to read, re-read, and engage with a text at their own pace
- Allows learners to choose what they want to read about and, so, motivates them to read
- Impacts language development in the areas of vocabulary and syntax
- Impacts knowledge of sight words and phonics
- Is important for second language learners as it provides a wealth of real language input

Reading for pleasure should be encouraged concurrently with teaching reading and basic literacy. Reading for pleasure is therapeutic, enlightening and paves the way for developing a culture of reading and life-long learning.

SKILL J: **Uses various instructional strategies to enhance students' reading comprehension**

Research in the area of comprehension, especially in early literacy, indicates that comprehension can be developed and that the following six strategies are particularly useful for teaching comprehension:

1. Monitor comprehension— See Competency 4.H.
2. Use graphic or semantic organizers—Graphs, word maps, and diagrams can help students identify their comprehension goals and illustrate the relationship between various concepts presented in the text.
3. Answer questions—Knowing that there are questions to answer following reading a text helps direct the purpose of reading to specific knowledge areas, and it helps students to actively think while they read.

4. Generate questions—When students create their own questions from material read, they are clarifying their own understanding of the material as well as becoming even more active in their reading by integrating material from all sections of the text.

5. Recognize story structure—Helping students recognize basic story structure (introduction, plot development, character development, and plot resolution) increases a student's appreciation of the story as well as his or her memory of the story.

6. Summarize—Have students identify the main or most important points of a text and then restate those points in their own words. This activity helps students focus on the important information, integrate elements in the text, and, most of all, remember what they read.

To discover multiple layers of meaning in a literary work, the first step is a thorough analysis, examining such things as setting, characters and characterization, plot (focusing particularly on conflicts and pattern of action), theme, tone, figures of speech, and symbolism. It's useful in looking for underlying themes to consider the author's biography, particularly about setting and theme, as well as the date and time of the writing. Encourage students to pay attention to literary undercurrents at the time of writing as well as political and social milieu.

Once the analysis is complete and data is accumulated on the historical background, determine the overt meaning. What does the story say about the characters and their conflicts? Where does the climax occur? Is there a denouement? Once the forthright, overt meaning is determined, then begin to look for undercurrents, or sub-themes, that are related to the author's life and to what is going on in the literary, political, and social background at the time of writing.

See Competency 4.B.

SKILL K: **Knows how to provide students with direct, explicit instruction in the use of strategies to improve their reading comprehension**

Reading Emphasis in Middle School

Reading for comprehension of factual material - content area textbooks, reference books, and newspapers - is closely related to study strategies in the middle/junior high. Organized study models, such as the SQ3R method, a technique that makes it possible and feasible to learn the content of even large amounts of text (Survey, Question, Read, Recite, and Review Studying), teach students to locate main ideas and supporting details, to recognize sequential order, to distinguish fact from opinion, and to determine cause/ effect relationships.

Strategies

1. Teacher-guided activities that require students to organize and summarize information based on the author's explicit intent are pertinent strategies in middle grades. Evaluation techniques include oral and written responses to standardized or teacher-made worksheets.

2. Reading of fiction introduces and reinforces competencies in inferring meaning, narration, and description. Teacher-guided activities in the process of reading for meaning should be followed by cooperative planning of the competencies to be studied and the selection of reading resources. Many printed reading for comprehension instruments, as well as individualized computer software programs, exist to monitor the progress of acquiring comprehension competencies.

3. Older middle school students should be given opportunities for more student- centered activities such as individual and collaborative selection of reading choices based on student interest, small group discussions of selected works, and greater written expression. Evaluation techniques include teacher monitoring and observation of discussions and written work samples.

4. Certain students may begin some fundamental critical interpretation - recognizing fallacious reasoning in news media; examining the accuracy of news reports and advertising; and explaining their reasons for preferring one author's writing to another's. Development of these competencies may require a more learning-centered approach in which the teacher identifies many objectives and suggested resources from which the student may choose his course of study. Self-evaluation through a reading diary should be stressed. Teacher and peer evaluation of creative projects resulting from such study is encouraged.

5. Reading aloud before the entire class as a formal means of teacher evaluation should be phased out in favor of one-to-one tutoring or peer-assisted reading. Occasional sharing of favored selections by both teacher and willing students is a good oral interpretation basic.

SKILL L: **Uses various communication modes to promote students' reading comprehension**

When preparing to present a book analysis orally, the analyst should become acquainted with the elements of the story such as setting, characterization, style (language, both technically about dialect but also structurally with regard to use of description, length of sentences, phrases, etc.), plot (particularly conflicts and patterns), tone (what is the *attitude* of the writer toward characters, theme, etc.) and theme (the message or point the story conveys). It's not essential to know the writer's biography, but it is often helpful, especially in responding from the analyst's point of view.

Literature is written to evoke a personal response in readers. This is why so many books are sold. Once the analyst has a grip on the story, then an analysis of one's own response to it is in order. The following questions are useful:

1. Do you respond emotionally to one of the characters? Why? Is a character similar to someone you know or have known?
2. Is the setting evocative for you because of a place, situation, or milieu that you have experienced that had meaning for you? Why?
3. Did the vocabulary, descriptions, or short or long sentences have impact on you? Why? For example, short, simple sentence after short, simple sentence may be used deliberately, but do you find it annoying?
4. Do you agree with the author's attitude toward the characters, setting, story, etc.? For example, has a character been written unsympathetically that you felt deserved more consideration? Does the author demonstrate a distaste for the setting he has chosen, and do you feel he is being unjust? Or do you experience the same distaste?

Reading is personal. Responding to it personally adds important dimensions to an analysis for others.

SKILL M: **Understands levels of reading comprehension and how to model and teach literal, inferential, and evaluative comprehension competencies**

An argument is a generalization that is proven or supported with facts. If the facts are not accurate, the generalization remains unproven. Using inaccurate "facts" to support an argument is called a *fallacy* in reasoning.

Some factors to consider in judging whether the facts used to support an argument are accurate are as follows:

1. Are the facts current, or are they out of date? For example, if the proposition "birth defects in babies born to drug-using mothers are increasing," then the data must include the latest that is available.
2. Another important factor to consider in judging the accuracy of a fact is its source. Where were the data obtained, and is that source reliable?
3. The calculations on which the facts are based may be unreliable. It's a good idea to run one's own calculations before using a piece of derived information.

The importance or significance of a fact may not be sufficient to strengthen an argument. For example, of the millions of immigrants in the U.S., using a single family to support a solution to the immigration problem will not make much difference overall even though those single-example arguments are often used to support one approach or another. They may achieve a positive reaction, but they will not prove that one solution is better than another. If enough cases were cited from a variety of geographical locations, the information might be significant.

How much is enough? Three strong supporting facts are sufficient to establish the thesis of an argument.

For example:

Conclusion: All green apples are sour.

> When I was a child, I bit into a green apple from my grandfather's orchard, and it was sour.

> I once bought green apples from a roadside vendor, and when I bit into one, it was sour.

> My grocery store had a sale on green Granny Smith apples last week, and I bought several only to find that they were sour when I bit into them.

The fallacy in the above argument is that the sample was insufficient. A more exhaustive search of literature, etc., will probably turn up some green apples that are not sour.

A writer makes choices about which facts will be used and which will be discarded in developing an argument. Those choices may exclude anything that is not supportive of the point of view the arguer is taking. It's always a good idea for the reader to do some research to spot the omissions and to ask whether they have impact on acceptance of the point of view presented in the argument.

No judgment is either black or white. If the argument seems too neat or too compelling, there are probably facts that might be relevant that have not been included.

Literal Comprehension

Literal comprehension describes the Competency students possess when they are able to derive basic understanding from a text. As discussed throughout this book, vocabulary, fluency, and prior knowledge all play a role in helping students comprehend the basic concept of a text. Students should be taught how to look at text, understand its organization, and determine the main idea of the reading.

Determining Main Idea
You can find the main ideas by looking at the way in which paragraphs are written. A paragraph is a group of sentences about one main idea. Paragraphs usually have two types of sentences: a topic sentence which contains the main idea and two or more detail sentences which support, prove, provide more information, explain, or give examples.

A topic of a paragraph or story is what the paragraph or story is about. The main idea of a paragraph or story states the important idea(s) that the author wants the reader to know about a topic. The topic and main idea of a paragraph or story is sometimes directly stated. There are times, however, that the topic and main idea are not directly stated but simply implied.

Look at this paragraph.

> Henry Ford was an inventor who developed the first affordable automobile. The cars that were being built before Mr. Ford created his Model-T were very expensive. Only rich people could afford to have cars.

The topic of this paragraph is Henry Ford. The main idea is that Henry Ford built the first affordable automobile.

The topic sentence indicates what the passage is about. It is the subject of that portion of the narrative. The ability to identify the topic sentence in a passage will enable the student to focus on the concept being discussed and better comprehend the information provided.

Inferential Comprehension

See Competency 4.B.

In developing a line of reasoning, the choice will be either inductive, going from the specific to the general, or deductive, going from the general to the specific.

Flaws in argument, either intended or unintended, frequently have to do with generalizations and specifics. Are the specifics sufficient to prove the truth of the generality? Does a particular specific actually apply to this generalization? Many times it will depend on definitions. The question can always be asked: has the writer (or speaker) established the generalization?

Sometimes generalizations are cited on the assumption that they are commonly accepted and do not need to be supported. An example: all men die sooner or later. Examples wouldn't be needed because that is commonly accepted. Now, some people might require that "die" be defined, but even the definition of "die" is assumed in this generalization.

A common fallacy in reasoning is the *post hoc ergo propter hoc* ("after this, therefore because of this") or the false-cause fallacy. These occur in cause/effect reasoning which may either go from cause to effect or effect to cause. They happen when an inadequate cause is offered for a particular effect; when the possibility of more than one cause is ignored; and when a connection between a particular cause and a particular effect is not made.

An example of a *post hoc*: Our sales shot up thirty-five percent after we ran that television campaign; therefore, the campaign caused the increase in sales. It might have been a cause, of course, but more evidence is needed to prove it.

An example of an inadequate cause for a particular effect: An Iraqi truck driver reported that Saddam Hussein had nuclear weapons; therefore, Saddam Hussein is a threat to world security. More causes are needed to prove the conclusion.

An example of ignoring the possibility of more than one possible cause: John Brown was caught out in a thunderstorm, and his clothes were wet before he was rescued; therefore, he developed influenza the next day because he got wet. Being chilled may have played a role in the illness, but Brown would have had to contract the influenza virus before he would come down with it, whether or not he had gotten wet.

Here is an example of failing to make a connection between a particular cause and an effect assigned to it. Anna fell into a putrid pond on Saturday; on Monday, she came down with polio; therefore, the polio was caused by the pond. This, of course, is not acceptable unless the polio virus is found in a sample of water from the pond. A connection must be proven.

Critical Comprehension

Facts are statements that are verifiable. Opinions are statements that must be supported in order to be accepted. Facts are used to support opinions.

For example, "Jane is a bad girl" is an opinion. However, "Jane hit her sister with a baseball bat" is a *fact* upon which the opinion is based. Judgments are opinions - decisions or declarations based on observation or reasoning that express approval or disapproval. Facts report what has happened and come from observation, measurement, or calculation. Facts can be tested and verified, whereas opinions and judgments cannot. They can only be supported with facts.

Most statements cannot be so clearly distinguished. "I believe that Jane is a bad girl" is a fact. The speaker knows what s/he believes. However, it obviously includes a judgment that could be disputed by another person who might believe otherwise. Judgments are not usually so firm. They are, rather, plausible opinions that provoke thought or lead to factual development.

Evaluative Comprehension

Evaluative comprehension describes comprehension competencies that allow students to understand fact/opinion, assumptions, and persuasive elements and then evaluate the quality of the written argument.

SKILL N: **Knows how to provide instruction to help students increase their reading vocabulary**

Students will be better at comprehension if they have a stronger working vocabulary. Research has shown that students learn more vocabulary when it is presented in context rather than in vocabulary lists. Furthermore, the more students get to use particular words in context, the more they will remember each word and utilize it in the comprehension of sentences that contain the words.

The National Reading Panel has put forth the following conclusions about vocabulary instruction.

1. There is a need for direct instruction of vocabulary items required for a specific text.
2. Repetition and multiple exposures to vocabulary items are important. Students should be given items that will be likely to appear in many contexts.
3. Learning in rich contexts is valuable for vocabulary learning. Vocabulary words should be those that the learner will find useful in many contexts. When vocabulary items are derived from content learning materials, the learner will be better equipped to deal with specific reading matter in content areas.
4. Vocabulary tasks should be restructured as necessary. It is important to be certain that students fully understand what is asked of them in the context of reading rather than focusing only on the words to be learned.
5. Vocabulary learning is effective when it entails active engagement in learning tasks.
6. Computer technology can be used effectively to help teach vocabulary.
7. Vocabulary can be acquired through incidental learning. Much of a student's vocabulary should be learned while doing things other than explicit vocabulary learning. Repetition, richness of context, and motivation may also add to the efficacy of incidental learning of vocabulary.
8. Dependence on a single vocabulary instruction method will not result in optimal learning. A variety of methods should be used effectively with emphasis on multimedia aspects of learning, richness of context in which words are to be learned, and the number of exposures to words that learners receive.

The Panel found that a critical feature of effective classrooms is the instruction of specific words that includes lessons and activities where students apply their vocabulary knowledge and strategies to reading and writing. Included in the activities were discussions where teachers and students talked about words, their features, and strategies for understanding unfamiliar words.

There are many methods for directly and explicitly teaching words. In fact, the Panel found twenty-one methods that have been found effective in research projects. Many emphasize the underlying concept of a word and its connections to other words such as semantic mapping and diagrams that use graphics. The keyword method uses words and illustrations that highlight salient features of meaning. Visualizing or drawing a picture either by the student or by the teacher was found to be effective.

See Competencies 1.C, 3.M, 3.N, and 4.Q

SKILL O: **Understands reading comprehension issues for students with different needs and knows effective reading strategies for those students**

See Competencies 2.K. 3.G, and 4.C.

SKILL P: **Knows the difference between guided and independent practice in reading and provides students with frequent opportunities for both**

It is important when providing students with reading instruction to begin new conceptual lessons with specific guided practice before asking the students to move to the independent stage. In guided reading, the teacher actively participates in the application of the Competency. This may be completed through modeling, think alouds, or other direct approaches. This approach gives the teacher the ability to monitor students closely. The teacher is able to determine which students are ready to move to the next level, independent practice.

Students should not move to the independent stage until they are at least 95% accurate at demonstrating the Competency. It is important for teachers to hold true to this percentage, as students who are less successful at demonstrating the specific Competency may practice inappropriately. As practice is to reinforce and provide more opportunities to learn the Competency, it is crucial the student practices correctly. Each incorrect practice would then have to be unlearned and relearned. This process takes significantly longer and requires more repetitions.

See Competencies 4.I and 5.P.

SKILL Q: **Knows how to promote students' development of an extensive reading and writing vocabulary by providing them with many opportunities to read and write**

Young children enter school as excited and self-confident learners. They are inquisitive and excited about learning to read and write, and they are extremely proud of their accomplishments. However, children often lose that self-confidence and enthusiasm. Students who are not confident in their reading and writing abilities often make excuses in order to avoid looking dumb by forgetting their homework or by playing the class clown in order to distract attention from their lack of understanding of the assignment.

Teachers can promote a student's confidence in their abilities by giving them choices in their selection of reading activities. Allowing students to choose a less difficult writing assignment that is within their scope of abilities enables the student to succeed. This success, reflected in better grades, will bolster their self- confidence. The teacher can then give the more difficult assignments at a later date. Students can be given short range goals that are easily accomplishable allowing them to increase their confidence to attempt and accomplish even harder goals. Students should be given critical instruction in private and congratulatory praise in public. This allows students to maintain a sense of well-being and self-confidence.

Exposing Students to Literacy

Having words from a familiar rhyme or poem in a pocket chart lends itself to an activity where the students arrange the words in the correct order and then read the rhyme. This is an instructional strategy that reinforces directionality of print. It also reinforces punctuation, capitalization, and matching print to speech.

Using highlighters or sticky tabs to locate letters or specific words can help students isolate words and learn about the structure of language they need to have for reading.

There should be plenty of books in the classroom for children to read on their own or in small groups. As you observe each of these groups, take note of how the child holds the book in addition to how he/she tracks and reads the words.

The use of a word or vocabulary wall is a great teaching tool for words in isolation and with writing. Each of the letters of the alphabet is displayed with words under each one that begin with that letter. Students can find the letter on the wall and read the words under each one. For vocabulary, teachers can arrange words by unit, theme, or root word.

Students should be exposed to daily opportunities for viewing and reading texts. Teachers can do this by engaging the students in discussions about books during shared, guided, and independent reading times. The teacher should draw the students' attention to the conventions of print and discuss with them the reasons for choosing different books. For example, teachers should let the students know that it is perfectly acceptable to return a book and select another if they think it is too hard for them.

Some things for teachers to observe during reading:

- Students' responses during reading conferences
- Students' knowledge about where they should begin reading and how to stop or pause depending on the punctuation
- Students' behavior when holding a book (e.g., holding the book right side up or upside down, reading from left to right, stopping to look at the pictures to confirm meaning)

Activities which can be completed to provide numerous opportunities for reading and writing include:

- Journal Writing
- Writing Workshops
- Reader response journals
- Reading Bookmarks
- Vocabulary Builder Charts
- Pen Pals
- Emails
- Games such as Scrabble©, Boggle©, etc…
- Mad Libs
- Specific Assigned Writing Activities (narratives, expository, persuasive, etc…)
- Jr. Great Books
- Reading Book Clubs
- Library Visitations
- Peer Tutoring

COMPETENCY 005   READING APPLICATIONS

SKILL A: **Understands competencies and strategies for understanding, interpreting, and evaluating different types of written materials, including narratives, expository texts, technical writing, and content-area textbooks**

To *interpret* means, essentially, to read with understanding and appreciation. It is not as daunting as it is made out to be. Simple techniques for interpreting literature are as follows:

- **Context:** This includes the author's feelings, beliefs, past experiences, goals, needs, and physical environment. Incorporate an understanding of how these elements may have affected the writing to enrich an interpretation of it
- **Symbols:** Also referred to as a sign, a symbol designates something which stands for something else. In most cases, it is standing for something that has a deeper meaning than its literal denotation. Symbols can have personal, cultural, or universal associations. Use an understanding of symbols to unearth a meaning the author might have intended, but not expressed, or even something the author never intended at all
- **Questions:** Asking questions, such as "How would I react in this situation?" may shed further light on how you feel about the work.

Elements of Fiction

It's no accident that plot is sometimes called action. If the plot does not *move*, the story quickly dies. Therefore, the successful writer of stories uses a wide variety of active verbs in creative and unusual ways. If readers are kept on their toes by the movement of the story, the experience of reading it will be pleasurable. That reader will probably want to read more of this author's work. William Faulkner is a good example of a successful writer whose stories are lively and memorable because of his use of unusual active verbs.

In analyzing the development of plot, it's wise to look at the verbs. However, the development of believable conflicts is also vital. If there is no conflict, there is no story. What devices does a writer use to develop the conflicts, and are they real and believable?

Character is portrayed in many ways including description of physical characteristics, dialogue, interior monologue, the thoughts of the character, the attitudes of other characters toward this one, etc. Descriptive language depends on the ability to recreate a sensory experience for the reader. If the description of the character's appearance is a visual one, then the reader must be able to *see* the character. What's the shape of the nose? What color are the eyes? How tall or how short is this character? How does the character move? How does the character walk? Terms must be chosen that will create a picture for the reader. It's not enough to say the eyes are blue, for example. What shade of blue?

A good test of characterization is the level of emotional involvement of the reader in the character. If the reader is to become involved, the description must provide an actual experience—seeing, smelling, hearing, tasting, or feeling.

Dialogue will reflect characteristics. Is it clipped? Is it highly dialectal? Does a character use a lot of colloquialisms? The ability to portray the speech of a character can make or break a story. The kind of person the character is in the mind of the reader is dependent on impressions created by description and dialogue. How do other characters feel about this one as revealed by their treatment of him/her, their discussions of him/her with each other, or their overt descriptions of the character? In analyzing a story, it's useful to discuss the devices used to produce character.

Setting may be visual, temporal, psychological, or social. Descriptive words are often used here also. In Edgar Allan Poe's description of the house in "The Fall of the House of Usher" as the protagonist/narrator approaches it, the air of dread and gloom that pervades the story is caught in the setting and sets the stage for the story. A setting may also be symbolic, as it is in Poe's story, where the house is a symbol of the family that lives in it. As the house disintegrates, so does the family.

The language used in all of these aspects of a story—plot, character, and setting—work together to create the mood of a story. Poe's first sentence establishes the mood of the story: "During the whole of a dull, dark, and soundless day in the autumn of the year, when the clouds hung oppressively low in the heavens, I had been passing alone, on horseback, through a singularly dreary tract of country; and at length found myself, as the shades of the evening drew on, within view of the melancholy House of Usher."

Good drama is built on conflict— an opposition of forces or desires that must be resolved by the end of the story. The conflict can be internal, involving emotional and psychological pressures, or it can be external, drawing the characters into tumultuous events.

These themes are presented to the audience in a narrative arc that looks roughly like this:

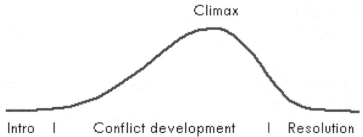

Following the Arc

Although any performance may have a series of rising and falling levels of intensity, in general, the opening should set in motion the events which will generate an emotional high toward the middle or end of the story. Then, regardless of whether the ending is happy, sad, bittersweet, or despairing, the resolution eases the audience down from those heights and establishes some sense of closure. Reaching the climax too soon undermines the dramatic impact of the remaining portion of the performance, whereas reaching it too late rushes the ending and creates a jarringly abrupt end to events.

For more information about fictional works, see Competency 5.K.

Reading Various Types of Texts

Discourse, whether in speaking or writing, falls naturally into four different forms: narrative, descriptive, expository, and persuasive. The first question to be asked when reading a written piece, listening to a presentation, or writing is "What's the point?" This is usually called the thesis. If you are reading an essay, when you've finished, you want to be able to say, "The point of this piece is…."

Persuasion is a piece of writing which attempts to change the minds of the audience members or to get them to do something. This is achieved in many ways:

- The credibility of the writer/speaker might lead the listeners/readers to a change of mind or a recommended action
- Reasoning is important in persuasive discourse. No one wants accept a new viewpoint or go out and take action just because s/he likes and trusts the person who recommended it. Logic comes into play in reasoning that is persuasive
- The third and most powerful force that leads to acceptance or action is emotional appeal. Even if a person has been persuaded logically or reasonably that s/he should believe in a different way, s/he is unlikely to act on it unless moved emotionally. Sermons are good examples of persuasive discourse

Persuasive writing often uses all forms of discourse. The introduction may be a history or background of the idea being presented (exposition). Details supporting some of the points may be stories (narration). Descriptive writing will be used to make sure the point is established emotionally.

Exposition is discourse whose only purpose is to inform. Expository writing is not interested in changing anyone's mind or getting anyone to take a certain action. It exists to give information. Some examples are driving directions to a particular place or the directions for putting together a toy that arrives unassembled. The writer doesn't care whether you do or don't follow the directions. S/he only wants to be sure you have the information in case you do decide to use it.
Narration is discourse that is arranged chronologically—something happened, then something else happened, and then something else happened. It is also called a story. News reports are often narrative in nature as are records of trips, etc. Memoirs are a form of narrative writing.

Description is discourse which makes an experience available through one of the five senses—seeing, smelling, hearing, feeling (as with the fingers), and tasting. Descriptive words are used to make it possible for the reader to "see" with her own mind's eye, hear through her own mind's ear, smell through her own mind's nose, taste with her own mind's tongue, and feel with her own mind's fingers. This is how language moves people. Only by experiencing an event can the emotions become involved. Poets are experts in descriptive language.

Technical Writing

As students progress in age, they will be required to read more complex types of documents. When completing research or other activities, it may be necessary for the students to read technical pieces. When reading technical pieces, students will need to expand their expository reading competencies. Typically, technical pieces include larger vocabulary terms with which the students may be unfamiliar.

In this respect, it is important that students are familiar with and understand how to find and use the glossary. Also, teaching the students to use highlighting and to write brief summaries after reading specific parts of the paper can be helpful tools.

Content-area Textbooks

Content areas become highly dependent on reading as they become more complex. In this respect, it is essential that students have specific strategies to use to ensure their understanding of the materials so they can participate in the classes.

Content texts typically have numerous subtitles or section headers which can provide the student with a good tool for organizing their thoughts, finding answers to specific questions, or to aid in guiding their reading. Also, most texts highlight key vocabulary words in bold. Teaching students the relationship between bolded words and their importance can provide students with a greater understanding of the topics being studied. Outlines, highlighting, and note-taking are also strategies which can be beneficial for students when reading content area texts.

For more information on optimizing textbook use, see Competency 5.7.

SKILL B: Understands different purposes for reading and related reading strategies

The question to be asked first when approaching a reading task is what is my objective? What do I want to achieve from this reading? How will I use the information I gain from this reading? Do I only need to grasp the gist of the piece? Do I need to know the line of reasoning—not only the thesis but the subpoints? Will I be reporting important and significant details orally or in a written document?

A written document can be expected to have a thesis—either expressed or derived. To discover the thesis, the reader needs to ask what point the writer intended to make? The writing can also be expected to be organized in some logical way and to have subpoints that support or establish that the thesis is valid. It is also reasonable to expect that there will be details or examples that will support the subpoints. Knowing this, the reader can decide about reading techniques required for the purpose that has already been established.

If the reader only needs to know the gist of a written document, speed-reading skimming techniques may be sufficient by using the forefinger, moving the eyes down the page, picking up the important statements in each paragraph and deducing mentally that this piece is about such-and-such. If the reader needs to get a little better grasp of how the writer achieved his/her purpose in the document, a quick and cursory glance—a skimming—of each paragraph will yield what the subpoints are, the topic sentences of the paragraphs, and how the thesis is developed, yielding a greater understanding of the author's purpose and method of development.

In-depth reading requires the scrutiny of each phrase and sentence with care, looking for the thesis first, and then the topic sentences in the paragraphs that provide the development of the thesis. The reader will also be looking for connections, such as transitional devices, that provide clues to the direction the reasoning is taking.

Sometimes rereading is necessary in order to make use of a piece of writing for an oral or written report upon a document. If this is the purpose of reading it, the first reading should provide a map for the rereading. The second time through should follow this map, and those points that are going to be used in a report or analysis will be focused upon on more carefully. Some new understandings may occur in this rereading, and it may become apparent that the "map" that was derived from the first reading will need to be adjusted. If this rereading is for the purpose of writing an analysis or using material for a report, either highlighting or note-taking is advisable.

See Competency 4.K for more information on reading of factual material, as well as strategies for improving comprehension competencies.

SKILL C: Knows and teaches strategies to facilitate comprehension of different types of text before, during, and after reading

Metacognitive reading development strategies can help students engage effectively with their reading materials across the curriculum. The sample strategies below can be employed through structured activities that occur before, reading, and after reading.

Before reading

- Incorporate prior knowledge: Draw a connection between students' previous experiences – both personal and educational – and the topic at hand. A student who has helped out in the family garden, for example, will have a visual and basic vocabulary starting point for the study of plant physiology
- Make predictions about what will be learned: Encourage students to identify what they think they will learn from the text based on cues in the material (e.g., book titles, chapter headings, pictures, etc.)
- Prepare questions: Write specific questions to be answered during reading

During reading:

- Use context cues: Utilize other words and concepts in the same sentence or paragraph to determine the meaning of an unfamiliar word
- Reread challenging text: Practice rereading a selection of text to check for understanding
- Use visualizing techniques: Mental pictures formed during the reading of text can aid in comprehension and retention of information. Read alouds, followed by a discussion of how these mental pictures factually reflect the text, provide opportunity for practicing and reinforcing this technique at all grade levels
- Make inferences: Much of human communication relies on our ability to "read between the lines" of explicit statements and make logical guesses

that fill in the blanks of information not provided. Similarly, for textbooks, making inferences means making connections to information extending beyond the text and subject matter at hand. For example, a geography book making the simple declaration that Brazil has a tropical climate can allow the student to deduce a wealth of information not stated in the text (e.g., tropical climates have warm, year-round temperatures and high precipitation levels, therefore certain crops will grow quite successfully and can positively impact the local economy, etc.)

- Check the predictions made before reading: Use the text to confirm earlier predictions about content and answer the questions posed prior to reading

After reading:

- Summarize information: Students who understand the information they have read should be able to restate what they have learned in an organized manner. This activity can be practiced in both written and oral forms
- Make critical evaluations: Encourage students to respond to the text with the ideas and opinions they've formed during reading. Facilitate discussions by devising questions that lead students to make qualitative and evaluative judgments about the content they've read

SKILL D: **Provides instruction in comprehension competencies that support students' transition from "learning to read" to "reading to learn" (e.g., matching comprehension strategies to different types of text and different purposes for reading).**

One of the most significant changes in academic Competency that occurs from early childhood through grade four is the development of reading ability. From early childhood to grade four, children go from not knowing how to read to reading for pleasure and new knowledge. The old saying is that kids go from "learning to read" to "reading to learn" in this critical time period.

Children will start with basic book competencies (such as knowing how to hold a book) and move to phonetic competencies (phonics, phonemic awareness) within the first couple of years of school. As the development of literacy competencies occur, there is a significant shift in the purpose for reading. Typically, beginning in third grade, students begin to make the shift from learning to read to reading to learn. In this way, students are no longer bogged down with decoding the text but can, instead, focus their mental energies on understanding what is being read. By fourth grade, students typically should not have to work rely on phonics. By that time, they should focus on learning how to read and make sense of informational, functional, and more complicated fictional texts using the many reading competencies they have acquired.

This change occurs at different times for different students but, within the classrooms, teachers shift most their reading instruction to comprehension strategies. Building and using personal schema, making inferences, summarizing, using contextual clues, making comparisons, visualization and making personal connections are all comprehension strategies taught through the middle grades.

SQR3 (Survey, Question, Read, Recite, Review) is a comprehension activity many middle grade teachers utilize to help students make sense of readings. This method helps students identify which questions are literal (in that they may be found directly in the text) and which are not literal and require the student to put information together. When putting information together, students will begin to understand that they must combine their own knowledge with that presented by the author to be able to accurately answer the questions.

Combing all of the comprehension strategies, teachers help students to understand how to gather information from reading. This is, of course, the major approach to reading throughout life.

SKILL E: **Understands the importance of reading as a competency in all content areas**

In the past, the content of the curriculum has often been divided into separate subjects for science, social studies, art, music, reading, spelling, handwriting, etc.; however, this often promotes the fragmentation of knowledge. These various subject matter areas can often be combined into themes or units, and instruction in oral language and reading is a major factor in practically every content area.

Students can have discussions and debates about a subject in the news that correlates with a social studies theme. They can orally present their reactions to observations about a science experiment. Teachers may even have students orally explain how they found the answers to certain math problems. Giving speeches and sharing personal experiences can also be related to themes and units.

Content areas such as science, mathematics, history and social studies rely on textbooks and other printed materials that use primarily expository text to introduce, explain, and illustrate new subject matter. From a reading perspective, students face several challenges when approaching these texts, such as deciphering unfamiliar vocabulary and adapting to new structures of content organization. These challenges directly impact students' ability to understand, synthesize, and apply the information contained therein.

Students lacking a solid foundation of reading strategies will likely experience difficulties in developing the competencies needed to master a subject area's academic requirements. At the secondary level, reading and understanding is only the beginning. Students are expected to absorb, evaluate, and form opinions and theories about topics within the subject matter and then discuss, write about, and apply what they've learned on a high level.

It is important for teachers to evaluate each student's reading and oral language development. Often, reading challenges and oral language impediments may show up, and this will allow the teacher to further assist the students with often hidden speaking difficulties.

SKILL F: **Understands the value of using dictionaries, glossaries, and other sources to determine the meanings, pronunciations, and derivation of unfamiliar words and teaches students to these sources**

Students need to understand how to utilize dictionaries or, in nonfiction pieces, glossaries to help them understand and interpret information they may be reading. There are many techniques which need to be specifically taught to students in order to ensure they can adequately use a dictionary or glossary to gain the necessary information. Some of these strategies include:

Explaining and Exploring the Distribution of Letters

It's not always easy to find a word in the dictionary, but there are a number of things that are there to help your students. To familiarize students with the distribution of letters and to save them time and frustration when they look words up, you can do the following exercise:

Hold a dictionary in front of you so that all the class can see it. Open it, and ask them to guess which letter appears on that page. Try this a few times and then get them to do it in pairs.

You can also ask questions such as:

- What do you think the first word in the dictionary is?
- What is the last word?
- Which letter starts the most words in English?
- How many pages do you think it takes up in the dictionary?

Remind Students of Guide Words

Students often ignore the two guide words at the top of each dictionary page. Point out to them that these words are there to tell them which is the first and last word on the open pages. Practice using the help these words offer with the following short exercises:

- On the page *lilac* to *limit*, which of the following words would you find? *limb, like, lime-green, lily, limp*
- Suggest two other words that could be on that page
- On the page *smell* to *smoke*, which of the following words would not be there? *smart, smile, smoked, smog, smoker*

When students are ready, ask them to compare their answers with the dictionary.

Focus on Pronunciation

It is important for students to understand the way pronunciation is shown in the dictionary. Practice using the phonetics symbols in a playful way. Here are a couple of exercises to show you what you can do in class:

- Ask the class to work in teams and give each team three different words that they don't know. Ask each team to choose a word and write the word in three phonetic spellings, two of which are incorrect. When they are ready, ask each team to say and write its word as if they all could be correct. The other teams try to deduce or guess the correct pronunciation without using the dictionary
- Do the same activity but, this time, ask the teams to find three stress patterns for their word. Ask students to find a word of three or more syllables. When they are ready, have teams write the word on the board, in normal spelling, and then say each of the three pronunciations aloud. The other teams try to guess which stress pattern is most probable, and then have the students check with their dictionaries

Learn about Phrases and Idioms

Point out to students that words rarely appear in isolation and that dictionaries are a valuable source of phrases and idioms. Make sure that students know where these phrases and idioms are listed in an entry and encourage them to use them appropriately. You can practice with this exercise:
In the entry for the noun *name*, find the following:

- a phrase that means 'to remember the name of someone you recognize'
- a phrase that means 'to do something that shows that someone is not guilty of something wrong or illegal that they have been accused of'
- a phrase that means 'to use a particular name, especially when it is not your real name'

Explore Phrasal Verbs

Phrasal verbs are often difficult for students. They do not always realize how many different meanings they have. Look at an entry for a common verb (e.g., *come, give*), and spend some time exploring it, ensuring that students discover in which part of the entry they can find phrasal verbs. Do the following exercise to help students practice finding the phrasal verb they are looking for:

Have students look up the phrasal verbs for *stand* in their dictionaries and ask questions such as:

- How many different phrasal verbs does *stand* have?
- How many senses are there for *stand for*?
- Which sense of *stand out* means 'to be much more impressive or important than others?'

Use the Examples

The examples in modern dictionaries are taken from natural written or spoken English. Use these as your source for grammar or vocabulary work in the classroom. For example, take a frequent word you want your class to study, and find the examples that are given for each meaning of that word in the dictionary. Remove the word itself from the examples leaving a blank. Where there is more than one meaning, provide examples for each meaning, with the word itself taken out. Read or show the examples with blanks to the class and invite students to discuss them and guess the blank word, explaining their choice.

Focus on Frequent Words

Most modern dictionaries provide extra information on aspects of English such as correct usage, common errors, synonyms, metaphors, differences between American and British English, and information on what the most frequently encountered words are. Explore the dictionary drawing students' attention to this type of information, and create classroom activities around them. To focus on frequent words, you can do the following activities:

- Choose the three words from the page *operetta* to *opportunity* that are used the most frequently: *opinion, opinionated, opportunist, opportunity, ophthalmologist*
- List three words that you think are marked as the most frequent ones on the page *reach* to *read*. Then check your answers in the dictionary.

SKILL G: **Knows how to teach students to interpret information presented in various formats and how to locate, retrieve, and retain information from a range of texts and technologies**

For information on interpreting, see Competency 5.A.

Locating and Interpreting Information

Quantitative data is often easily presented in graphs and charts in many content areas. However, if students are unable to decipher the graph, their use becomes limited to students. Since information can clearly be displayed in a graph or chart form, accurate interpretation of the information is an important Competency for students.

Some possibilities for the analysis of data whether presented in tables, charts, graphs, maps, or other illustrations are as follows:

- Qualitative descriptions—drawing conclusions about the quality of a particular treatment or course of action as revealed by the illustration
- Quantitative descriptions—how much do the results of one particular treatment or course of action differ from another one, and is that variation significant?
- Classification—is worthwhile information derived from breaking the information down into classifications?
- Estimations—is it possible to estimate future performance on the basis of the information in the illustration?
- Comparisons—is it useful to make comparisons based on the data?
- Relationships—are relationships between components revealed by the scrutiny of the data?
- Cause-and-effect relationships—is it suggested by the data that there were cause-and-effect relationships that were not previously apparent?
- Mapping and modeling—if the data were mapped and a model drawn up, would the point of the document be demonstrated or refuted?

Graphs & Charts

Graphs also present data in visual form. Whereas tables are useful for showing large numbers of specific, related facts or statistics in a brief space, trends, movements, distributions, and cycles are more readily apparent in a graph. However, although graphs can present statistics in a more interesting and comprehensible form than tables, they are less accurate. For this reason, the two will often be shown together.

For graphs, students should be taught to evaluate all the features of the graph, including the main title, what the horizontal and vertical axes represent. Also, students should locate and evaluate the graph's key (if there is one) in the event there is more than one variable on the graph. For example, line graphs are often used to plot data from a scientific experiment. If more than one variable was used, a key or legend would indicate what each line on the line graph represented. Then, once students have evaluated the axes and titles, they can begin to assess the results of the experiment.

There are two good reasons for using a graph:

1. To present a model or theory visually in order to show how two or more variables interrelate
2. To present real world data visually in order to show how two or more variables interrelate

Graphs are most useful when one wishes to demonstrate the sequential increase or decrease of a variable or to show specific correlations between two or more variables in each circumstance. In all graphs, an upward sloping line represents a direct relationship between the two variables. A downward slope represents an inverse relationship between the two variables. In reading any graph, you must always be very careful to understand what is being measured, what can be deduced, and what cannot be deduced from the given graph.

For charts (such as a pie chart), the process is similar to interpreting bar or line graphs. The key which depicts what each section of the pie chart represents is very important to interpreting the pie chart. Be sure to provide students with lots of assistance and practice with reading and interpreting graphs and charts so their experience with and confidence in reading them develops.

To use charts correctly, you should remember the reasons for using graphs. The general ideas are similar. It is usually a question as to which is more capable of adequately portraying the information you want to illustrate. You can see the difference between them and realize that in many ways graphs and charts are interrelated.

Maps

Information can be gained looking at a map that might take hundreds of words to explain otherwise. To show such a variety of information, maps are made in many ways. Because of this variety, maps must be understood in order to make the best sense of them. Once they are understood, maps provide a meaningful and useful tool in communicating a point of view. Teachers need to model how to use the map's legend, title, and representations to decipher information from a map.

While the most obvious use for maps is to locate places geographically, they can also show specific geographic features such as roads, mountains, rivers, etc. They can also show information per geographic distribution such as population, housing, manufacturing centers, etc.

Tables

Tables that simply store descriptive information in a form available for general use are called repository tables. They usually contain primary data which simply summarizes raw data. They are not intended to analyze the data, so any analysis is left to the reader or user of the table. A good example of a repository table would be a report of birth statistics by the federal Health and Human Services Department.

An analytical table, on the other hand, is constructed from some sort of analysis of primary or secondary data, possibly from a repository table or from the raw data itself. An example of an analytical table would be one that compares birth statistics in 1980 to birth statistics in 2005 for the country at large. It might also break the data down into comparisons by state.

To interpret data in tables, we read across rows and down columns. Each item of interest has different data points listed under different column headings.

Table 1. Sample Purchase Order

Item	Unit	$/Unit	Qty.	Tot. $
Coffee	lb.	2.79	45	125.55
Milk	gal.	1.05	72	75.60
Sugar	lb.	0.23	150	34.50

In Table 1 (above), the first column on the left contains the items in a purchase order. The other columns contain data about each item labeled with column headings. The second column from the left gives the unit of measurement for each item. The third column gives the price per unit. The fourth column gives the quantity of each item ordered, and the fifth column gives the total cost of each item.

Illustrations

A wide range of illustrations may be used to illuminate the text in a document. They may also be a part of a graphic layout designed to make the page more attractive.

Here are some questions to ask regarding an illustration: Why is the illustration in this document? What was the writer's purpose in putting it in the document and why at this particular place? Does it make a point clearer? What implications are inherent in a table that shows birth statistics in all states or even in some selected states? What does that have to do with the point and purpose of this piece of writing? Is there adequate preparation in the text for the inclusion of the illustration? Does the illustration underscore or clarify any of the points made in the text? Is there a clear connection between the illustration and the subject matter of the text?

SKILL H: **Knows how to help students comprehend abstract content and ideas in written materials**

When students are reading, they will often be presented with ideas which are quite abstract to them. Sometimes the content, itself, will be quite abstract while, other times, it is due to a lack of personal experience or background knowledge related to the information which impairs the students. In this case, it is imperative that the teacher take the time to explain, explore, and provide specific connections to information with which the learner is familiar. It is through connections that information can be moved into long term memory.

Other times, it can be quite helpful for the students to summarize the reading in their own words. Simplifying the language can provide students with a much greater chance at comprehending the materials. In some cases, this summary may need to be provided to the students by the teacher. Outlines can also be helpful to students. Teachers can provide completed outlines or provide partially completed outlines to help guide students through the material.

Identification of key vocabulary terms is critical for understanding complex content. Utilization of glossaries and dictionaries can be helpful in providing the students with definitions of these key terms. However, if students need to look up a large number of words, they will continue to have difficulty understanding the material. Therefore, it may be helpful to teach key terms before the students are expected to read the more abstract content.

Finally, tying the abstract to the concrete as often as possible will provide the students with the best opportunity to acquire the new information. Games, puzzles, models, flash cards, drawings, mind maps, and graphic organizers are all examples of tools which can be utilized to help students take abstract concepts and make them more concrete to increase understanding.

See Competency 5.B.

SKILL I: **Knows literary genres and their characteristics**

The major literary genres include those listed below:

Allegory: A story in verse or prose with characters representing virtues and vices. There are two meanings, symbolic and literal. John Bunyan's *The Pilgrim's Progress* is one of the most renowned of this genre.

Autobiography: A form of biography, but it is written by the subject himself or herself. Autobiographies can range from the very formal to intimate writings made during one's life that were not intended for publication. These include letters, diaries, journals, memoirs, and reminiscences.

Ballad: An *in medias res* story told or sung, usually in verse and accompanied by music. Literary devices found in ballads include the refrain, or repeated section, and incremental repetition, or anaphora, for effect. Earliest forms were anonymous folk ballads.

Biography: A form of nonfiction literature, the subject of which is the life of an individual. The earliest biographical writings were probably funeral speeches and inscriptions, usually praising the life and example of the deceased. Early biographies evolved from this and were almost invariably uncritical, even distorted, and always laudatory.

Epic: A long poem, usually of book length, reflecting values inherent in the generative society. Epic devices include an invocation to a Muse for inspiration, purpose for writing, universal setting, protagonist and antagonist who possess supernatural strength and acumen, and interventions of a God or the gods. Understandably, there are very few epics: Homer's *Iliad* and *Odyssey*, Virgil's *Aeneid*, Milton's *Paradise Lost*, Spenser's *The Fairie Queene*, Barrett Browning's *Aurora Leigh*, and Pope's mock-epic, *The Rape of the Lock* are some examples.

Epistle: A letter that is not always originally intended for public distribution but, due to the fame of the sender and/or recipient, becomes public domain. Paul wrote epistles that were later placed in the Bible.

Essay: Typically a limited length prose work focusing on a topic and propounding a definite point of view and authoritative tone. Great essayists include Carlyle, Lamb, DeQuincy, Emerson, and Montaigne, who is credited with defining this genre.

Fable: Terse tale offering up a moral or exemplum. Chaucer's "The Nun's Priest's Tale" is a fine example of a *bete fabliau,* or beast fable, in which animals speak and act characteristically human, illustrating human foibles.

Informational books and articles: Make up much of the reading of modern Americans. Magazines began to be popular in the 19th century in this country and, while many of the contributors to those publications intended to influence the political/social/religious convictions of their readers, many also simply intended to pass on information. A book or article whose purpose is simply to be informative, that is, not to persuade, is called exposition. An example of an expository book is the *MLA Style Manual*. The writers do not intend to persuade their readers to use the recommended stylistic features in their writing; they are simply making them available in case a reader needs such a guide.

Legend: A traditional narrative or collection of related narratives, popularly regarded as historically factual but, actually, a mixture of fact and fiction.

Myth: Stories that are more or less universally shared within a culture to explain its history and traditions.

Newspaper accounts of events: Expository in nature, of course, a reporting of a happening. That happening might be a school board meeting, an automobile accident that sent several people to a hospital and accounted for the death of a passenger, or the election of the mayor. They are not intended to be persuasive although the bias of a reporter or an editor must be factored in. A newspapers' editorial stance is often openly declared, and it may be reflected in such things as news reports. Reporters are expected to be unbiased in their coverage, and most of them will defend their disinterest fiercely, but what a writer *sees* in an event is inevitably shaped, to some extent, by the writer's beliefs and experiences.

Novel: The longest form of fictional prose containing a variety of characterizations, settings, local color, and regionalism. Most have complex plots, expanded description, and attention to detail. Some of the great novelists include Austin, Twain, Tolstoy, Hugo, Hardy, Dickens, Hawthorne, Forster, and Flaubert.

Poem: The only requirement is rhythm. Sub-genres include fixed types of literature such as the sonnet, elegy, ode, pastoral, and villanelle. Unfixed types of literature include blank verse and dramatic monologue.

Romance: A highly imaginative tale set in a fantastical realm dealing with the conflicts between heroes, villains, and/or monsters. "The Knight's Tale" from Chaucer's *Canterbury Tales* and Keats' "The Eve of St. Agnes" are prime representatives.

Short Story: Typically, a terse narrative with less developmental background about characters. Short stories may include description, author's point of view, and tone. Poe emphasized that a successful short story should create one focused impact. Considered to be great short story writers are Hemingway, Faulkner, Twain, Joyce, Shirley Jackson, Flannery O'Connor, de Maupassant, Saki, Poe, and Pushkin.

Dramatic Texts

Theatre: Plays – comedy, modern, or tragedy - typically in five acts. Traditionalists and neoclassicists adhere to Aristotle's unities of time, place, and action. Plot development is advanced via dialogue. Literary devices include asides, soliloquies, and the chorus representing public opinion. One of the greatest of all dramatists/playwrights is William Shakespeare. Other dramaturges include Ibsen, Williams, Miller, Shaw, Stoppard, Racine, Moliére, Sophocles, Aeschylus, Euripides, and Aristophanes.

Comedy: The comedic form of dramatic literature is meant to amuse and, often, ends happily. It uses techniques such as satire or parody and can take many forms, from farce to burlesque.

Tragedy: Tragedy is comedy's other half. It is defined as a work of drama written in either prose or poetry, telling the story of a brave, noble hero who, because of some tragic character flaw, brings ruin upon himself. It is characterized by serious, poetic language that evokes pity and fear. In modern times, dramatists have tried to update its image by drawing its main characters from the middle class and showing their nobility through their nature instead of their standing in the community.

Drama: In its most general sense, a drama is any work that is designed to be performed by actors onstage. It can also refer to the broad literary genre that includes comedy and tragedy. Contemporary usage, however, denotes drama as a work that treats serious subjects and themes but does not aim for the same grandeur as tragedy. Drama usually deals with characters of a less stately nature than tragedy.

Dramatic Monologue/Soliloquy: A dramatic monologue is a speech given by an actor directed at an individual or group whereas a soliloquy is a theatrical device in which a character speaks to him or herself. Both reveal key aspects of the character's psyche and shed insight on the situation at hand. The audience takes the part of the silent listener, passing judgment and giving sympathy at the same time. Shakespeare's Hamlet has one of the most famous soliloquies in literature, "To be or not to be." Victorian poet, Robert Browning helped establish and perfect the dramatic monologue.

SKILL J: Recognizes a wide range of literature and other texts appropriate for students

Adolescent literature, because of the age range of readers, is extremely diverse. Fiction for the middle group, usually ages ten/eleven to fourteen/fifteen, deals with issues of coping with internal and external changes in their lives. Because children's writers in the twentieth century have produced increasingly realistic fiction, adolescents can now find problems dealt with honestly in novels.

Teachers of middle/junior high school students experience the greatest change in interests and reading abilities. Fifth and sixth graders, included in elementary grades in many schools, are viewed as older children while seventh and eighth graders are considered preadolescent. Ninth graders, included sometimes as top dogs in junior high school and sometimes as underlings in high school, definitely view themselves as teenagers. Their literature choices will often be governed more by interest than by ability, thus, the wealth of high-interest, low readability books that have flooded the market in recent years. Tenth through twelfth graders will still select high-interest books for pleasure reading but are also easily encouraged to stretch their literature muscles by reading more classics.

Because of the rapid social changes, topics that once did not interest young people until they reached their teens - suicide, gangs, homosexuality - are now subjects of books for even younger readers. The plethora of high-interest books reveals how desperately schools have failed to produce on-level readers and how the market has adapted to that need. However, these high-interest books are now readable for younger children whose reading levels are at or above average. No matter how tastefully written, some content is inappropriate for younger readers.

The problem becomes not so much steering students toward books that they have the reading ability to handle but encouraging them toward books whose content is appropriate to their levels of cognitive and social development. A fifth-grader may be able to read V.C. Andrews book *Flowers in the Attic* but not possess the social/moral development to handle the deviant behavior of the characters. At the same time, because of the complex changes affecting adolescents, the teacher must be well versed in learning theory and child development as well as competent to teach the subject matter of language and literature.

Most seventh and eighth grade students, according to learning theory, are still functioning cognitively, psychologically, and morally as sixth graders. As these are not inflexible standards, there are some twelve and thirteen-year-old students who are much more mature socially, intellectually, and physically than the younger children who share the same school. They are becoming concerned with establishing individual and peer group identities that present conflicts with breaking from authority and the rigidity of rules. Some at this age are still tied firmly to the family and its expectations, while others identify more with those their own age or older.

Enrichment reading for this group must help them cope with life's rapid changes or provide escape and, thus, must be either realistic or fantastic depending on the child's needs. Adventures and mysteries (the *Hardy Boys* and *Nancy Drew* series) are still popular today. These preteens also become more interested in biographies of contemporary figures rather than legendary figures of the past.

Reading level 6.0 to 6.9

Barrett, William. *Lilies of the Field*
Cormier, Robert. *Other Bells for Us to Ring*
Dahl, Roald. *Danny, Champion of the World; Charlie and the Chocolate Factory*
Lindgren, Astrid. *Pippi Longstocking*
Lindbergh, Anne. *Three Lives to Live*
Lowry, Lois. *Rabble Starkey*
Naylor, Phyllis. *The Year of the Gopher, Reluctantly Alice*
Peck, Robert Newton. *Arly*
Speare, Elizabeth. *The Witch of Blackbird Pond*
Sleator, William. *The Boy Who Reversed Himself*

Reading level 7.0 to 7.9

Armstrong, William. *Sounder*
Bagnold, Enid. *National Velvet*
Barrie, James. *Peter Pan*
London, Jack. *White Fang, Call of the Wild*
Lowry, Lois. *Taking Care of Terrific*
McCaffrey, Anne. The *Dragonsinger* series
Montgomery, L. M. *Anne of Green Gables* and sequels
Steinbeck, John. *The Pearl*
Tolkien, J. R. R. *The Hobbit*
Zindel, Paul. *The Pigman*

Reading level 8.0 to 8.9

Cormier, Robert. *I Am the Cheese*
McCullers, Carson. *The Member of the Wedding*
North, Sterling. *Rascal*
Twain, Mark. *The Adventures of Tom Sawyer*
Zindel, Paul. *My Darling, My Hamburger*

SKILL K: **Provides multiple opportunities for students to listen and respond to a wide variety of children's and young people's literature, both fiction and nonfiction, and to recognize characteristics of various types of narrative and expository texts**

Teachers should select a variety of texts to give students a broad experience in the reading process. Exposure to both narrative and expository texts allows them to build and expand their knowledge base, identify and distinguish genres, learn how different texts are structured, and experience a variety of authors' writing styles, ideas, and language usage across eras.

Fiction

Fiction is the opposite of fact and, simple as that may seem, it's the major distinction between fictional works and nonfictional works. Fiction is the result of imagination and is recorded for the purpose of entertainment in addition to giving the author the ability to control the message.

A work of fiction typically has a central character, called the protagonist, and a character that stands in opposition, called the antagonist. The antagonist might be something other than a person. In Stephen Crane's short story, *The Open Boat*, for example, the antagonist is a hostile environment, a stormy sea. Conflicts between protagonist and antagonist are typical of a work of fiction, and climax is the point at which those conflicts are resolved. The plot has to do with the form or shape that the conflict takes as the story moves toward resolution. A fiction writer artistically uses devices labeled characterization to reveal character. Characterization can depend on dialogue, description, or the attitude or attitudes of one or more characters toward another.

Enjoying fiction depends upon the ability of the reader to suspend belief, to some extent. The reader makes a deal with the writer that for the time it takes to read the story, his/her own belief will be put aside, replaced by the convictions and reality that the writer has written into the story. This is not true in nonfiction. The writer of nonfiction declares in the choice of that genre that the work is reliably based upon reality.

Students should read an assortment of fiction works to provide opportunities to learn about character and plot development in the various genres, the role of setting and dialogue, themes and narrative story structure, as well as the ability to define and identify elements of fiction (e.g., tone, mood, foreshadowing, irony, symbolism). Types of texts to be included in the reading curriculum are folktales, myths, legends, short stories, mysteries, historical fiction, science fiction, plays, and general-interest novels. See Competency 5.1 for basic information on fictional works.

Some (not all) types of nonfiction:

- Almanac
- Autobiography
- Biography
- Blueprint
- Book report
- Diary
- Dictionary
- Documentary film
- Encyclopedia
- Essay
- History
- Journal
- Letter
- Philosophy
- Science book
- Textbook
- User manual

Nonfiction

The earliest nonfiction came in the form of cave-paintings, the record of what prehistoric man caught on hunting trips. On the other hand, we don't know that some of it might be fiction—that is, what they would like to catch on future hunting trips. Cuneiform inscriptions, which hold the earliest writings, are probably nonfiction, having to do with conveying goods such as oxen and barley and dealing with the buying and selling of these items. It's easy to assume that nonfiction, then, is pretty boring, since it simply serves the purpose of recording everyday facts.

Appropriate selection of nonfiction materials provides the opportunity to practice and reinforce the complex reading comprehension competencies necessary to succeed across the curriculum. Topics should contain a high level of detail, covering diverse topics which encourage active discussion, questioning, synthesizing, and evaluation of the information presented. Readers should be exposed to complex content structures and be required to apply critical reading competencies to evaluate the quality of information. Text selection should include textbooks, autobiographies/biographies, informational books, Web sites, newspapers, magazines, encyclopedias, and brochures.

Some (not all) genres of fiction:

- Action-adventure
- Crime
- Detective
- Fable
- Fantasy
- Horror

- Mystery
- Romance
- Science fiction
- Thriller
- Western

For more information on responding to literature, see Competency 4.L.

For information on narrative texts and expository texts, see Competency 5.A.

SKILL L: **Understands and promotes students' development of literary response and analysis, including teaching students elements of literary analysis and providing students with opportunities to apply comprehension competencies to literature**

Before responding to a literary piece, be it short story, novel, or poetry, there must be analysis. For fiction, the first step is to identify the protagonist, the conflicts, and the pattern of action. Are the conflicts resolved? Do they remain unresolved? If so, what is the redeeming quality of the plot? Remember that readers like resolution, which is the reason many people read and can often be the compelling reason that a work becomes a best-seller or endures for generations. In order for the resolution to be that satisfying, the conflicts must be particularly engaging.

In Mitch Albom's *The Five People You Meet in Heaven*, which remained at the top of all best-seller lists for months, the conflicts were between a competency fully-written protagonist and a hostile world, including an abusive father. The resolution of those conflicts involves a twist, at the end, where it is revealed to the character that his life has, in fact, been lived meaningfully to protect and save children even though he had been denied parenthood. This story struck a chord with readers because of the depth of satisfaction that comes with the resolution of intense and engaging conflicts.

An analysis of characterization may be appropriate in writing about a piece of fiction. The devices a writer uses to reveal character may be uniquely artistic and worth writing about. Setting is often an important device for adding depth and meaning to a story. The Albom story is set in a seaside recreation park, and it plays an important role in the development of the story and, particularly, in the long ending where the purpose of the protagonist's life is revealed. Setting may, itself, play a role as a character in a story.

What about the writer's life and times adds interest to the story? Albom's story is set in World War II and the years following, but the long ending reaches into the past in order to add depth and meaning to the resolution. A writer's use of language may be unique. Ernest Hemingway established new approaches to dialogue and description with his spare and economical pared-down use of words.

When writing about poetry, many of the same factors may be useful. What is the statement the poet wishes to make? Why is it relevant or meaningful? What is unique about the use of words, particularly descriptive ones? How does the form chosen by this poet add strength and meaning to this particular poem? Or is there dissonance? Does the form contradict the theme? Does the sound of the words create cacophony? Remember that poetry is meant to be read aloud, so sounds should be uppermost when analyzing a poem.

Responding to Literature

Responding to literature through art, writing, and drama helps children to reflect on the books they have read and make them a part of their lives. The following list suggests just a few of the extending activities teachers can facilitate using children's books to make them come alive:

- Have younger children make puppets to retell the story
- Allow children to act out the story with the teacher as the first narrator. Books like John Burningham's *Mr. Gumpy's Outing* work well for this

- Complete an art project using the same artistic medium as was in the book, such as a collage after reading Ezra Jack Keats or Eric Carle
- Have children create a tableau (a montage of still figures) that captures a critical scene from a book
- Use the interlocking structure of Bill Martin's *Brown Bear, Brown Bear* as the template for a new story in which the children draw new characters. This can be made into a classroom Big Book
- After reading a book like *The Village of Round and Square Houses*, have the children create a village of box sculptures
- Have children create a story map to show critical places in the setting
- Ask students to write telegraphs or emails to characters explaining how to handle a problem
- Encourage older children to retell a story from another character's point of view as in Jon Scieszka's *The True Story of the Three Little Pigs* which is told from the point of view of the wolf
- Children can create a newspaper based on a book, such as the multiple perspectives in Anthony Browne's *Voices in the Park*
- In writing, have children connect a book to their own lives. For example, after reading *Jamaica's Friend*, write about something you and your best friend do together

Further Evaluating Literature and Poetry

At the middle school level, students should be provided with opportunities to evaluate literature, including considering the historical context within which the text was written. Students should learn to ask questions such as: What does the fictional work of a foreign culture or distant period tell us about those who constructed the fiction? What are the cultural needs such stories answered? Are there fundamental anthropological premises which make us create fictional worlds? Did these fictions entertain, divert, and instruct? Did they—as one could assume when reading ancient and medieval myths—just provide a substitute for better, more scientific knowledge, or did they add to the luxuries of life a particular culture enjoyed?

A novel must be adjudged by the period in which it was created. The sentimentalism of an earlier period might not be appealing to a 21st century reader or critic; nevertheless, these books were probably appropriate in the period in which they were written. If they have endured and have continued to be read and enjoyed, then time has proven their worth.

At the most basic level, all poetry can be measured by certain standards: A bad poem tends to be stereotyped, while an excellent poem tends to be considered unique. What is the poem trying to do, and does it succeed? Before judging a poem, one must understand it, although an obscure poem that demands much from the reader may be worthwhile for that very reason.

A good poem should have a significant theme, although that is not enough to make it great. Even not-so-good poems can have admirable themes. A great poem shocks us into another order of perception, helps us know ourselves, and points beyond words to something still more essential. The best poem ushers us into an experience so profoundly moving that we feel changed. A bad or indifferent poem fails to do so. Different periods will judge the same poem differently. It's useful to read what earlier critics have said about a poem and measure their conclusions against those of a different era, as well as critiques of the current understanding to see if what is valuable and what is not has changed over time.

See Competency 5.O.

SKILL M: **Selects and uses a variety of materials to teach students about authors and about different purposes for writing**

A piece of writing is an integrated whole. It's not enough to just look at the various parts; the total entity must be examined. It should be considered in two ways:

- As an emotional expression of the author
- As an artistic embodiment of a meaning or set of meanings

This is what is sometimes called "**tone**" in literary criticism.

It's important to remember that the writer is a human being with his/her own individual bents, prejudices, and emotions. A writer is telling the readers about the world as he/she sees it and will give voice to certain phases of his/her own personality. By reading a writer's works, we can know the personal qualities and emotions of the writer embodied in the work itself. However, it's important to remember that not all of the writer's characteristics will be revealed in a single work. People change and may have very different attitudes at different times in their lives. Sometimes, a writer will be influenced by a desire to have a piece of work accepted or to appear to be current based on the interests and desires of the readers he/she hopes to attract. This can destroy a work or make it less than it might be. Sometimes, the best works are not commercial successes in the time they were written but are discovered at a later time and by another generation.

There are three places to look for tone:

- Choice of form: tragedy or comedy; melodrama or farce; parody or sober lyric
- Choice of materials: characters that have human qualities that are attractive; others that are repugnant. What an author shows in a setting will often indicate his/her interests

- The writer's interpretation: it may be explicit—telling us how he/she feels
- The writer's implicit interpretations: the author's feelings for a character come through in the description. For example, the use of "smirked" instead of "laughed" or "marched" instead of "walked"

The reader is asked to join the writer in the feelings expressed about the world and the things that happen in it. The tone of a piece of writing is important in a critical review of it.

Style, in literature, means a distinctive manner of expression and applies to all levels of language, beginning at the phonemic level—word choices, alliteration, assonance. Next is the syntactic level—length of sentences, choice of structure and phraseology, patterns. The next level extends even beyond sentences to paragraphs and chapters. What is distinctive about this writer's use of these elements?

In Steinbeck's *Grapes of Wrath*, for instance, the style is quite simple in the narrative sections, and the dialogue is dialectal. Because the emphasis is on the story—the narrative—his style is straightforward, for the most part. He just tells the story.

However, there are interior chapters where Steinbeck varies his style. He uses symbols and combines them with realistic descriptions. He sometimes shifts to a crisp, repetitive pattern to underscore the beeping and speeding of cars. By contrast, some of those inter chapters are lyrical, almost poetic. These shifts in style reflect the attitude of the author toward the subject matter. He intends to make a statement, and he uses a variety of styles to strengthen the point.

SKILL N: **Provides students with opportunities to engage in silent reading and extended reading of a wide range of materials, including expository texts and various literary genres**

For information on silent reading, see Competency 4.I.

For information on various literary genres, see Competency 5.I.

SKILL O: **Engages students in varied reading experiences and encourages students to interact with others about their reading**

See Competency 5.L.

Reading literature involves a reciprocal interaction between the reader and the text.

Types of Responses

Emotional
The reader can identify with the characters and situations so as to project himself into the story. The reader feels a sense of satisfaction by associating aspects of his own life with the people, places, and events in the literature. Emotional responses are observed in a reader's verbal and non-verbal reactions - laughter, comments on its effects, and retelling or dramatizing the action.

Interpretive
Interpretive responses result in inferences about character development, setting, plot, analysis of style elements (metaphor, simile, allusion, rhythm, tone), outcomes derivable from information provided in the narrative, and assessment of the author's intent. Interpretive responses are made verbally or in writing.

Critical
Critical responses involve making value judgments about the quality of a piece of literature. Reactions to the effectiveness of the writer's style and language use are observed through discussion and written reactions.

Evaluative
Some reading response theory researchers also add a response that considers the readers consideration of such factors as how well the piece of literature represents its genre and reflects the social/ ethical mores of society in addition to how well the author has approached the subject for freshness and slant.

Levels of Response

Middle school readers will exhibit both emotional and interpretive responses. Naturally, making interpretive responses depends on the degree of knowledge the student has of literary elements. A child's being able to say why a particular book was boring or why a particular poem made him sad evidences critical reactions on a fundamental level. Adolescents in ninth and tenth grades should begin to make critical responses by addressing the specific language and genre characteristics of literature. Evaluative responses are harder to detect and are rarely made by any but a few advanced high school students. However, if the teacher knows what to listen for, she can recognize evaluative responses and incorporate them into discussions.

For example, if a student says, "I don't understand why that character is doing that," he is making an interpretive response to character motivation. However, if he goes on to say, "What good is that action?" he is giving an evaluative response that should be explored in terms of "What good should it do, and why isn't that positive action happening?"

COMPTENCY 6.0   **WRITTEN LANGUAGE—WRITING CONVENTIONS**

SKILL A: **Knows predictable stages in the development of writing conventions and recognizes that individual variations occur**

Even though learning to write is generally a sequential process, it is an individual process for each child. Some children find learning to write harder than others. There is a continuous growth in writing, but children vary in the development of these stages. A child's writing may show evidence of more than one stage. Children may even skip levels on their way to developing writing competency.

Children progress as writers from one phase to the next, with one set of competencies building on the competencies acquired earlier. Writing, however, combines many competencies and relies on development in many areas not specific to writing. A child's fine motor control and vocabulary, for example, must improve in order for writing to progress normally. In order for children to write correctly, they must first develop their fine motor competencies. Before being required to manipulate a pencil, children should have dexterity and strength in their fingers, which helps them to gain more control of small muscles. Writing begins as scribbles and progresses to the formation of letters and then words. The words then form sentences, and the rules of grammar and punctuation need to be incorporated for formal writing to be produced.

Children in early elementary school will begin to string words together into sentences. Their vocabulary is going to be limited. These age groups enjoy writing about topics of their own choice as well as imitating favorite authors and stories. School children should also be encouraged to keep journals and to write to each other. Children may still use invented spellings, but teachers will need to encourage them to begin to follow the conventions of standard written English.

Writing is a process that flows gradually. Younger children will use simple sentences. A good place to begin to raise the level of writing is to encourage the use of descriptive language and adjectives. Teachers should encourage the use of detail. As writing improves, teachers can introduce concepts such as main ideas, topic sentences, and revising for clarity. As students receive time to explore and experiment with writing, teachers will see evidence of growth.

By the time they reach middle school, children are quite adept at forming sentences. They have also developed an expanded vocabulary, so they can make themselves understood when writing and speaking. They can write on favorite topics at length but often have difficulty coming up with ideas on their own. While there may still be invented spelling, for the most part, middle school students have a good grasp on conventional spelling of commonly used words. They do have knowledge of some of the conventions of standard written English but still need instruction in the more advanced conventions.

Instruction in writing in the middle school grades includes teaching students how to make their writing more descriptive. They are familiar with the steps of the writing process by this point in their schooling, but they are often reluctant to use them because they want to get the writing finished quickly and move on to more exciting things. As students receive time to explore and experiment with writing, teachers will see evidence of growth. Since writing is a process and stages are connected, students may show evidence of more than one stage in a single piece of writing

Children develop writing competencies through a series of steps. The steps and their characteristics are:

Role Play Writing
In this stage, the child writes in scribbles and assigns a message to the symbols. Even though an adult would not be able to read the writing, the child can "read" what is written although it may not be the same each time. The child will be able to read back the writing because of prior knowledge that print carries a meaning. The child will also dictate to adults who can write a message or story.

Experimental Writing
In this stage, the child writes in simple forms of language. The words usually contain letters according to the way they sound. For instance, the word "are" may be written as "r". However, the child does display a sense of sentence formation and writes in groups of words with a period at the end. There is evidence of an awareness of the correspondence between written words and oral language.

Early Writing
Children start to use a small range of familiar text forms and sight words in their writing. The topics they choose for writing are those that have some importance for them, such as their family, friends or pets. Because they are used to hearing stories, they do have a sense of how a story sounds, and children will begin to write simple narratives. They learn that they do have to correct their writing so that others can easily read it.

Conventional Writing
By the time students reach this stage of writing, they have a sense of audience and purpose for writing. They are able to proofread their writing and edit it for mistakes. They have gained the ability to transfer between reading and writing so that they can get ideas for writing from what they have read. By this time, students also have a sense of what correct spelling and grammar look like, and they can change the order of events in the writing so that it makes sense for the reader.

Review the chart below for a summary of writing abilities with respect to the stages of the developing writer:

	Spelling	Penmanship	Print/mechanics Concepts	Content
Role Play Writer	Scribbles and uses writing-like behavior; scribbles to represent word; no phonetic association	Develops pencil position and traces words and letters	Develops awareness of environmental print	Uses pictures and scribble writing
Emergent Writer	Writes initial consonants; correlates some letter/sounds; knows each syllable has a letter	Can write on line; incorrectly mixes upper and lower case letters	Makes some letters and words; attempts to write name	Copies words and uses pattern sentences
Developing Writer	Left/right correspondence; invented spelling with initial/final consonants; few vowels	Correctly uses upper and lowercase letters	Directional writing and one-to-one writing/reading words; writes word patterns	Uses invented spelling and simple sentences
Beginning Writer	Correct spelling for most words; uses resources and decoding for spelling	Sentence structure; only focuses on one writing component at a time, i.e., spelling or punctuation	Chooses personally significant topics for writing assignments	Organizes paragraphs using complete sentences
Expanding Writer	Edits for mechanics during and after writing	Varies writing components based on writing task	Uses organization and a variety of word choices	Writes in a variety of formats: poetry, stories, reports, etc.

SKILL B: **Knows and applies appropriate instructional strategies and sequences to teach writing conventions and their applications to all students, including English Language Learners**

Sentence Structure

Students need to avoid fragments and run-on sentences. In order to do so, they must be able to identify and recognize simple, compound, complex, and compound-complex sentences. Teachers need to introduce students to the concepts of dependent (subordinate) and independent clauses correctly to create these sentence structures.

Simple	Joyce wrote a letter.
Compound	Joyce wrote a letter, and Dot drew a picture.
Complex	While Joyce wrote a letter, Dot drew a picture.

Compound/Complex
When Mother asked the girls to demonstrate their newly-found competencies, Joyce wrote a letter, and Dot drew a picture.

Simple sentence with compound subject
<u>Joyce</u> and <u>Dot</u> wrote letters.

The <u>girl</u> in row three and the <u>boy</u> next to her were passing notes across the aisle.

Simple sentence with compound predicate
Joyce <u>wrote letters</u> and <u>drew pictures</u>.

The captain of the high school debate team <u>graduated with honors</u> and <u>studied broadcast journalism in college</u>.

Simple sentence with compound object of preposition
Coleen graded the students' essays for <u>style</u> and <u>mechanical accuracy</u>.

Types of Clauses

Clauses are connected word groups that are composed of *at least* one subject and one verb. (A subject is the doer of an action or the element that is being joined. A verb conveys either the action or the link.) In the following examples, the subjects are underlined, and the verbs are in italics.

<u>Students</u> *are waiting* for the start of the assembly.

At the end of the play, <u>students</u> *wait* for the curtain to come down.

Clauses can be independent or dependent.

(In the following example sentences, the dependent clause is underlined once, and the independent clause is underlined twice.)

Independent clauses can stand alone or can be joined to other clauses.

<u>Kathy likes ice cream as a treat</u>, and <u>Shannon prefers brownies</u>.

Dependent clauses, by definition, contain at least one subject and one verb. However, they cannot stand alone as a complete sentence. They are structurally dependent on the main clause.

There are two types of dependent clauses: (1) those with a subordinating conjunction, and (2) those with a relative pronoun.

Sample coordinating conjunctions:	Sample relative pronouns:
Although When If Unless Because	Who Whom Which That

Unless a cure is discovered, many more people will die of the disease.

The White House has an official website, *which contains* press releases, news updates, and biographies of the President and Vice-President.
(relative pronoun in italics)

Misplaced and Dangling Modifiers

Particular phrases that are not placed near the one word they modify often result in misplaced modifiers. Phrases that do not relate to the subject being modified result in dangling modifiers.

Error: Weighing the options carefully, a decision was made regarding the punishment of the convicted murderer.

Problem: Who is weighing the options? No one capable of weighing is named in the sentence; thus, the participle phrase weighing the options carefully dangles. This problem can be corrected by adding a subject of the sentence capable of doing the action.

Correction: Weighing the options carefully, the judge made a decision regarding the punishment of the convicted murderer.

Error: One damaged house stood only to remind townspeople of the hurricane.

Problem: The placement of the misplaced modifier only suggests that the sole reason the house remained was to serve as a reminder. The faulty modifier creates ambiguity.

Correction: Only one damaged house stood, reminding townspeople of the hurricane.

Spelling

See Competency 6.G.

Capitalization

Capitalize all proper names of persons (including specific organizations or agencies of government); places (countries, states, cities, parks, and specific geographical areas); things (political parties, structures, historical and cultural terms, and calendar and time designations); and religious terms (any deity, revered person or group, and sacred writings).

> Percy Bysshe Shelley, Argentina, Mount Rainier National Park, Grand Canyon, League of Nations, the Sears Tower, Birmingham, Lyric Theater, Americans, Midwesterners, Democrats, Renaissance, Boy Scouts of America, Easter, God, Bible, Dead Sea Scrolls, Koran

Capitalize proper adjectives and titles used with proper names.

> California gold rush, President John Adams, French fries, Homeric epic, Romanesque architecture, Senator John Glenn

Note: Some words that represent titles and offices are not capitalized unless used with a proper name.

Capitalized	Not Capitalized
Congressman McKay	the congressman from Florida
Commander Alger	commander of the Pacific Fleet
Queen Elizabeth	the queen of England

Capitalize all main words in titles of works of literature, art, and music.

The candidate should be cognizant of proper rules and conventions of punctuation, capitalization, and spelling. Competency exams will generally test the ability to apply the more advanced competencies; thus, a limited number of more frustrating rules is presented here. Rules should be applied according to the American style of English, i.e., spelling *theater* instead of *theatre* and placing terminal marks of punctuation almost exclusively within other marks of punctuation.

Punctuation

Using terminal punctuation in relation to quotation marks

In a quoted statement that is either declarative or imperative, place the period inside the closing quotation marks.

> "The airplane crashed on the runway during takeoff."

If the quotation is followed by other words in the sentence, place a comma inside the closing quotations marks and a period at the end of the sentence.

> "The airplane crashed on the runway during takeoff," said the announcer.

In most instances in which a quoted title or expression occurs at the end of a sentence, the period is placed before either the single or double quotation marks.

> "The middle school readers were unprepared to understand Bryant's poem 'Thanatopsis.'"

There is an instance in which the final quotation mark would precede the period - if the content of the sentence were about a speech or quote so that the understanding of the meaning would be confused by the placement of the period.

> The first thing out of his mouth was "Hi, I'm home."
> *but*
> The first line of his speech began "I arrived home to an empty house".

In sentences that are interrogatory or exclamatory, the question mark or exclamation point should be positioned outside the closing quotation marks if the quote itself is a statement or command or cited title.

> Who decided to lead us in the recitation of the "Pledge of Allegiance"?

> I was embarrassed when Mrs. White said, "Your slip is showing"!

In sentences that are declarative but the quotation is a question or an exclamation, place the question mark or exclamation point inside the quotation marks.

> The hall monitor yelled, "Fire! Fire!"

> "Fire! Fire!" yelled the hall monitor.

> Cory shrieked, "Is there a mouse in the room?" (In this instance, the question supersedes the exclamation.)

ENG. LANG-ARTS & READING 4-8   121

Using periods with parentheses or brackets

Place the period inside the parentheses or brackets if they enclose a complete sentence, independent of the other sentences around it.

> Stephen Crane was a confirmed alcohol and drug addict. (He admitted as much to other journalists in Cuba.)

If the parenthetical expression is a statement inserted within another statement, the period in the enclosure is omitted.

> Mark Twain used the character Indian Joe (He also appeared in *The Adventures of Tom Sawyer*) as a foil for Jim in *The Adventures of Huckleberry Finn*.

When enclosed matter comes at the end of a sentence requiring quotation marks, place the period outside the parentheses or brackets.

> "The secretary of state consulted with the ambassador [Albright]."

Using commas

Separate two or more coordinate adjectives modifying the same word and three or more nouns, phrases, or clauses in a list.

> Maggie's hair was dull, dirty, and lice-ridden.

> Dickens portrayed the Artful Dodger as competency of pickpocket, loyal follower of Fagin, and defendant of Oliver Twist.

> Ellen daydreamed about getting out of the rain, taking a shower, and eating a hot dinner.

Use commas to separate antithetical or complimentary expressions from the rest of the sentence.

> The veterinarian, not his assistant, would perform the delicate surgery.

> The more he knew about her, the less he wished he had known.

> Randy hopes to, and probably will, get an appointment to the Naval Academy.

> His thorough, though esoteric, scientific research could not easily be understood by high school students.

Using double quotation marks with other punctuation

Quotations - whether words, phrases, or clauses - should be punctuated according to the rules of the grammatical function they serve in the sentence.

"You'll get my money," the old man warned, "when 'Hell freezes over'."

Sheila cited the passage that began "Four score and seven years ago...." (Note the ellipsis followed by an enclosed period.)

"Old Ironsides" inspired the preservation of the U.S.S. Constitution.

Use quotation marks to enclose the titles of shorter works: songs, short poems, short stories, essays, and chapters of books.

"The Tell-Tale Heart"   "Casey at the Bat"   "America the Beautiful"

Using semicolons

Use semicolons to separate independent clauses when the second clause is introduced by a transitional adverb. (These clauses may also be written as separate sentences, preferably by placing the adverb within the second sentence.)

The Elizabethans modified the rhyme scheme of the sonnet; thus, it was called the English sonnet.

or

The Elizabethans modified the rhyme scheme of the sonnet. It thus was called the English sonnet.

Use semicolons to separate items in a series that are long and complex or have internal punctuation.

The Italian Renaissance produced masters in the fine arts: Dante Alighieri, author of the *Divine Comedy;* Leonardo da Vinci, painter of *The Last Supper;* and Donatello, sculptor of the *Quattro Coronati,* the four saints.

The leading scorers in the WNBA were Haizhaw Zheng, averaging 23.9 points per game; Lisa Leslie, 22; and Cynthia Cooper, 19.5.

Using colons

Place a colon at the beginning of a list of items. (Note its use in the sentence about Renaissance Italians in the previous paragraph.)

> The teacher directed us to compare Faulkner's three symbolic novels: *Absalom, Absalom; As I Lay Dying;* and *Light in August*.

Do **not** use a comma if the list is preceded by a verb.

> Three of Faulkner's symbolic novels are *Absalom, Absalom; As I Lay Dying,* and *Light in August*.

Using dashes

Place dashes to denote sudden breaks in thought.

> Some periods in literature - the Romantic Age, for example - spanned different time periods in different countries.

Use dashes instead of commas if commas are already used elsewhere in the sentence for amplification or explanation.

> The Fireside Poets included three Brahmans - James Russell Lowell, Henry David Wadsworth, Oliver Wendell Holmes - and John Greenleaf Whittier.

Using italics

Use italics to punctuate the titles of long works of literature, names of periodical publications, musical scores, and works of art, motion picture television, and radio programs. (When unable to write in italics, students should be instructed to underline in their own writing where italics would be appropriate.)

The Idylls of the King	*Hiawatha*	*The Sound and the Fury*
Mary Poppins	*Newsweek*	*The Nutcracker Suite*

See Competency 7.C for information regarding further developing students' writing competencies.

SKILL C: **Knows informal and formal procedures for assessing students' use of writing conventions and uses multiple, ongoing assessments to monitor and evaluate students' development in this area**

Assessment for writing means using both informal and formal assessment methods. Informal testing should always precede formal testing. Teachers can start the year by having the students write a demand piece of a topic. This will not be used for grading purposes. It is an assessment to see where the students are in writing development and to assess their needs for further instruction. The teacher then plans writing instruction based on the students' strengths and weaknesses.

Throughout the instruction, teachers can give mini-lessons on certain aspects of writing either to the whole class or to small groups of students with similar needs. Through one-on-one conferencing, the teacher can assess how well students are improving. The use of checklists and anecdotal records helps teachers know how students are developing with each stage of the writing process.

Portfolio assessment throughout the course helps both students and teachers understand the amount of progress being made. Students should include drafts of writing so the teacher can provide comments and examples at all stages. It is important for teachers to note that not all writing will be developed to the published stage. Students often get bored with writing a piece over and over. It is not the actual piece of writing that needs to be assessed, but the improvements that students are making to demonstrate their learning.

Teachers need to use exemplars to show students what good and bad writing looks like. This can be a collection of writings from students of previous years or from another class with the names deleted. It is important not to use writing from the current class because students at this age level whose writing is really good will recognize their own piece and tell others that it is their writing. The same thing applies to students who are experiencing difficulty. While they will not tell the other students it is their writing, they will feel ridiculed by the teacher, and this will bring down their self-confidence in writing.

Rubrics are used for assessing writing. Students should know what these rubrics are so that they can informally assess their own writing to make sure they meet the criteria.

Formal assessment for writing can take the form of having students write a demand piece in one sitting or have them work through a process piece over the course of a week. The teacher will then use a rubric to grade the writing. When giving the students a grade, the teacher should pass back the writing along with the rubric so that students can see where they made mistakes. They should then engage in reflection on their writing and set goals for improving in the next assignment.

When beginning a class in writing, teachers should assess for certain things in each piece of writing rather than expect students to master everything overnight. For example, in the first piece of writing, the teacher might be looking for evidence that students use complete sentences and varied sentence structure. In another piece of writing, the teacher might concentrate on editing for spelling and grammar mistakes. Eventually, the assessment will include all aspects of writing.

Assessment Methods

- Have students write a short story, essay, or other specified genre of writing
- Observe ability to use language resources appropriate for the required task.
- Use a rating system. For example, a scale from 1 to 4 (where 1=unsatisfactory and 4=excellent).
- Monitor their use of source material
- Evaluate the structure and development of their writing
- Ensure that writing style is appropriate for the task assigned
- Check for grammatical correctness
- Provide follow-up support for any weaknesses detected

SKILL D **Uses ongoing assessment of writing conventions to determine when a student needs additional help or intervention to bring the student's performance to grade level, based on state content and performance standards for writing in the Texas Essential Knowledge and Competencies (TEKS)**

See Competencies 6.B and 6.C.

SKILL E **Analyzes students' errors in applying writing conventions and uses the results of this analysis as a basis for future instruction**

See Competency 6.B.

SKILL F **Knows writing conventions and appropriate grammar and usage and provides students with direct instruction and guided practice in these areas**

See Competency 6.B.

SKILL G: **Understands the contribution of conventional spelling toward success in reading and writing**

Spelling in English is complicated by the fact that it is not phonetic—that is, it is not based on the one-sound/one letter formula used by many other languages. The reason for this is that it is based on the Latin alphabet. The Latin alphabet, which originally had twenty letters, consisted of the present English alphabet minus J, K, V, W, Y, and Z. The Romans added K to be used in abbreviations and Y and Z in words that came from the Greek. This 23-letter alphabet was adopted by the English, who developed W as a ligatured doubling of U and later J and V as consonantal variants of I and U. The result was our alphabet of 26 letters with upper case (capital) and lower case forms.

Oral Language and Spelling

Phonological awareness leads children to the understanding of the sounds that make up spoken words. This is a necessary prelude to the production of written words. More specifically, children come to understand that words are made up of distinct phonemes, and that these sounds are correlated to letters which comprise written words. The letters in written words correspond to the phonemes in spoken ones. Phonemic awareness is a crucial Competency that underlies literacy and spelling.

Correct spelling makes it easier to read the written language. When words are constantly misspelled, the reader often gives up because reading becomes too frustrating. When students read words spelled correctly, they get a sense of how these words should be spelled. When children are learning new words they will, of course, make mistakes and use invented spelling.

Teachers should teach the rules of conventional spelling and teach students to use the dictionary to correct their spelling mistakes. However, teachers should not automatically correct the misspelled words for the students. They should point out the words they need to take a second look at and let the students find the correct spelling. "Have a Go" sheets are just as useful in middle school as they are in primary and elementary grades. Standard spelling develops more effectively when it is taught within the realm of the students' own writing. They are using words of their own and, therefore, words they need to know how to spell. The spelling instruction provided should help them acquire a variety of strategies for figuring out how words are spelled.

One example of teaching students the importance of using conventional spelling in their writing is to have them edit pieces of writing with many misspellings. Have them discuss the difficulty of reading the pieces. As they work through the editing, they will be more cognizant of their own spelling mistakes and take the time to make sure they use conventional spelling.

See Competencies 3.C and 6.A.

SKILL H: **Understands stages of spelling development and how and when to support students' development from one stage to the next**

There are five developmental stages in learning to spell:

1) **Pre-phonemic spelling**—Children know that letters stand for a message, but they do not know the relationship between spelling and pronunciation.

2) **Early phonemic spelling**—Children are beginning to understand spelling. They usually write the beginning letter correctly with the rest consonants or long vowels.

3) **Letter-name spelling**—Some words are consistently spelled correctly. The student is developing a sight vocabulary and a stable understanding of letters as representing sounds. Long vowels are usually used accurately, but silent vowels are omitted. The child spells unknown words by attempting to match the name of the letter to the sound.

4) **Transitional spelling**—This phase is typically entered in late elementary school. Short vowel sounds are mastered, and some spelling rules are known. The students are developing a sense of which spellings are correct and which are not.

5) **Derivational spelling**—This is usually reached from high school to adulthood. This is the stage at which spelling rules are mastered.

Effective spelling strategies should emphasize these principles:

- knowledge of patterns, sounds, letter-sound association, syllables
- memorizing sight words
- writing those words correctly many times
- writing the words in personal writing

As teachers observe students in the classroom, conference with them about their writing, and correct written assignments, they will have a good idea of where the students are in their spelling development. Arriving at the point where one spells words correctly most of the time is a process that evolves over time. Spelling should not be taught as a separate subject but should be an integral part of Language Arts classes. Students immersed in reading and writing, together with mini-lessons on aspects of conventional spelling, will become increasingly aware of how words should be spelled.

Students who seem to be encountering difficulty should have instruction tailored to their needs. The teacher can do this on an individual basis or by providing instruction to small groups of students with similar needs. For many students, the difficulty may arise if they do not have the background knowledge in the rules of standard written English. These students may need some instruction in specific rules, such as rules for making words plural. As teachers assess students while they are writing, they will see instructional opportunities for teaching spelling, and they should incorporate this into their planning. See Competency 6.A.

SKILL I: **Provides systematic spelling instruction and gives students opportunities to use and develop spelling competencies in the context of meaningful written expression**

Basic Spelling Instruction

Concentration in this section will be on spelling plurals and possessives. The multiplicity and complexity of spelling rules based on phonics, letter doubling, and exceptions to rules - not usually mastered until adulthood - should be aided with the use of a good dictionary.

Most plurals of nouns that end in hard consonants or hard consonant sounds followed by a silent *e* are made by adding *s*. Some words ending in vowels only add *s*.

fingers, numerals, banks, bugs, riots, homes, gates, radios, bananas

Nouns that end in soft consonant sounds *s, j, x, z, ch,* and *sh*, add *es*. Some nouns ending in *o* add es.

dresses, waxes, churches, brushes, tomatoes, potatoes

Nouns ending in *y* preceded by a vowel, just add *s*.

boys, alleys

Nouns ending in *y* preceded by a consonant, change the *y* to *i* and add *es.*

babies, corollaries, frugalities, poppies

Some nouns plurals are formed irregularly or remain the same.

sheep, deer, children, leaves, oxen

Some nouns derived from foreign words, especially Latin, may make their plurals in two different ways. Sometimes, the meanings are the same. Other times, the two plurals are used in slightly different contexts. It is always wise to consult the dictionary.

      appendices, appendixes   criterion, criteria
      indexes, indices   crisis, crises

Make the plurals of closed (solid) compound words in the usual way except for words ending in *ful* which make their plurals on the root word.

      timelines, hairpins, cupsful

Make the plurals of open or hyphenated compounds by adding the change in inflection to the word that change in number.

      fathers-in-law, courts-martial, masters of art, doctors of medicine

Make the plurals of letters, numbers, and abbreviations by adding *s*.

      fives and tens, IBMs, 1990s, *p*s and *q*s (Note that letters are italicized.)

Spelling Activities

Spelling Bee
Have students practice their spelling words before having the actual test.

Newspaper Spelling
Have students find their spelling word in an article in the newspaper. Circle the spelling, and then make a list.

Weekly Spelling Story
Post a picture or illustration on the board. Have the students write a short paragraph or several sentences (depending on the level of ability) to narrate the picture.

Spelling Poems
Have students write a short poem that includes their weekly spelling words.

Students often vary in their learning styles. A visual child will be more able to learn from textbooks and worksheets. Some are auditory, learning best from hearing the rules and words. A kinesthetic child will want to feel and move, retaining information through hands-on experiences. Having a broad range of learning materials will enable students to learn at their own optimum learning level.

Spelling competencies should develop as part of an overall language arts phonemic awareness, phonics , reading comprehension, vocabulary and reading fluency, grammar, reading, and writing program. Students should (with help from their teacher) develop their foundational spelling competencies through an interest in words, regular writing, constant reading, a study of spelling rules, and playing of spelling games. Skilled, fluent readers are the culmination of the successful learning of a broad array of pre-reading and reading competencies. Irrespective of family background, learning to be a skilled speller is often not a trouble-free process. Spelling programs, personalized tutoring, reading workbooks, spelling games, and structured computer spelling programs can help teach or reinforce these competencies.

Some children need spelling practice, while others need more intensive remedial spelling programs. Teachers can help their students with the spelling process by providing high-quality educational materials, establishing a pattern of daily spelling and reading, instructing through guided spelling activity, creating a rich language environment, and discussing a child's progress with parents.

COMPETENCY 007   WRITTEN LANGUAGE—COMPOSITION

SKILL A: **Knows predictable stages in the development of written language and recognizes that individual variations occur**

See Competency 6.A

Oral Language and Writing

Many early play experiences can support a young child's emerging literacy competencies. Sorting, matching, classifying, and sequencing materials such as beads, a box of buttons, or a set of colored cubes, contribute to children's emerging literacy competencies of written forms. Rolling play dough and doing finger plays help children to strengthen and improve the coordination of the small muscles in their hands and fingers. They use these same muscles to control writing tools such as crayons, pencils, markers, and paint brushes.

Use of invented spelling encourages a child's phonemic awareness. Young children can use invented spelling to write a grocery list at the same time as a parent is writing his or her own list. By watching an adult write, they are introduced to the conventions of writing. By signing their names with a scribble, a drawing, or even some of the letters, children are learning that their names represent them. They begin to understand that writing involves utilizing written symbols which serves as a purposeful way of communicating their needs and wishes.

As children develop, they begin to learn that adults use written symbols to read and write, and those are the 26 upper and lower case letters of the alphabet. Children soon begin to learn the conventional rules governing how to write letters and form words which includes writing letters so they face in the correct direction, using upper and lower case versions, spelling words correctly, and putting spaces between words.

The development of thinking and reasoning abilities soon begins to help children understand how to read and write unfamiliar words. A child might use the meaning of a previous word, look at a familiar prefix or suffix, or use prior knowledge to recall how to pronounce a letter combination that appeared in another word.

Early emergent writing students:

- can read and retell familiar stories
- use predicting and questioning strategies for comprehension
- use reading and create/write their own stories
- practice oral reading to enhance fluency
- use letter-sound associations, word parts, and context to identify new words

- learn to identify an increasing number of words by sight
- sound out the spelling of a word
- attempt to use some punctuation and capitalization

SKILL B: **Promotes student recognition of the practical uses of writing, creates an environment in which students are motivated to express ideas in writing, and models writing as an enjoyable activity and a tool for lifelong learning**

Writing, however academic it may seem, is one of life's most basic competencies. The practical uses are endless: thank you letters, stories, journals, to-do lists, etc. Therefore, a teacher should foster that practicality in the classroom by calling attention to writing in its most basic and enjoyable forms. Remind students that writing can allow them to express thoughts they might not otherwise put forth. Furthermore, when those thoughts are put down on paper, the choice is up to them whether they want to share them with their peers or keep them as private notes. Allow students to have occasional free-writing periods, and inform them that they need not turn in their work. This breaks down the inhibitions that most students have when writing in a classroom setting. Encourage students to save their writing, describing the enjoyment they will have when looking back on it at an older age.

Many students see writing as a painful task, but they should be reminded that writing is not used solely for essays and reports. Think about signing yearbooks, writing screen plays, writing to pen pals, or writing an angry note to vent frustration (whether it is ever sent or not). Finally, stress the idea that the more one writes, the better that writer gets each time.

When teaching writing, it is important for teachers to make the activity an enjoyable one for students. When students enjoy writing in school, they will continue to view it as an enjoyable activity in their adult years. Students and teachers must recognize that writing is messy, and the students should be allowed to mark up their first and second drafts so that they can revise and edit without having to rewrite everything.

Students enjoy writing about topics that have relevance in their lives. When they see the teacher is interested in knowing about their experiences, they are eager to write. Teaching revising and editing is often difficult because middle school students, especially, want to write one draft and be finished with it. One way to help them over this hurdle is to choose one aspect of the writing for them to edit, such as finding words misspelled in the writing or finding sentence fragments. On the next piece of writing, teachers can remind them of this editing and then add a new aspect for students to edit for. Thus, students will not become bored as easily as they do when they have to work at the same piece of writing for a long time.

For information on practical uses of writing, see Competency 6.P.

SKILL C: **Knows and applies appropriate instructional strategies and sequences to develop students' writing competencies**

Stories

It seems simplistic, yet it's an often-overlooked truism: the first and most important measure of a story is the story itself. However, a good story must have certain characteristics. Without conflict there is no story, so determining what the conflicts are should be a priority for the writer. Once the conflicts are determined, the outcome of the story must be decided. Who wins? Who loses? And what factors go into making one side of the equation win out over the other? The pattern of the plot is also an important consideration. Where is the climax going to occur? Is denouement necessary? Does the reader need to see the unwinding of all the strands? Many stories fail because a denouement is needed but not supplied.

Characterization, the choice the writer makes about the devices he/she will use to reveal character, requires an understanding of human nature, as well as an artistic Competency to convey a personality to the reader. This is usually accomplished subtly through dialogue, interior monologue, description, and the character's actions and behavior. In some successful stories, the writer comes right out and tells the reader what this character is like. However, sometimes there will be discrepancies between what the narrator tells the reader about the character and what is revealed to be true.

Point of view is a powerful tool not only for the writer but is also important for the enjoyment and understanding of the reader. The writer must choose among several possibilities: first-person narrator objective, first-person narrator omniscient, third-person objective, third-person omniscient, and third-person limited omniscient. The most successful story-writers use point of view very creatively to accomplish their purposes. If a writer wishes to be successful, he/she must develop point-of-view competencies.

Style—the unique way a writer uses language—is often the writer's signature. The writer must be cognizant of his/her own strengths and weaknesses and continually work to hone the way sentences are written, words are chosen, and descriptions are crafted until they are razor-sharp. The best advice to the aspiring writer: read the works of successful writers. If a writer wants to write a best-seller, then that writer needs to be reading best-sellers.

Poetry

Writing poetry in the 21st century is quite a different thing from writing it in earlier periods. There was a time when a poem was required to fit a certain pattern or scheme. Poetry was once defined as a piece of writing that was made up of end-rhymes. Today, the rhymed poem makes up only a small percentage of worthwhile and successful poems.

The first Competency to work on for the budding poet is descriptive writing – writing defined as language that appeals to one or more of the five senses. A good poem makes it possible for the reader to experience an emotional event (for example, seeing a mountain range as the sun dawns, watching small children on a playground, smelling the fragrance of a rose, or feeling fine silk under one's fingers). Creating language that makes that experience available to the readers is only the first step, however, because the ultimate goal is to evoke an emotional response. Feeling the horror of the battleground, weeping with the mother whose child was drowned, exulting with a winning soccer team. It's not enough to tell the reader what it's like. It's the *showing* that is necessary.

The aspiring poet should know the possibilities as well as the limitations of this genre. A poem can tell a story, for instance, but the emotional response is more important than the story itself.

Play Writing

Play writing uses many of the same competencies that are necessary for successful story writing. However, in addition to those competencies, there are many more required of the writer who wishes his/her story to be told on stage or film. The point of view, of course, is always objective unless the writers uses the Shakespearean device of the soliloquy, where a player steps forward and gives information about what's going on. The audience must figure out the meaning of the play on the basis of the actions and speeches of the actors.

The plot of most plays is rising; that is, the conflicts are introduced early in the play and continue to develop and intensify over the life of the play. As a general rule, the climax is the last thing that happens before the final curtain falls, but not necessarily. Plots of plays demonstrate the same breadth of patterns that are true of stories.

A successful playwright is an expert in characterization as described above under "Story." What a character is like is determined by dialogue, appearance (costume, etc.), behavior, and actions. A successful playwright also understands motivation. If a character's behavior cannot be traced to motivating circumstances, the audience will probably find the action incoherent—a major barrier to positive reception of the play.

The writing must be very carefully honed. Absolutely no excess words can be found in a successful play. It takes very little time to lose an audience, so every word counts. The playwright should concentrate on saying the most possible with the fewest words.

Setting is an important feature of the play. Many plays have only one setting because changing settings in the middle is difficult and disrupting. This calls for a very special kind of writing. The entire action of the play must either take place within the setting or be brought forth in that setting by the reporting or recounting of what is going on outside of the setting by one or more of the characters.

Improving Organization, Clarity and Focus of Writing

Introductions

It's important to remember that in the writing process, the introduction should be written last. Until the body of the paper has been determined—the thesis and its development—it's difficult to make strategic decisions regarding the introduction. The basic purpose of the introduction is to lead the audience into the discourse. It can let the reader know what the purpose of the discourse is, and it can condition the audience to be receptive to what the writer wants to say. It can be very brief, or it can take up a large percentage of the total word count. Aristotle said that the introduction could be compared to the flourishes that flute players make before their performance—an overture in which the musicians display what they can play best in order to gain the favor and attention of the audience for the main performance.

In order to do this, we must first of all know what we are going to say; who the readership is likely to be; what the social/political/economic climate is; what preconceived notions the audience is likely to have regarding the subject; and how long the discourse is going to be.

There are many ways to do this:

- Show that the subject is important
- Show that although the points we are presenting may seem improbable, they are true
- Show that the subject has been neglected, misunderstood, or misrepresented
- Explain an unusual mode of development
- Forestall any misconception of the purpose
- Apologize for a deficiency
- Arouse interest in the subject with an anecdotal lead-in
- Ingratiate oneself with the readership
- Establish one's own credibility

The introduction often ends with the thesis (the point or purpose of the paper). However, this is not set in stone. The thesis may open the body of the discussion, or it may conclude the discourse. The most important thing to remember is that the purpose and structure of the introduction should be deliberate if it is to serve the purpose of "leading the reader into the discussion."

Conclusions

It's easier to write a conclusion after the decisions regarding the introduction have been made. Aristotle taught that the conclusion should strive to do five things:

1. Inspire the reader with a favorable opinion of the writer.
2. Amplify the force of the points made in the body of the paper.
3. Reinforce the points made in the body.
4. Rouse appropriate emotions in the reader.
5. Restate in a summary way what has been said.

The conclusion may be short, or it may be long depending on its purpose in the paper. Recapitulation, a brief restatement of the main points or certainly of the thesis, is the most common form of effective conclusions.

Text Organization

In studies of professional writers and how they produce their successful works, it has been revealed that writing is a process that can be clearly defined. In practice, however, it must have enough flexibility to allow for creativity. The teacher must be able to define the various stages that a successful writer goes through in order to make a statement that has value. There must be a discovery stage when ideas, materials, supporting details, etc., are deliberately collected. These may come from many possible sources: the writer's own experience and observations, deliberate research of written sources, interviews of live persons, television presentations, or the Internet.

Organization is where the purpose, thesis, and supporting points are determined. Most writers will put forth more than one possible thesis, and the writing of the paper will settle on one as the result of trial and error. Once the paper is written, effective editing is necessary. At this point, decisions must be made regarding whether the reasoning is cohesive, arranged well, and clear.

It's important to remember that the best writers engage in all of these stages recursively. They may go back to discovery at any point in the process. They may also go back and rethink the organization, etc. To help students become effective writers, the teacher needs to give them adequate practice in the various stages and encourage them to engage deliberately in the creative thinking that makes writers successful.

Techniques to Maintain Focus

- **Focus on a main point.** The point should be clear to readers, and all sentences in each paragraph should relate to the topic of that paragraph
- **Start the paragraph with a topic sentence.** This should be a general, one-sentence summary of the paragraph's main point, relating both back toward the thesis and toward the content of the paragraph. (A topic

sentence is sometimes unnecessary if the paragraph continues to develop an idea clearly introduced in a preceding paragraph or if the paragraph appears in a narrative of events where generalizations might interrupt the flow of the story)

- **Stick to the point.** Eliminate sentences that do not support the topic sentence
- **Be flexible.** If there is not enough evidence to support the claim your topic sentence is making, do not fall into the trap of wandering or introducing new ideas within the paragraph. Either find more evidence or adjust the topic sentence to coordinate with the evidence that is available

Enhancing Interest

- Start out with an attention-grabbing introduction. This sets an engaging tone for the entire piece and will be more likely to pull in the reader
- Use dynamic vocabulary and varied sentence beginnings. Keep the readers on their toes. If they can predict what you are going to say next, switch it up
- Avoid using clichés (as cold as ice, the best thing since sliced bread, nip it in the bud). These are easy shortcuts, but they are not interesting, memorable, or convincing

Ensuring Understanding

- Avoid using the words, "clearly," "obviously," and "undoubtedly." Often, things that are clear or obvious to the author are not as apparent to the reader. Instead of using these words, make your point so strongly that it is clear on its own
- Use the word that best fits the meaning you intend, even if it is longer or a little less common
- When in doubt, explain further

SKILL D: **Knows characteristics and uses of informal and formal written language assessments, and uses multiple, ongoing assessments to monitor and evaluate students' writing development**

See Competencies 6.C and 6.D.

SKILL E: **Uses assessment results to plan focused instructions to address the writing strengths, needs and interests of all individuals and groups, including English-language learners.**

See Competencies 6.C and 6.D.

- Keep an idea book so that they can jot down ideas that come to mind
- Write in a daily journal
- Write down whatever comes to mind - this is called free writing. Students do not stop to make corrections or interrupt the flow of ideas. A variation of this technique is focused free writing - writing on a specific topic - to prepare for an essay
- Make a list of all ideas connected with their topic - this is called brainstorming. Make sure students know that this technique works best when they let their minds work freely. After completing the list, students should analyze the list to see if a pattern or way to group the ideas emerges
- Ask the questions Who? What? When? Where? When? and How? Help the writer approach a topic from several perspectives
- Create a visual map on paper to gather ideas. Cluster circles and lines to show connections between ideas. Students should try to identify the relationship that exists between their ideas. If they cannot see the relationships, have them pair up, exchange papers, and have their partners look for some related ideas
- Observe details of sight, hearing, taste, touch, and taste
- Visualize by making mental images of something and write down the details in a list

After they have practiced with each of these writing strategies, ask students to pick out the ones they prefer, and ask them to discuss how they might use the techniques to help them with future writing assignments. It is important to remember that they can use more than one writing strategy at a time. Also, they may find that different writing situations may suggest certain techniques.

| SKILL F: | Uses ongoing assessment of written language to determine when a student needs additional help or intervention to bring the student's performance to grade level, based on state content and performance standards for writing in the Texas Essential Knowledge and Competencies (TEKS). |

When assessing and responding to student writing, there are several guidelines to remember.

Responding to non-graded writing (formative)

1. Avoid using a red pen. Whenever possible use a #2 pencil.
2. Explain the criteria that will be used for assessment in advance.
3. Read the writing once while asking the question, "Is the student's response appropriate for the assignment?"
4. Reread and make note at the end whether the student met the objective of the writing task.

5. Responses should be non-critical and use supportive and encouraging language.
6. Resist writing on or over the student's writing.
7. Highlight the ideas you wish to emphasize, question, or verify.
8. Encourage your students to take risks.

Responding to and evaluating graded writing (summative)

1. Ask students to submit prewriting and rough-draft materials including all revisions with their final draft.
2. For the first reading, use a holistic method, examining the work as a whole.
3. When reading the draft for the second time, assess it using the standards previously established.
4. Responses to the writing should be written in the margin and should use supportive language.
5. Make sure you address the process as well as the product. It is important that students value the learning process as well as the final product.
6. After scanning the piece a third time, write final comments at the end of the draft.

Sometimes revising their work is seen by students as simply catching errors in spelling or word use. Students need to reframe their thinking about revising and editing. Some questions that need to be asked:

- Is the reasoning coherent?
- Is the point established?
- Does the introduction make the reader want to read this discourse?
- What is the thesis? Is it proven?
- What is the purpose? Is it clear? Is it useful, valuable, interesting?
- Is the style of writing so wordy that it exhausts the reader and interferes with engagement?
- Is the writing so sparse that it is boring?
- Are the sentences too uniform in structure?
- Are there too many simple sentences?
- Are too many of the complex sentences the same structure?
- Are the compounds truly compounds, or are they unbalanced?
- Are parallel structures truly parallel?
- If there are characters, are they believable?
- If there is dialogue, is it natural or stilted?
- Is the title appropriate?
- Does the writing show creativity, or is it boring?
- Is the language appropriate? Is it too formal? Too informal? If jargon is used, is it appropriate?

Studies have clearly demonstrated that the most fertile area in teaching writing is revision. If students can learn to revise their own work effectively, they are well on their way to becoming effective, mature writers. Word processing is an important tool for teaching this stage in the writing process. Microsoft Word has tracking features that make the revision exchanges between teachers and students more effective than ever before.

See Competencies 6.C and 6.D.

SKILL G: **Understands the use of self-assessment in writing and provides opportunities for students to self-assess their writing (e.g., for clarity, interest to audience, comprehensiveness) and their development as writers.**

When teaching writing, teachers must provide many opportunities for the children to write. In fact, writing should be a daily activity in the classroom, just as reading is. As the children are writing, teachers need to engage in ongoing assessment to determine the strengths and needs of the students. For some strategies, the teacher might need to teach or re-teach specific competencies to a small group of students. At other times, there may be a need for whole class instruction.

Motivating students to write means helping them find topics that are of interest to them. By having students complete an interest survey, teachers will get an idea of what they like to read and write about. Before beginning any writing program, the teacher could ask the student to brainstorm a list of topics they could write about during the year and keep this list in their writing folders. As teachers work with the students through the stages of the writing process, teacher-student conferences provide the best information on the students' progress. Instead of letting students work all the way through a piece of writing and then grading the final copy, teachers should conference with each student through every stage. This way, the teacher will learn where students need intervention as well as which students would make the best peer editors for other students.

Students that struggle with editing and revising need constant praise to keep them motivated. They often become overwhelmed with having to edit a large piece of text, especially if there are a lot of mistakes. Teachers could ask the student to edit for capitalization only, which will make it easier for the students. Teachers can also assess students' writing by reading over the drafts, making notes as to what corrections should be made, and giving the students another chance to improve the writing before they receive a final grade.

Monitoring Writing Development

Teachers need to continually monitor students' writing development throughout the school year. Aside from formal state and classroom assessments, teachers can gather information about students' writing progress in informal ways, too.

Some of these ways include:

- Writer's workshop portfolios
- Running records
- Portfolio assessment
- Journal writing
- Assignments scored with rubrics
- Application of writing to other subject areas and projects

Together with formal assessments, these methods can help teachers and parents watch students' writing develop throughout the year.

Viewing writing as a process allows teachers and students to see the writing classroom as a cooperative workshop where students and teachers encourage and support each other in each writing endeavor.

Listed below are some techniques that help teachers facilitate and create a supportive classroom environment.

1. Create peer response/support groups that are working on similar writing assignments. The members help each other in all stages of the writing process (prewriting, writing, revising, editing, and publishing).
2. Provide several prompts to give students the freedom to write on a topic of their choice. Writing should be generated out of personal experience, and students should be introduced to in-class journals. One effective way to get into writing is to let them write often and freely about their own lives, without having to worry about grades or evaluation.
3. Respond in the form of a question whenever possible. The teacher/facilitator should respond non-critically and use positive, supportive language.
4. Respond to formal writing by acknowledging the student's strengths and by focusing on the composition competencies demonstrated by the writing. A response should encourage the student by offering praise for what the student has done well. Give the student a focus for revision, and demonstrate that the process of revision has applications in many other writing situations.
5. Provide students with readers' checklists so that students can write observational critiques of others' drafts. Then they can revise their own papers at home using the checklists as a guide.
6. Pair students so that they can give and receive responses. Pairing students keeps them aware of the role of an audience in the composing process and in evaluating stylistic effects.
7. Focus critical comments on aspects of the writing that can be observed in the writing. Comments like, "I noticed you use the word 'is' frequently" will be more helpful than "Your introduction is dull" and will not demoralize the writer.

8. Provide the group with a series of questions to guide them through the group writing sessions.

SKILL H: **Understands differences between first-draft writing and writing for publication and provides instruction in various stages of writing, including prewriting, drafting, editing, and revising.**

The Writing Process

Writing is a recursive process. As students engage in the various stages of writing, they develop and improve not only their writing competencies but their thinking competencies as well. Students must understand that writing is a process and typically involves many steps when writing quality work. No matter the level of writer, students should be experienced in the following stages of the writing process.

Prewriting

Prior to writing, students will need to prewrite for ideas and details as well as decide how the essay will be organized. In the hour they have to write, students should spend no more than 5-10 minutes prewriting and organizing ideas. As they prewrite, students should remember to include at least three main points and at least two to three details to support each main idea.

Prewriting may include clustering, listing, brainstorming, mapping, free writing, and charting. Providing many ways for a student to develop ideas on a topic will increase his/her chances for success. Remind students that as they prewrite, they need to consider their audience and purpose.

Prewriting strategies assist students in a variety of ways. Listed below are the most common prewriting strategies students can use to explore, plan, and write on a topic. It is important to remember when teaching these strategies that not all prewriting must eventually produce a finished piece of writing. In fact, in the initial lesson of teaching prewriting strategies, it might be more effective to have students practice prewriting strategies without the pressure of having to write a finished product.

See Competency 6.J.

There are several types of graphic organizers that students can use to prepare for the essay portion of a test.

VISUAL ORGANIZER: GIVING REASONS

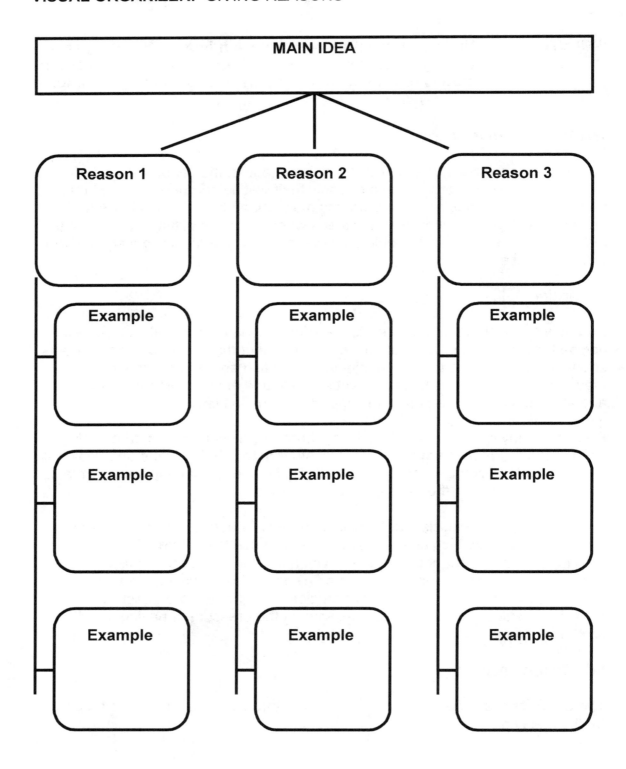

After students have completed a graphic organizer, they need to decide how to organize their essays. Students might consider one of the following patterns to structure their essays.

1. Examine individual elements such as plot, setting, theme, character, point of view, tone, mood, or style.

   SINGLE ELEMENT OUTLINE
   Intro - main idea statement
   Main point 1 with at least two supporting details
   Main point 2 with at least two supporting details
   Main point 3 with at least two supporting details
   Conclusion (restates main ideas and summary of main points)

2. Compare and contrast two elements.

POINT-BY-POINT	BLOCK
Introduction Statement of main idea about A and B	Introduction Statement of main idea about A and B
Main Point 1 Discussion of A Discussion of B	Discussion of A Main Point 1 Main Point 2 Main point 3
Main Point 2 Discussion of A Discussion of B	Discussion of B Main Point 1 Main Point 2 Main Point 3
Main Point 3 Discussion of A Discussion of B	Conclusion Restate main idea
Conclusion Restatement or summary of main idea	

PRACTICE:
Using the cluster on the next page, choose an organizing chart and complete it for the topic.

VISUAL ORGANIZER: GIVING INFORMATION

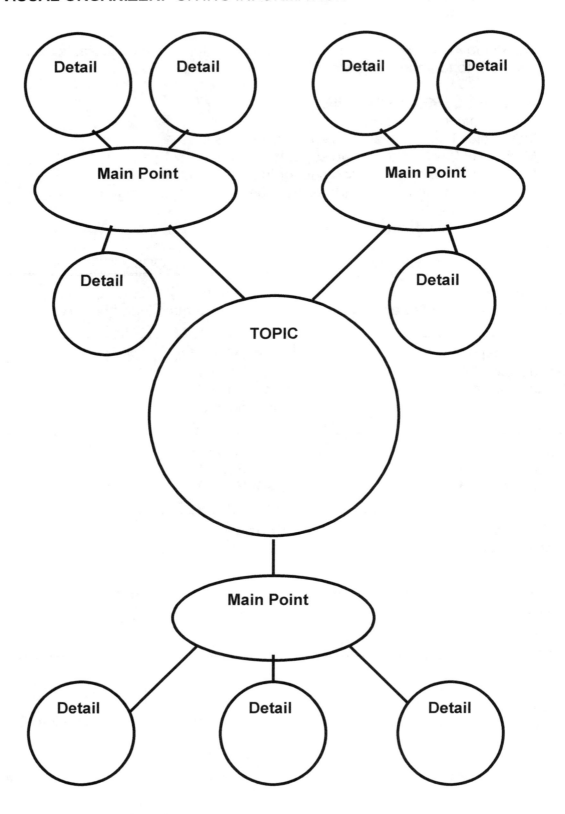

Seeing writing as a process is very helpful in saving preparation time, particularly in the taking of notes and the development of drafts. Once a decision is made about the topic to be developed, some preliminary review of literature is helpful in thinking about the next step, which is to determine what the purpose of the written document will be.

For example, if the topic is immigration, a cursory review of the various points of view in the debate going on in the country will help the writer decide what this particular written piece will try to accomplish. The purpose could just be a review of the various points of view, which would be an informative purpose. On the other hand, the writer might want to take a point of view and provide proof and support with the purpose of changing the reader's mind. The writer might even want the reader to take some action as the result of reading. Another possible purpose might be simply to write a description of a family of immigrants.

Once that cursory review has been completed, it's time to begin research in earnest and prepare to take notes. If the thesis has been clearly defined and some thought has been given to what will be used to prove or support it, a tentative outline can be developed. A thesis plus three points is typical. Decisions about the introduction and conclusion should be deferred until the body of the paper is written. Note-taking is much more effective if the notes are being taken to provide information for an outline. There is much less danger that the writer will go off on time-consuming tangents.

Formal outlines inhibit effective writing. However, a loosely constructed outline can be an effective device for note-taking that will yield the information for a worthwhile statement about a topic. Sentence outlines are better than topic outlines because they require the writer to do some thinking about the direction a subtopic will take.

Drafting
Once this preliminary note-taking phase is over, the first draft can be developed. The writing at this stage is likely to be highly individualistic. However, successful writers tend to just write, keeping in mind the purpose of the paper, the point that is going to be made in it and the information that has been turned up in the research. Student writers need to understand that this first draft is just that—the first one. It takes more than one draft to write a worthwhile statement about a topic. This is what successful writers do. It's sometimes helpful to have students read the various drafts of a story by a well-known writer.

Revision and Editing
Once the draft is on paper, revision/editing occurs. With word processors, this is much more easily achieved than in the past. Sections can be deleted, words can be changed, and additions can be made without doing the entire project over a second time.

Revise comes from the Latin word *revidere*, meaning, "to see again." Revision is probably the most important step for the writer in the writing process. Here, students examine their work and make changes in wording, details, and ideas. So many times, students write a draft and then feel they're done. On the contrary, students must be encouraged to develop, change, and enhance their writing as they go as well as once they've completed a draft.

Revision is slightly different than editing. Both teachers and students should be aware of the difference between these two writing processes. Revising typically entails making substantial changes to a written draft, and it is during this process that the look, idea, and feel of a draft may be altered, sometimes significantly. Like revising, editing continues to make changes to a draft. However, the changes made during the editing process do more to enhance the ideas in the draft, rather than change or alter them.

Effective teachers realize that revision and editing go hand-in-hand, and students often move back and forth between these stages during the course of one written work. Also, these stages must be practiced in small groups, pairs and/or individually. Students must learn to analyze and improve their own work as well as the works of their peers. Some methods to use include:

- Have students, working in pairs, analyze sentences for variety
- Have students, working in pairs or groups, ask questions about unclear areas in the writing or help students add details, information, etc.
- Have students perform final edit

To help students revise, provide students with a series of questions that will assist them in revising their writing.

- Do the details give a clear picture? Add details that appeal to more than just the sense of sight
- How effectively are the details organized? Reorder the details if it is needed
- Are the thoughts and feelings of the writer included? Add personal thoughts and feelings about the subject

Many teachers introduce Writer's Workshop to their students to maximize learning about the writing process. Writer's Workshops vary across classrooms, but the main idea is for students to become comfortable enough with the writing process to produce written work. A basic Writer's Workshop will include a block of classroom time committed to writing various projects (i.e., narratives, memoirs, book summaries, fiction, book reports, etc.). Students use this time to write, meet with others to review/edit writing, make comments on writing, revise their own work, proofread, meet with the teacher, and publish their work.

Teachers who facilitate effective Writer's Workshops are able to meet with students one at a time and can guide that student in their individual writing needs. This approach allows the teacher to differentiate instruction for each student's writing level.

Students need to be trained to become effective at proofreading, revising, and editing strategies. Begin by training them using both desk-side and scheduled conferences. Listed below are some strategies to use to guide students through the final stages of the writing process (and these can easily be incorporated into a Writer's Workshop).

- Provide some guide sheets or forms for students to use during peer responses
- Allow students to work in pairs
- Model the use of the guide sheet or form for the entire class
- Give students a time limit or number of written pieces to be completed in a specific amount of time
- Have the students read their partners' papers, and ask at least three who, what, when, why, and how questions. The students answer the questions and use them as a place to begin discussing the piece

Proofreading
Proofreading is the stage where grammatical and technical errors are addressed. Students proofread the draft for punctuation and mechanical errors. There are a few key points to remember when helping students learn to edit and proofread their work.

- It is crucial that students are not taught grammar in isolation but in the context of the writing process
- Ask students to read their writing and check for specific errors such as whether or not every sentence starts with a capital letter and has the correct punctuation at the end
- Provide students with a proofreading checklist to guide them as they edit their work

Publishing
Students may have their work displayed on a bulletin board, read aloud in class, or printed in a literary magazine or school anthology.

SKILL I: **Understands the development of writing in relation to the other language arts and uses instructions strategies that connect these various aspects of language.**

The last twenty years have seen great change in instruction in the English classroom. Gone are the days when literature is taught on Monday, Wednesday is grammar day, and Friday you assign writing. Integrating reading, writing, speaking, listening, and viewing allows students to make connections between each aspect of language development during each class.

Suggestions for Integrating Language Arts

- Use pre-reading activities such as discussion, writing, research, and journals; use writing to tap into prior knowledge before students read; engage students in class discussions about themes, issues, and ideas explored in journals; encourage predicting the outcome and exploring related information
- Use prewriting activities such as reading model essays, researching, interviewing others, combining sentences, and other prewriting activities. Remember that developing language proficiency is a recursive process and involves practice in reading, writing, thinking, speaking, listening, and viewing
- Create writing activities that are relevant to students by having them write and share with real audiences
- Connect correctness - including developing competencies of conventional usage, spelling, grammar, and punctuation - to the revision and editing stage of writing. Review of mechanics and punctuation can be done with mini-lessons that use sentences from student papers, sentence combining strategies, and modeling passages of skilled writers
- Connect reading, writing, listening, speaking, and viewing by using literature read as a springboard for a variety of activities

See Competency 5.E.

SKILL J: **Understands similarities and differences between language (e.g., syntax, vocabulary) used in spoken and written English and helps students use knowledge of these similarities and differences to enhance their own writing.**

Strategies for promoting awareness of the relationship between spoken and written language

- The teacher writes down what the children are saying on a chart
- Highlight and celebrate the meanings, uses, and print products found in the classroom. These products include: posters, labels, yellow sticky pad notes, labels on shelves and lockers, calendars, rule signs, and directions.
- The intentional reading of big-print and oversized books to teach print conventions such as directionality

- Practice exercises in reading to others
- Search and discuss adventures in word awareness and close observation where children are challenged to identify and talk about the length,

appearance, and boundaries of specific words and the letters which comprise them

- Have children match oral words to printed words by forming an echo chorus. As the teacher reads the story aloud, they echo the reading. Often this works best with poetry or rhymes
- Have the children combine, manipulate, switch, and move letters to change words and spelling pattern
- Work with letter cards to create messages and respond to the messages that they create

Student's developmental writing competencies parallel their reading development. Print awareness develops in young children as a result of listening to a story read to them by adults and recognizing that words on a page symbolize meaning. Print awareness is the realization that writing is created with instruments such as pens, pencils, crayons, and markers. Children began to imitate the shapes and letters they see in a book or in text. Children soon learn that the power of writing is expressing one's own ideas in print form and can be understood by others.

Due to the social nature of children's learning, early instruction must provide rich demonstrations, interactions, and models of literacy. Children learn about the relation between oral and written language and the relation between letters, sounds, and words. Classrooms should include a wide variety of print and writing activities that involve talking, reading, writing, playing, and listening to one another. Books, papers, writing tools, and functional signs should be visible everywhere in the classroom so that children can see and use literacy for multiple purposes.

Sitting down with a child and discussing ideas for writing helps in organizing thoughts. This also gives the student the opportunity to state the ideas out loud before writing them out on paper. Allow students who have difficulty with writing to respond by using art (drawing their favorite part or character) or drama (rehearsing the story) to aid them. This extra time allows writers to rehearse their ideas before putting them on paper. Most importantly, respect a student's writing. All students need to feel that their work is valued.

See Competency 1.l.

SKILL K: **Understands writing for a variety of audiences, purposes and settings and provides students with opportunities to write for various audiences, purposes, and settings.**

In the past, most teacher-assigned writing had the teacher as the sole audience for the assignments, and the purpose of the assignment was usually to inform. However, for students to be meaningfully engaged in their writing, they must write for a variety of reasons and audiences. Writing for different audiences and aims allows students to be more involved in their writing. If they write for the same audience and purpose, they will continue to see writing as just another assignment. Listed below are suggestions that give students an opportunity to write in more creative and critical ways.

- Write letters to the editor, to a college, to a friend, or to another student that would be sent to the intended audience
- Write stories that would be read aloud to a group (the class, another group of students, a group of elementary school students) or published in a literary magazine or class anthology
- Write plays that would be performed
- Have students discuss the parallels between the different speech and writing styles for different readers or audiences
- Allow students to write a particular piece for different audiences
- As part of the prewriting, have students identify the audience
- Expose students to writing that is on the same topic but intended for various audiences; have students identify the variations in sentence structure and style
- Remind your students that it is not necessary to identify all the specifics of the audience in the initial stage of the writing process but that at some point they must make some determinations about audience

Make sure students consider the following when analyzing the needs of their audience.

1. Why is the audience reading my writing? Do they expect to be informed, amused, or persuaded?
2. What does my audience already know about my topic?
3. What does the audience want or need to know? What will interest them?
4. What type of language suits my readers?

It may seem, sometimes, that the business letter is a thing of the past. Although much business letter writing has been relegated to email communications, letters are still a valuable form of communication. A carefully-written letter can be powerful. It can alienate, convince, persuade, entice, motivate, and/or create good-will.

As with any other communication, it's worthwhile to learn as much as possible about the receiver. This may be complicated if there will be more than one receiver of the message; in these cases, it's best to aim for the lowest common denominator if that can be achieved without "writing down" to any of those who will read and be affected or influenced by the letter. It may be better to send more than one form of the letter to the various receivers in some cases.

Purpose is the most powerful factor in writing a business letter. What is the letter expected to accomplish? Is it intended to get the receiver to act or to act in a specific manner? Are you hoping to see some action take place as the result of the letter? If so, students should clearly define what the purpose is before crafting the letter.

Reasons for choosing the letter as the channel of communication include the following:

1. It's easy to keep a record of the transaction.
2. The message can be edited and perfected before it is transmitted.
3. It facilitates the handling of details.
4. It's ideal for communicating complex information.
5. It's a good way to disseminate mass messages at a relatively low cost.

Business letters typically use formal language. They should be straightforward, concise, and courteous. Clarity is also very important. Otherwise, it may take more than one exchange of letters or phone calls to get the message across.

A complaint is a different kind of business letter. It can come under the classification of a "bad news" business letter, and there are some guidelines that are helpful when writing this kind of letter. A positive writing style can overcome much of the inherent negativity of a letter of complaint. Maintaining self-control and courtesy is more likely to be effective and helps to avoid demeaning or blaming language. Abruptness, condescension, or harshness of tone will not help achieve your purpose, particularly if you are requesting a positive response such as reimbursement for a bad product or some help in righting a wrong. It's important to remember the goal is a solution to the specific problem.

News articles are written in the "inverted pyramid" format and are deductive in nature. The opening statement is the point of the article, and everything else is details. "Who, what, why, when, and where" are usually the questions to be answered in a news article.

A formal essay, on the other hand, may be persuasive, informative, descriptive, or narrative in nature. The purpose should be clearly defined, and development must be coherent and easy to follow.

Email has revolutionized business communications. It has most of the advantages of business letters and the added benefits of immediacy, lower cost, and convenience. Even very long reports can be attached to an email. On the other hand, a two-line message can be sent and a response received immediately bringing together the features of a postal system and the telephone. Instant messaging goes even one step further. It can do all of the above—send messages, attach reports, etc.—and still have many of the advantages of a telephone conversation. Email has an unwritten code of behavior that includes restrictions on how informal the writing can be. The level of accepted business conversation is usually also acceptable in emails. Capital letters and bolding are considered shouting and are usually frowned on.

SKILL L: **Knows how to write using voices and styles appropriate for different audiences and purposes, and provides students with opportunities to write using various voices and styles.**

The more information a speaker has about an audience, the more likely he/she is to communicate effectively. Several factors figure into the speaker/audience equation: age, ethnic background, educational level, knowledge of the subject, and interest in the subject.

For example, one must consider age when writing or speaking about computers to senior citizens because they will likely have, at best, rudimentary knowledge about the way computers work. Perhaps handing out a glossary of terms would be useful for this audience. On the other hand, the average high-school student has more experience with computers than most adults, and that should be considered. Writing for computer systems engineers requires a rather thorough understanding of the jargon related to the field.

However, in considering the audience, it's best not to make blanket assumptions. The gathering of senior citizens might include retired systems engineers or people who have made their livings using computers, so research about the audience is important. It might not be wise to assume that high-school students have a certain level of understanding, either.

It's unwise to "speak down" to an audience; they will almost certainly be insulted. On the other hand, writing or speaking to an audience of college graduates will require different competencies than writing or speaking to an audience of people who have never attended college.

Finally, the reason the audience has assembled is important. Has the audience come because of an interest in the topic or because they have been influenced or forced to come to the presentation? If the audience comes with an interest in the subject already, efforts to motivate or draw them into the discussion might not be needed. On the other hand, if the speaker knows the audience does not have a high level of interest in the topic, it would be wise to use devices to draw them into it, to motivate them to listen.

Informal and formal language is a distinction made based on the occasion as well as the audience. At a "formal" occasion, for example, a meeting of executives or government officials, even conversational exchanges are likely to be more formal. A cocktail party or a golf game are both examples where the language is likely to be informal. Formal language uses fewer or no contractions, less slang, longer sentences, and more organization in longer segments.

Speeches or writing delivered to executives, college professors, government officials, etc., are likely to be formal. Speeches and writing presented to fellow employees are likely to be informal. Sermons tend to be formal; Bible lessons tend to be informal.

Jargon is a specialized vocabulary. It may be the vocabulary peculiar to a industry such as computers or a field such as education. It may also be the vocabulary of a social group. The speaker must be knowledgeable about and sensitive to the jargon peculiar to the audience. That may require some research and some vocabulary development on the speaker's part.

Technical language is a form of jargon. It is usually specific to an industry, profession, or field of study. Sensitivity to the language familiar to the audience is important.

Slang is lower in prestige than Standard English. It tends to first appear in the language of groups with low status, and it is often taboo and unlikely to be used by people of high status. Slang also tends to displace conventional terms, either as shorthand or as a defense against perceptions associated with the conventional terms.

Regionalisms are those usages that are peculiar to a part of the country. The speaker/writer should be cognizant of the various terms that are specific to a region when presenting a speech or writing to maximize clarity.

Vocabulary also varies from region to region. A small stream is a "creek" in some regions but "crick" in others. In Boston, soft drinks are generically called "tonic," but it becomes "soda" in other parts of the northeast. It is "liqueur" in Canada, and "pop" when you get very far west of New York.

SKILL M: **Understands the benefits of technology for teaching writing and writing for publication, and provides instruction in the use of technology to facilitate written communication.**

The Internet has transformed all kinds of communications all over the world. Very few people write letters in the 21st century that will be delivered physically to an individual's mailbox. However, there are still important reasons for writing letters. For one thing, letters are more personal and convey a quite different message from an e-mail, especially if they are handwritten. For another, not everybody has and uses e-mail regularly.

A high percentage of communications between individuals, groups, and businesses is conducted nowadays over the Internet. It has even replaced many telephone calls. Internet language should be courteous, free of words that might be offensive, and clear. In the early days of e-mail, a writer was censured for using bold or capital letters. That has relaxed somewhat. Nowadays, almost anything goes, although it's generally accepted that restrained language is assumed for business people and personal communications. The blog, where a person has his/her own website and uses it to send messages, is a new wrinkle. Chat is available on most blogs as well as other Internet sites. The language and the messages tend to be unrestrained there.

Some people use the same styles for letters via e-mail that are recommended for paper letters; however, the formatting has tended to become less and less formal. It is not uncommon for thank-you letters and invitations to be sent via e-mail. One important feature of the Internet that makes it so valuable is that it has the potential to reach everywhere—to small communities, all the way across the country, and overseas. It's possible to dash off an e-mail note to a person or business or several persons or businesses in Europe as quickly as to a person in the next office, and it costs no extra money beyond the cost of equipment and Internet services.

The fax machine is yet another dimension of electronic communications. At first, it was used primarily by businesses, but it has become so affordable that many people have them in their homes. The fax makes possible an actual picture of a document. This may be preferable to retyping a document or sending it by paper mail because it can go immediately. Sometimes, people who are exchanging contracts will use the fax to cut down on the time it takes to get them signed and sent back and forth. The scanner will do the same thing but will produce a document that can be e-mailed.

Using Technology to Help Students Write

Teachers and students have been suddenly projected into a world where many of the activities of the writing classroom of the past have vanished. It's important to remember that the students sitting in your writing class are going to be required to have the competencies to write clearly and succinctly and to think critically in the world they will soon be entering. Even those who will not be going on to college will be required to use technological tools in their worlds. They will be filling out forms on a computer and communicating with many people via web sites and e-mail. The demands on the writing teacher are no longer simply teaching thinking/writing competencies but also teaching students competencies that will connect them to the technological world of the 21st century.

There are many aspects of technology that help students learn how to write effectively. Since most students today type their assignments on the computer using a word processing program, the software typically highlights sections of the text that are not grammatically correct and words that are misspelled. The students can then get help as to how to make the corrections. Using the Spell Check feature of the software also proofreads the document for them and lets them see where they may have made certain mistakes. Teachers should provide instruction for students so that they know how to use all the features of a word processing program, such as how to use a Thesaurus to find more precise words and how to insert graphics into the document.

Other types of software, such as Kidspiration, allow students to insert different types of graphics that help them brainstorm a topic or include pictures with their writing.

Students need to know how to get on the Internet; where to find e-mail (multiple programs are available); how to compose an e-mail in order to be understood; and the etiquette required for effective e-mail communications. Job and college applications are often completed on a website. They also need to know how to conduct searches, so they need to be aware of what "search" means, what Boolean terms are, what the major search engines are, and how to use them. In most colleges nowadays, themes are exchanged on a website set up specifically for the school. The students need to be prepared to present their themes electronically and exchange messages with their teachers in this way, so they need to understand Microsoft Word well enough to be able to read and respond to comments on Word's tracking function and to create a "clean version" of a paper while retaining the one from the teacher with edits and comments.

COMPETENCY 8.0   VIEWING AND REPRESENTING

SKILL A: **Knows grade-level expectations in the Texas Essential Knowledge and Competencies (TEKS) and procedures for assessing students' competencies in interpreting, analyzing, evaluating, and producing visual images, messages, and meanings**

With the passage of the Texas Essential Knowledge and Competencies (TEKS) in 1997, a new strand in the English Language Arts TEKS known as Viewing and Representing was introduced. Because society is flooded with media of various types, teachers must help students become critical viewers and consumers of media.

Viewing refers to understanding and interpreting visual communications that are conveyed non-verbally. Representing refers to expressing one's understanding by producing some type of visual media.

The Viewing and Representing TEKS are comprised of three components: Understanding and Interpreting, Analyzing and Critiquing, and Producing.

The competencies required by the V/R TEKS are designed to promote media literacy. Media literacy is the informed, critical understanding of media, including news, entertainment, and advertising. It involves the ability to analyze and deconstruct media messages.

It's important to teach media literacy because:

- Media dominate our lives
- Media provide models for our values and behavior; and
- Media literacy increases our understanding, appreciation, and enjoyment of media

The Texas Essential Knowledge and Competencies (TEKS) are listed below:

(22) Viewing/representing/interpretation. The student understands and interprets visual images, messages, and meanings. The student is expected to:

[A] describe how illustrators' choice of style, elements, and media help to represent or extend the text's meanings (4-8);
[B] interpret important events and ideas gathered from maps, charts, graphics, video segments, or technology presentations (4-8); and
[C] use media to compare ideas and points of view (4-8).

(23) Viewing/representing/analysis. The student analyzes and critiques the significance of visual images, messages, and meanings. The student is expected to:

[A] interpret and evaluate the various ways visual image makers such as illustrators, documentary filmmakers, and political cartoonists represent meanings (6-8);

[B] compare and contrast print, visual, and electronic media such as film with written story (4-8);

[C] evaluate the purposes and effects of varying media such as film, print, and technology presentations (6-8); and

[D] evaluate how different media forms influence and inform (6-8).

(24) Viewing/representing/production. The student produces visual images, messages, and meanings that communicate with others. he student is expected to:

[A] select, organize, or produce visuals to complement and extend meanings (4-8);

[B] produce communications using technology or appropriate media such as developing a class newspaper, multimedia reports, or video reports (4-8); and

[C] assess how language, medium, and presentation contribute to the message (6-8).

For these expectations to be met in the middle school environment, sixth grade students will evaluate the purposes and effects of film, print, and technology presentations. In Grade 7, students will refine and master previously learned knowledge and competencies in increasingly complex presentations, reading selections, and written compositions. Seventh grade students will also analyze a speaker's persuasive techniques and credibility and evaluate a spoken message in terms of its content, credibility, and delivery. Eighth grade students will present oral and written reports, including presentations strengthened by visuals and media.

Students' competency in these areas would be assessed in a variety of ways. Some ideas are listed below:

- Take notes while viewing a film documentary
- Read and respond to various texts, such as novels, speeches, letters, poetry, and newspaper articles
- Through discussion and written responses, determine authors' purpose, such as to inform, influence, express, and/or entertain
- Use a Venn diagram to compare/contrast different points of view in various forms of media such as films, photographs, recorded speeches
- Determine how different media forms are used to influence and inform

SKILL B: **Uses ongoing assessment and knowledge of grade-level expectations in the Texas Essential Knowledge and Competencies (TEKS) to identify students' needs regarding the interpretation, analysis, evaluation, and production of visual images, messages, and meanings and to plan instruction**

See Competency 8.A.

SKILL C: **Understands characteristics and functions of different types of media and knows how different types of media influence and inform**

Media's impact on today's society is immense and ever-increasing. As children, we watch programs on television that are amazingly fast-paced and visually rich. Parent's roles as verbal and moral teachers are diminishing in response to the much more stimulating guidance of the television set. Adolescence, which used to be the time for going out and exploring the world first hand, is now consumed by the allure of MTV, popular music, and video games. Young adults are exposed to uncensored sex and violence.

But media's effect on society is beneficial and progressive at the same time. Its effect on education, in particular, provides special challenges and opportunities for teachers and students.

Thanks to satellite technology, instructional radio and television programs can be received everywhere from urban classrooms to rural villages. CD-ROMs allow students to learn information through a virtual reality experience. The Internet allows instant access to unlimited data and connects people across all cultures through shared interests. Educational media, when used in a productive way, enriches instruction and makes it more individualized, accessible, and economical.

Conventions for language that appears in print have been developed over several centuries; they change somewhat from generation to generation but, compared to the use of language in electronic media, they are fairly static. On the other hand, language use in radio and television has undergone rapid changes. Listening to a radio show from the thirties is a step back in time. The intonation had its own peculiar qualities.

The same is true of television. Listening to early television news shows—Edward R. Murrow, for example—reminds us instantly of an earlier time. It followed in the style of the radio shows. It was declamatory in nature and sounded more like an announcement than a conversation.

Radio and television speech, nowadays, is much more conversational in tone. In fact, on many of the news shows, there are two or more news people who will carry on a conversation before, after, and between the news stories. This would have seemed peculiar to earlier listeners.

The use of language on the Internet is quite a different thing. In the early days of email, there were unspoken/unwritten rules of conduct that were based on good manners. One was not to use all capital letters or bold letters because that was the same as shouting. E-mail writers who ignored the rules were severely criticized and shunned. The Internet was to be used only for polite conversations. This stage did not last long. Now, just about anything goes.

Before accepting as gospel anything that is printed in a newspaper or advertising or presented on radio, television, or the Internet, it is wise to first of all consider the source. Even though news reporters and editors claim to be unbiased in the presentation of news, they often take an editorial point of view. A newspaper may avow that it is Republican or conservative in nature and may even make recommendations at election time, but it will still claim to present the news without bias. Sometimes this is true, and sometimes it is not. For example, Fox News declares itself to be conservative and to support the Republican Party. Its presentation of news often reveals that bias. When Vice President Cheney made a statement about his shooting of a friend in a duck-hunting accident, it was only made available to Fox News.

On the other hand, CBS has tended to favor more liberal politicians although it avows that it is even-handed in its coverage. Dan Rather presented a story critical of President Bush's military service that was based on a document that could not be validated. His failure to play by the rules of certification of evidence cost him his job and his career. Even with authentication, such a story would not have gotten past the editors of a conservative-leaning news system.
Even politicians usually play by the rules of fairness in the choices they make about going public. They usually try to be even-handed. However, some channels and networks will show deference to one politician over another. Advertising, whether in print or electronic media, is another thing. Will using a certain toothpaste improve a person's love life? Is a satellite dish better than cable? The best recourse a reader/viewer has is to ask around and find someone who has experience that is relevant or do research and conduct interviews of users of both so they can determine the answer for themselves.

Tips for using print media and visual aids

- Use pictures over words whenever possible
- Present one key point per visual
- Use no more than three or four colors per visual to avoid clutter and confusion
- Use contrasting colors such as dark blue and bright yellow

- Use a maximum of 25-35 numbers per visual aid
- Use bullets instead of paragraphs when possible
- Make sure it is student-centered not media-centered. Delivery is just as important as the media presented

Tips for using film and television

- Study programs in advance
- Obtain supplementary materials such as printed transcripts of the narrative or study guides
- Provide your students with background information, explain unfamiliar concepts, and anticipate outcomes
- Assign outside readings based on their viewing
- Ask cuing questions
- Watch along with students
- Observe students' reactions
- Follow up viewing with discussions and related activities

See Competency 8.D.

SKILL D: **Compares and contrasts print, visual, and electronic media**

Media that are used to send a message from one person to another

- Letter
- Telephone
- E-mail

Media that are used for entertainment

- TV shows, like situation comedies and dramas
- Novels
- Video games
- Movies

Media that are used to provide information to a large group of people

- Books
- Newspapers
- Radio news
- Web sites

Media that are used to persuade

- Advertising
- Infomercials
- Direct marketing (junk mail)
- Telemarketing (phone calls from salespersons)

See Competency 8.G.

SKILL E: **Evaluates how visual image makers represent messages and meanings and provides students with varied opportunities to interpret and evaluate visual images in various media**

More money is spent each year on advertising aimed toward children than education. Thus, the media's strategies are considerably well thought out and effective. They employ large, clear letters; bold colors; simple line drawings; and popular symbols to announce upcoming events, push ideas, and advertise products. By using attractive photographs, brightly colored cartoon characters, or instructive messages, advertising can increase sales, win votes or stimulate learning. The graphics are designed to communicate messages clearly, precisely, and efficiently. Some even target subconscious yearnings for sex and status.

Because so much effort is being spent on influencing students through media tactics, just as much effort should be devoted to educating those students about media awareness. A teacher should explain that artists and the aspect they choose to portray, as well as the ways in which they portray them, reflect their attitude and understanding of those aspects. The artistic choices they make are not entirely based on creative license—they also reflect an imbedded meaning the artist wants to represent. Colors, shapes, and phrases are meant to arouse basic instincts for food, sex, and status, and are often used to sell cars, clothing, or liquor.

To stimulate analysis of media strategies, ask students such questions as:

- Where/when do you think this picture was taken/film was shot/piece was written?
- Would you like to have lived at this time in history or in this place?
- What objects are present?
- What do the people presented look like? Are they happy or sad?
- Who is being targeted?
- What can you learn from this piece of media?
- Is it telling you something is good or bad?
- What message is being broadcasted?

To determine whether the information in an advertisement is a statement of fact or someone's subjective opinion, ask these two questions.

Is the statement general or specific?
Statements of opinion in advertising claims often include sweeping generalizations or exaggerations. Facts are often highly specific.

Can the claim be measured or tested?
Factual claims are measurable. They can be tested and proven as either true or false. Opinion claims can't be measured and, therefore, can't be proven either true or false.

Give students familiar advertising slogans and ask them to decide if the slogan is factual or subjective. Examples: "Bet you can't eat just one." (Lay's Potato Chips) and "Nobody does it like Sara Lee. " (Sara Lee Desserts)

SKILL F: **Knows how to teach students to analyze visual image makers' choices and evaluate how these choices help to represent or extend meaning**

See Competency 8.E.

SKILL G: **Provides students with opportunities to interpret events and ideas based on information from maps, charts, graphics, video segments, and technology presentations and to use media to compare ideas and points of view**

The old adage that a picture is worth a thousand words is never more evident than in the use of charts, graphs, and tables in expository writing. It's one thing to say that the GDP of the United States rose fifteen percentage points in the last five years, but it's an entirely different thing to show a graph that depicts that rapid rise. If the point being made is that the increase in the GDP is better than it has ever been in the past fifty years, then a graph showing that growth cinches the point. If the point being made is that the growth in the GDP corresponds to the growth of the stock market for the same period, then that also can be graphed.

It's important that data in charts and graphs be simple and comprehensive. Also, they should only be used if they do, in fact, display the information more effectively than words alone. However, graphs and charts should also be able to stand alone. If two or more charts or tables are used within a work, they should be consistent in style. Whatever a graphic is used, elements of the same kind must always be represented in the same way. This is not a time to be artistic graphically; visual effects should be used only for the purpose of making the point, not for variety.

In graphs, both the horizontal and vertical axes should be labeled. In a column, both column heads and stubs should be labeled. In a graph, the vertical axis is always read from the bottom up, and curves or bars should be graphically distinct (color or dotted lines, for example), and all elements should be clearly identified in a key. If abbreviations are used, care should be taken to make them easily recognizable unless they are explained in the key or in the caption.

A table can often give information that would take several paragraphs to present and can do so more clearly. Tables should be as simple as the material allows, and they should be understandable without explanation. Only necessary explanations should be presented in the text; the table should be able to stand alone.

The advent of word processing makes the creation and insertion of charts, graphs, and tables much more practical than ever before. It takes very little knowledge or competency to create these illustrative devices, and helping students develop those competencies is a valuable enhancement to a writing course.

For more information on interpreting maps and charts, see Competency 5.G.

See Competency 5.R.

Using Media when Comparing Points of View

Students can also be asked to compare and contrast two different media messages. Here are some examples of appropriate pairs of "texts" for students to analyze:

- A TV ad and a print ad for the same product
- A newspaper article and a magazine article about the same news event
- A web site and a TV news program about the same issue
- Two reviews of a film or a TV show from different publications

Students are aware that adults and teachers watch different kinds of TV shows, read different magazines, and use the Internet for different purposes. Students may have expectations about how teachers will respond to their media use. Some students fear that teachers will demean or trivialize their interests in certain kinds of TV shows, web sites, musicians, and movies. They may be aware of some beliefs or attitudes that teachers and adults have about the media and attempt to imitate those attitudes.

To explore media issues in an authentic way, students need to feel "safe" in sharing their genuine pleasures and dissatisfactions with media and technology. Teachers can support this by providing a balance of both support for students' ideas and observations and questions that provide insight on the interpretation of media messages. This blend of support and challenge helps deepen the level of discussion.

SKILL H: **Knows steps and procedures for producing visual images, messages, and meaning to communicate with others**

These ideas are the main principles of media literacy:

1. All messages are constructions
Messages are created by authors who select the ideas, images, words, sounds, and music to convey meanings. We don't always notice the way in which authors carefully make choices about each story element, each word in a book, and each image in a TV commercial. Constructing a media message takes creativity, planning, teamwork, and persistence.

2. Messages are representations
Messages provide us with information about people, places, events, and ideas, but because media messages are selective and incomplete, they can't provide an accurate picture of reality in all its complexity. Media messages about families, for example, leave out many important elements of ordinary family life. Detecting stereotyping is one way to explore how media messages may distort, mislead, and oversimplify.

3. Messages have economic purposes
Media messages that rely on advertising must attract large audiences. Newspapers, magazines, TV, radio, and the Internet use advertising to subsidize media products. The industry's economic goals of reaching large audiences affect us as consumers. Financial goals shape the content, quality, and diversity of media messages we receive for both entertainment and information.

4. Individuals interpret messages differently
People find meaning in media messages when they can connect the message to their life experiences and their understanding of the world. It's important to respect people's unique interpretations and pleasures as they read, view, and listen.

5. Unique characteristics of media
It's not fair to say that some forms of communication are inherently better than others. Each form of media has strengths and weaknesses, depending on your purpose, point of view, and goals as a communicator. People should be able to use a wide range of symbols, tools, and technologies for self-expression and communication.

Subtexts

All media messages have a subtext, an unstated message that is implied or suggested though the use of symbols (characters, words, images, music, special effects, and more). The author composes the message with a certain subtext in mind. The reader or viewer interprets the subtext by carefully studying the construction of the message.

Appeals

Ads use a set of common strategies to get the attention of the audience and convince them to accept the persuasive message. Here are three common appeals:

- **The Testimonial Advertisement:** A celebrity or authority figure promotes a product. The subtext strategy is if the audience likes or believes the spokesperson, then they will transfer that acceptance of the person to the product
- **The Lifestyle Advertisement:** An advertisement provides a glimpse from a particular lifestyle or way of living. The subtext strategy is if the audience desires the lifestyle, then they'll transfer that longing to the product
- **The Slice of Life Advertisement:** The advertisement is a mini-story with characters, conflict and the advertiser's product. The subtext strategy is if the audience understands or relates to the character and the conflict, then they will transfer that good feeling from the story to the product

Targets

All advertisements have a target audience. This is the group of people the advertiser hopes to influence – either by shaping opinion or by motivating behavior. Advertisers categorize people by their demographic characteristics: their age, gender, race, class, and the geographic region where they live.

SKILL I:	Teaches students how to select, organize, and produce visuals to complement and extend meanings

The elements of design can be used to teach the ways that visual media influence our thinking when understanding and interpreting, analyzing and critiquing, and producing visual images, messages, and meanings.

There are five major elements of design:

- Shape
- Color
- Balance
- Lines
- Texture

These elements combine to convey a message to the viewer. The table below provides a more in-depth discussion for these five elements.

ART ELEMENT	DEFINITION	USES	ASSESSMENT
Line	A stroke or mark. Qualities include width, length, direction, and feeling (jagged, smooth, blurred etc.)	Focuses attention and creates the illusion of depth Can "frame" an object	How is line used to draw attention to the product?
Texture	The surface quality or appearance of an object	Makes an object look three dimensional Affects tone and perception: Consider a smooth, glossy marble versus a fuzzy blanket	What textures are suggested? How does texture draw attention to the product?
Shape/ Form	**Shape:** the external outline of an object **Form:** a three dimensional object	Organic shapes appear natural and living. Geometric shapes are inorganic and appear man-made.	What shapes are organic? Which are more geometric? What is the effect of the combination of both?
Size	How large or small a form or shape appears in relation to others	Size helps create perspective and depth (small objects placed high in the frame appear farther away.) Larger objects command more attention	What is the largest form in the image? Why do you think that is true?
Space	**Positive** space is occupied by a shape or form **Negative** space is empty space	Objects can be arranged in space in a uniform pattern or randomly The arrangement affects perception, from crowded and claustrophobic to alone and isolated	How does the arrangement of objects highlight the product?
Color	**Hue:** Primary colors: Red, Yellow, Blue Secondary colors: Orange, Green, Violet **Intensity:** The brightness or dullness of a color	**Warm Colors** • May speed up our perception of time • More readily draw the eye • Associated with happiness and comfort **Cool colors** • Can slow down our perception of time • Recede into the distance and are very suitable for backgrounds • Associated with feelings of peace and contentment or sometimes sadness, depression and melancholy	

Tips for creating visual media

- Limit your graph to just one idea or concept
- Keep the content simple and concise (avoid overusing lines, words, or pictures)
- Balance substance and visual appeal
- Make sure the text is large enough for the class to read
- Match the information to the format that will fit it best

Show students a Power Point slide or other visual containing text and graphics on a topic familiar to students. Discuss design features of the slide, including:

- amount of text per slide
- content of the text
- use of graphics to illustrate the main idea
- use of organizational features for clarity
- use of font
- use of size of print

Then show examples of graphics with too much information and discuss why there is too much and what elements could be simplified or eliminated.

CRITICAL QUESTIONS TO CONSIDER:

- Who made this message and what is the purpose?
- What techniques are used to attract and hold your attention?
- What meaning does the message have for you, and how might others interpret it differently?
- What point of view is represented in this message?
- What information or points of view may be missing from this message?

SKILL J: **Provides students with opportunities to use technology to produce various types of communications and helps students analyze how language, medium, and presentation contribute to the message**

See Competencies 6.R and 8.C.

COMPETENCY 9.0 STUDY AND INQUIRY COMPETENCIES

SKILL A: **Understands study and inquiry competencies and knows the significance of these competencies for student learning and achievement**

Effective, research-proven study competencies include goal-setting, organization and time management, learning styles, note-taking competencies, information gathering and research competencies, memory competencies, and test-taking competencies. An informative website with information on all these topics is: http://www.how-to-study.com

Goal-Setting

Students must learn the difference between a goal and wishful thinking. It's been said that the greatest enemy of action is the lack of a plan, but the inverse is also true. The greatest enemy of a plan is lack of action. Goals are merely wishful thinking unless you further define them as *objectives* with specific measurements and act upon them. A goal is specific, attainable, and measurable, and it must be tied to a specific time frame.

Organization and Time Management

Students with organizational competencies are more productive, happier, and less stressed. Organizational competencies require a person to set priorities. You must know the things that you need to accomplish and set the level of their importance.

To master time management, a schedule of long-term, intermediate, and short-term activities must be arranged and planned accordingly per week. Long-term activities include obligations or activities that are regularly accomplished every week. The intermediate activities are major events that need to be accomplished within the week. Students should write down the things that they need to do along with the timetable.

You can find an excellent lesson on time management at the following website: http://pbskids.org/itsmylife/school/time/article5.html

Note-Taking Competencies

Note-taking is a competency that must be taught. The following is a list of tactics that should be shared with students. It might be beneficial to occasionally test the students and allow them to use their notes only. After the test, explain why the questions chosen are important and how the student can recognize important facts when taking notes. The goal is for students to take notes which provide information for every question on the test. In this way, students will develop note-taking competencies as another approach to studying which is the purpose of taking notes in the first place.

- Don't write every word
- Use your own form of shorthand, including abbreviations, symbols, diagrams and drawings
- Try to draw parallels between your own experience and knowledge and the lecture
- Look for a structure in t lecture. If he or she says there were three main issues at stake in the Civil War, look for those three issues to be clearly defined, and listen for details about each one
- Try to review your notes as soon as you can after class, mark the most important points, and do a little reorganization if you need to. For instance, you might draw an arrow from a topic that belongs in a different spot than where you have it written

See Competency 9.C.

Research Competencies

Research presentations are structured similarly to essays. They often present a thesis or over-arching claim/argument. Then, they explain the thesis or argument with examples and details. The point of a research presentation is to provide an audience with enough details so that they will (a) remember the presentation, and (b) believe the argument.

The best place to start research is usually at your local library. Not only does it have numerous books, videos, and periodicals to use for references, the librarian is always a valuable resource for finding information.

Locating information for research projects and compiling research sources using both print and electronic resources is vital in the construct of written documents. The resources that are available in today's school communities include a large database of Internet resources and World Wide Web access that provides individual navigation for print and electronic information. Research sources include looking at traditional commercial databases and using The Electronic Library to print and cite a diversity of informational resources.

The vital aspect of the research process includes learning to analyze the applicability and validity of the massive amounts of accessible information in cyberspace. Verifying and evaluating electronic resources are part of the process of sorting through the downloaded hardcopies or scrolling through the electronic databases. In using a diversity of research sources, the user must be able to discern authentic sources of information from the mass collections of websites and information databases.

In primary research, selecting a topic and setting up an outline for research information precedes using the secondary research of both print and electronic resources. Using conceptual Venn diagrams to center the topic and brainstorm the peripheral information pertaining to the topic clarifies the purpose of the research.

There are two aspects of the secondary research:

- using print sources
- using electronic research tools

Print sources provide guides on locations for specific or general information resources. Libraries have designated areas dedicated to the collection of encyclopedias, specific resource manuals, card catalogs, and periodical indexes that will provide information on the projected topic. Electronic research tools include a listing of the latest and most effective search engines like Goggle, Microsoft, AOL, and Yahoo to find the topic of research, along with peripheral support information. Electronic databases that contain extensive resources will provide the user with selecting resources, choosing effective keywords, and constructing search strategies. The world of electronic research opens up a global library of resources for both print and electronic information.

The major online services such as Microsoft, Prodigy, and CompuServe provide users with access to specialized information that is either free or have a minimal charge assessed for that specific service or website. Online resources teach effective ways to bookmark sites of interest and how to cut and paste relevant information into word documents for citation and reference. Bookmarking favorite Internet searches that contain correct sources for reference can save a lot of research time.

The Internet is a multi-faceted goldmine of information, but students must be careful to discriminate between reliable and unreliable sources. Teachers should encourage students to stick to sites that are associated with an academic institution, whether it be a college or university or a scholarly organization.

Keep content and context in mind when researching. Remind students to avoid being so wrapped up in how to apply the resource that they miss the author's entire purpose or message. Remember that there are multiple ways to get the needed information. Read an encyclopedia article about the topic to get a general overview, and then focus in from there. Note important names of people associated with the subject, time periods, and geographic areas. Make a list of key words and their synonyms to use while searching for information. And finally, don't forget about articles in magazines, newspapers, or even personal interviews with experts related to the field of interest!

Memory Competencies

One of the most called upon resources of the human brain is memory. There are very few academic tasks that do not call upon our ability to remember. All tasks, from the simplest to the most complex in the classroom and social environments, ask students to use their memory. These memory tasks require auditory, visual, and/or kinesthetic remembering.

The following is a list of some common memory techniques:

- **List:** When memorizing dates, formulae, etc., some find useful the simplest method of all--the list. When memorizing the scientific names of different organisms for a biology class, for instance, a student could create two columns side by side--one listing the common names, the other listing the scientific names. By reading the list over several times and then covering up pieces of information so that you are forced to remember them, you can teach your brain to associate the two names more quickly

- **Flash cards:** Flash cards are a valuable resource as well. They work much like a list, but instead of putting the corresponding information in two columns, students can use index cards (or paper, etc.) and put matching information on either side. They can then look at one side of the card and try to recall the information on the other side. This method is very similar to the list but easier with which to quiz oneself. It does, however, require more preparation (in creating the cards)

- **Acronyms/acrostics:** Acronyms are valuable in memorizing information as well. An example of a useful acronym would be the construction HOMES. Each of the letters in HOMES begins the name of one of the Great Lakes (Huron, Ontario, etc.) By remembering HOMES, it becomes easier to list all five lakes. An acrostic is similar to an acronym but, instead of creating a word, one can create a sentence in which the first letters of all the words correspond with the first letters of the objects of memorization. For example, in the sentence "Please Excuse My Dear Aunt Sally," the first letters correspond to "parenthesis, exponents, multiplication, division, addition, subtraction," which is the order of operations in solving mathematic equations. Acronyms and acrostics will do little to help you unless you are already familiar with the terms you are attempting to recall

For more ideas on memory techniques, visit Mind Tools at
http://www.mindtools.com/memory.html

Test-Taking Competencies

Currently, there is a strong focus on standards and testing. When specific test-taking competencies are taught, practiced, and perfected, students will perform better on tests.

Many tests are timed; therefore, students need many experiences taking timed tests. Pacing is also important. Students should be instructed to keep going! If they don't know an answer, skip it. Do as many questions as they can. Then, go back and try to do the questions that were skipped. If there is extra time, check over answers.

Many students know the answers but are confused by formats and mark answers incorrectly. Look at the formats on the tests your students will take. Do they include multiple choice, filling in bubbles beside correct answers, or drawing lines to match questions and answers? Give students opportunities to practice using similar formats.

Words and phrases used on tests can also confuse students. They know the concepts, but the terminology on the tests gets in the way of understanding how to answer questions. Scan over tests to see if there are any words or phrases that will be unfamiliar to your students.

How Efficient Study and Research Competencies Affect Learning

Effective study competencies and strategies are the basis of effective learning, giving you an opportunity to approach learning tasks systematically and independently.

SKILL B: **Knows grade-level expectations for study and inquiry competencies in the Texas Essential Knowledge and Competencies (TEKS) and procedures for assessing students' development and use of these competencies**

Curriculum documents list the competencies students must know in order to receive a passing grade in the course. The scope and sequence documents for each course also describes the spiral nature of the curriculum and how competencies students develop in one grade level prepare them for the further development of these competencies in subsequent grades. Teachers should be knowledgeable about all areas of the curriculum so they will ensure they teach the student the inquiry competencies mandated by the curriculum.

Depending on the competency or inquiry level, the activities teachers plan as part of the lessons should address assessing the student development and use of these competencies. It is not enough for teachers to explain to students how they can do something. To determine whether or not students understand, they have to be able to do the competencies themselves. This is when the teacher assesses the students.

Although students may know how to conduct research or how to do a science experiment, it is not until they do these things that the teacher can determine how well developed they are in the competencies. The observations of the teacher will determine whether students need extra teaching as a whole group or if only a small number of students need re-teaching on a specific topic or competency.

According to the Texas Essential Knowledge and Competencies, expectations for study and inquiry are as follows. The student is expected to:

- read in varied sources such as diaries, journals, textbooks, maps, newspapers, letters, speeches, memoranda, electronic texts, and other media
- analyze the characteristics of clearly written texts, including the patterns of organization, syntax, and word choice
- evaluate the credibility of information sources, including how the writer's motivation may affect that credibility
- recognize logical, deceptive, and/or faulty modes of persuasion in texts

To meet the expectations for study and inquiry as outlined above, teachers must ensure students have access to the specific types of texts. They need to ensure that these texts are used in the classroom and that the students have experiences in using them. Mini-lessons must be taught on the characteristics of the texts so that students can distinguish between them and determine which ones best meet their needs for specific assignments.

The writer's craft is something that teachers need to incorporate into their lessons so that students can readily recognize the source of information. By exposing the students to different texts, having them analyze these texts, and discussing them in class, students will be better prepared to determine the credibility and fallibility of the texts.

SKILL C: **Knows and applies instructional practices that promote the acquisition and use of study and inquiry competencies across the curriculum by all students, including English Language Learners**

When you open a textbook or a resource book, there is a copious amount of information that unfolds within the pages or within the media sources. Organization and establishing basic criteria are crucial to create a more manageable mode of dealing with large amounts of information. Whether using note cards, index cards or search engine bookmarks for writing down the relevant bits of information, the organization of information provides a method of dealing with how to rearrange large amounts of research into relevant data bits of accessible information.

Having a notebook to create topic areas can create an avenue to brainstorm the information presented in texts and media. The notebook provides a specific place to organize and categorize information. The ability to get organized can further be processed in a notebook or word processing program by subject or topic areas.

Another strategy used in studying information involves the use of color-coded index tabs to create visual methods of organized information. When the information is presented in various areas of the text, index tabs can provide quick avenues to process similar topic areas. Visual tabs also create lists of inventory for future reading.

The ability to organize large amounts of information in text and other media creates a method of internalizing and processing smaller informational resources into usable pieces of useful data. When presented with text and media to evaluate, creating strategies to understand the theme and purpose of what is being presented helps the reader or learner organize that information into additional topic areas for research.

Another aspect to consider in studying information is asking why time should be spent engaged in the pursuit of understanding a specific topic area. With such a myriad of information gathered, the purpose and reason for engaging in a particular study should be obvious and applicable for the reader or researcher. When a person studies information or looks at media resources, it should be due to a choice in wanting to pursue additional knowledge on a subject. How the information is presented or written can either provide quick access to the information or a roadblock to access.

We live in an age of instant gratification which includes quick access of information and quicker access of understanding that information. The Internet and today's technology provides information with the click of a button and a connection to cyberspace. The ability to decipher and organize that information is still up to the user.

Note-taking and Outlining Competencies

Being effective note takers requires consistent development of technique whether the mode of note taking uses 5X7 note cards, lined notebooks, or a computer. Organizing all collected information per a research outline will allow the user to take notes on each section and begin the writing process. If the computer is used, then the actual format of the report can be word-processed to speed up the writing process of the final research report. Creating a title page and a bibliography page will allow each downloaded report to have its resources cited immediately in that section.

Note taking involves identification of specific resources that include the author's or organization's name, year of publication, title, publisher location, and publisher. When taking notes, whether on the computer or using note cards, use the author's last name and page number on cited information. In citing information for major categories and subcategories on the computer, create a file for notes that includes summaries of information and direct quotes. When direct quotes are put into a word file, the cut-and-paste process for incorporation into the report is quick and easy.

In outline information, it is crucial to identify the headings and subheadings for the topic being researched. When researching information, it is easier to cut-and-paste information under the indicated headings in creating a visual flow of information for the report. In the actual drafting of the report, the writer is able to lift direct quotations and citations from the posted information to incorporate in the writing.

See Competency 9.A.

SKILL D: **Knows how to provide students with varied and meaningful opportunities to learn and apply study and inquiry competencies to enhance their achievement across the curriculum**

Teaching organization and study skills is, in many ways, different from teaching a content course such as social studies or chemistry. Although study skills courses have content information, the actual task of the study skills teacher is more akin to that of a coach than a teacher. It is helpful to keep a box of study tools on hand to show students the latest marketed products that can help them get and stay organized. These items might include bookmarks, a wire-frame book holder, a timer, Post-It Flags as well as Post-It Notes, and any other supplies business people use that could be helpful for students. Below are some descriptions of good organizational materials:

- **File box:** This is to show students how and where to store schoolwork at home. One of the best is a file box with a latch and handle for easy portability, the dimensions being roughly 11" x 14". The box should be set up with at least five hanging folders (i.e., one for each potential class) labeled in the order of an "example" student's class schedule.
- **Supply Box:** This can be something like a tackle box. It should contain examples of all the potential supplies a student will need for studying at home, and the box and contents should be things the student could easily purchase (such as pens, pencils, pencil sharpener, three-hole punch, stapler, staples, Post-It Notes and Flags, etc.) or anything else students may need when they sit down to study. The supply box helps students keep everything easily accessible, fosters attention to the study tasks at hand and, thereby, shortens study time since they will not need to leave the study area to "find" something.

- **Three-ring Demonstration Binder:** This will serve as a "show and tell" model of how school notebooks can be set up. Although some schools have students use multiple binders, a one-notebook binder system helps everyone, and disorganized students in particular, reduce the number of items they must keep up with on a daily basis. When students carry one notebook, they feel less fragmented because they do not have to keep up with a myriad of items

- **A calendar planner:** This should have two types of pages: a week-at-a-glance for recording daily assignments and a month-at-a-glance for planning for future tests, papers, and projects. Recording social and family activities on the same weekly calendar can help students budget their time when they can see where extra-curricular obligations fall with respect to their academic obligations

- **A double-sided pocket folder:** One side labeled "homework to be done, papers to be signed" and the other side labeled "graded work." During class, graded homework is placed in the back pocket of the folder and then filed behind the correct tab in the notebook during the home study time

If possible, study skills curriculum should be taught as a complete unit or course that includes all the competencies students are likely to need to improve their learning and boost their academic success. This way, when students must use a specific competency such as lecture note taking, with a study coach's assistance, they can quickly review, practice, and extend the competency if need be.

Although a study skills course should cover the gamut of competencies in a relatively short time (a week to a half semester or so), some topics seem better suited to teaching immediately prior to their occurrence. How to plan and study for final exams is an example. About three weeks before the scheduled final exams, students should return to the study skills coach for a separate exam preparation session designed to take them step-by-step through the process of preparing for important, usually cumulative, exams.

How to use calendar planners both weekly and monthly, should be modeled for the student. The instructor should show how to break assignments down onto a calendar, how to plan for future projects, and how to manage time for daily homework as well as for future tests. A daily routine is established which is followed Monday through Thursday. The student may have to do additional homework or study on the weekend but should maintain this routine during the school week. The study routine goes like this: After taking a short break, the student goes to the study area and does three things.

1. Updates calendar by putting future assignments on the monthly calendar.
2. Files all papers by placing graded work in the school notebook, punching holes in papers, and filing them behind the appropriate subject tab.
3. Studies subject-by-subject in the order of the day.

This routine gives the student a place to begin so that homework is always completed. A five to ten-minute review in subjects where no homework has been assigned serves as a good review or enables students to get ahead.

See Competency 9.C.

SKILL E: **Uses ongoing assessment and knowledge of grade-level expectations in the Texas Essential Knowledge and Competencies (TEKS) to identify students' needs regarding study and inquiry competencies, to determine when a student requires additional help of intervention, and to plan instruction**

See Competency 2.I.

SKILL F: **Responds to students' needs by providing direct, explicit instruction to promote the acquisition and use of study and inquiry competencies**

See Competency 9.D.

In writing, students can be taught to express their points of view either implicitly or explicitly. Often, in a clear-cut argumentative essay, students should portray their points of view and opinions explicitly. In other words, they should make it very clear what their belief or argument is. However, in persuasive or critical essays that are intended to slowly draw someone from one perspective to the student's perspective, it is often a better idea to hide the argument within the examples and other areas of support.

In other words, with an audience that may already agree with the writer's perspective, it is useful to clearly state the argument. With an audience that may not agree with the writer's perspective, it is safer to ease the audience into the argument with examples and support first.

Logical organization for a supportive audience looks like this:

- Argument
- Weak example
- Adequate example
- Strong example

By organizing in this fashion, the writer clearly states the opinion up-front (to keep the audience interested). Then, the writer arranges the weakest arguments first so that the strong examples at the end assist in a strong, emphasis-filled conclusion.

Logical organization for a non-supportive audience looks like this:

- Example
- Example
- Example
- Argument

Or

- Argument (stated very lightly)
- Strong example
- Adequate example
- Weak example

The reason for this approach is that we want the audience to be drawn in by the facts of the case first. Then, once they have, in essence, agreed on the facts, the writer can suggest that, "If you believe X, you must also believe Y." And hence, Y is the argument that they first did not accept.

This type of approach works for persuasive writing, argumentation, critical analysis, and evaluation. In each type of writing, we are trying to convince the reader of our thesis. Even with critical analysis, where opinions might not be as heated, if we propose out of the ordinary ideas, we might be better off using the approach for a non-supportive audience.

Finally, to write—even for or against an idea—and not utilize biased language, we need to write as much as possible in an active voice as concisely as possible. I f a word is not needed, it should be eliminated. Writers can further remove bias by putting themselves in the frames of mind of various people for or against an issue and re-reading the essay. Even if we are arguing for a topic, we want to remain bias-free so that we look like we are simply presenting the best possible solution to any problem. Let's say we are arguing for gun control. We want to write it not as if we have always been gun control supporters but, rather, as un-biased people who have simply come to the best decision about the topic.

An easy and effective way of organizing information to be used in a work of nonfiction is by asking specific questions that are geared toward a mode of presentation. Some examples of useful research questions follow:

Asking Factual Questions

Assume your readers knows nothing about your subject. Try to tell them everything they need to know to understand what you will say in your project. Make a list of specific questions that ask: Who? What? When? Where? Why?

Example: For a report about President Abraham Lincoln's attitude and policies toward slavery, people must know: Who was Abraham Lincoln? Where and when was he born? To which political party did he belong? When was he elected president? What were the attitudes and laws about slavery during his lifetime? How did his actions affect slavery? Why might he have done the things he did?

Asking Interpretive Questions

These kinds of questions are the result of original thinking. They can be based on the preliminary research done on the chosen topic. Select one or two to answer in the presentation. They can be the basis of forming a thesis statement.

- **Hypothetical**: How would things be different today if something in the past had been different?

  Example: How would our lives be different today if the Confederate (Southern) states had won the United States Civil War? What would have happened to the course of World War II if the atomic bomb hadn't been dropped on Hiroshima and Nagasaki?

- **Prediction**: How will something look or be in the future based on the way it is now?

  Example: What will happen to sea levels if global warming due to ozone layer depletion continues and the polar caps melt significantly? If the population of China continues to grow at the current rate for the next fifty years, how will that impact its role in world politics?

- **Solution**: What solutions can be offered to a problem that exists today?

  Example: How could global warming be stopped? What can be done to stop the spread of sexually transmitted diseases among teenagers?

- **Comparison or Analogy**: Find the similarities and differences between your main subject and a similar subject or with another subject in the same time period or place.

  Example: In what ways is the Civil War in the former Yugoslavia similar to (or different from) the United States Civil War? What is the difference in performance between a Porsche and a Lamborghini?

- **Judgment**: Based on the information you find, what can you say is your informed opinion about the subject?

  Example: How does tobacco advertising affect teen cigarette smoking? What are the major causes of eating disorders among young women? How does teen parenthood affect the future lives of young women and men?

See Competencies 9.A and 9.C.

Sample Test

Essay Question

Read the passage below from *The Diary of Anne Frank* (1947) and then complete the exercise that follows.

Written on July 15, 1944, three weeks before the Frank family was arrested by the Nazis, Anne's diary entry explains her worldview and future hopes.

"It's difficult in times like these: ideals, dreams and cherished hopes rise within us, only to be crushed by grim reality. It's a wonder I haven't abandoned all my ideals; they seem so absurd and impractical. Yet I cling to them because I still believe, in spite of everything, that people are truly good at heart.

"It's utterly impossible for me to build my life on a foundation of chaos, suffering and death. I see the world being slowly transformed into a wilderness; I hear the approaching thunder that, one day, will destroy us, too. I feel the suffering of millions, and yet, when I look up at the sky, I somehow feel that everything will change for the better, that this cruelty too shall end, that peace and tranquility will return once more. In the meantime, I must hold on to my ideals. Perhaps the day will come when I will be able to realize them!"

Using your knowledge of literature, write a response in which you:

- Compare and contrast Anne's ideals with her awareness of the conditions in which she lives; and
- Discuss how the structure of Anne's writing—her sentences and paragraphs—emphasize the above contrast

Sample Weak Response

Anne Frank's ideals in this writing make readers clear on the point that she was strongly against Hitler and the Nazis. You can tell that she knows the Nazis are very dangerous and violent people who cause "the suffering of millions." Otherwise, why would she have written this? This fact of Nazis causing the suffering and deaths of millions of people, is a large contrast to how much she believes "that people are truly good at heart." Anne Frank is right about her ideals, and that is why her whole book is such a large contrast to the conditions in which she lived in WWII, when everything was going wrong in the world. You can also tell from this passage that she is a lot smarter than Hitler was. That is another big contrast in the book.

Anne's sentences and paragraphs emphasize the above contrast. They are not fiction; they are her own real thoughts, and these thoughts don't cause "a grim reality" of "cruelty" or the "absurd and impractical" things that she talks about as the war's fault. No, Anne's words cause us to see what is true and real in her writing and in her heart. She makes us see that love is not the fiction. Hitler and the Nazis are the ones who make the fiction. We can read this in between the lines, which sometimes has to be done.

Back when Anne Frank wrote her words down on paper, everything was going wrong around her, but she knew what to do, and she did it. She wrote a world classic story about her life. This story is a big contrast to what the Germans were doing.

Sample Strong Response

This excerpt from *The Diary of Anne Frank* reveals the inner strength of a young girl who refuses, despite the wartime violence and danger surrounding her, to let her idealism be overcome by hatred and mass killing. This idealism is reflected, in part, by her emphases on universal human hopes such as peace, tranquility, and goodwill. But Anne Frank is no dreamy Pollyanna. Reflecting on her idealism in the context of the war raging around her, she matter-of-factly writes, "my dreams, they seem so absurd and impractical."

This indicates Anne Frank's awareness of not only her own predicament but of human miseries that extend beyond the immediate circumstances of her life. For elsewhere she writes in a similar vein, "In times like these... I see the world being slowly transformed into a wilderness"; despite her own suffering she can "feel the suffering of millions."

And yet Anne Frank believes, "in spite of everything, that people are truly good at heart." This statement epitomizes the stark existential contrast of her worldview with the wartime reality that ultimately claimed her life.

The statement also exemplifies how Anne's literary form—her syntax and diction—mirror thematic content and contrasts. "In spite of everything," she still believes in people. She can "hear the approaching thunder...yet, when I look up at the sky, I somehow feel that everything will change for the better." At numerous points in this diary entry, first-hand knowledge of violent tragedy stands side-by-side with belief in humanity and human progress.

"I must hold on to my ideals," Anne concludes. "Perhaps the day will come when I'll be able to realize them!" In her diary she has done so and more.

Multiple Choice

1. **Which of the following is not true about English?**
(Competency 1.A, Easy)

   A. English is the easiest language to learn

   B. English is the least inflected language

   C. English has the most extensive vocabulary of any language

   D. English originated as a Germanic tongue

2. ***Students are fluent readers if they***
(Competency 1.A, Average)

   A. read texts fast enough with appropriate expression or prosody.

   B. read word-to-word and haltingly.

   C. must intentionally decode a majority of the words.

   D. write disorganized sentences.

3. **Which aspect of language is innate?**
(Competency 1.A, Rigorous)

   A. Biological capability to articulate sounds understood by other humans

   B. Cognitive ability to create syntactical structures

   C. Capacity for using semantics to convey meaning in a social environment

   D. Ability to vary inflections and accents

4. **All of the following techniques are used to conduct ongoing informal assessment of student progress except for**
(Competency 1.B, Average)

   A. analyzing the student work product at key stages

   B. collecting data from assessment tests

   C. posing strategic questions

   D. observing students as they work

5. **Which of the following sentences contains an error in agreement?**
    (Competency 1.C, Easy)

    A. Jennifer is one of the women who writes for the magazine.

    B. Each one of their sons plays a different sport.

    C. This band has performed at the Odeum many times.

    D. The data are available online at the listed website.

6. **A teacher should refer all of the following concerns to the appropriate expert except for**
    (Competency 1.E, Average)

    A. Auditory trauma.

    B. Ear infection.

    C. Vision problems.

    D. Underdeveloped vocabulary.

7. **In preparing a speech for a contest, your student has encountered problems with gender specific language. Not wishing to offend either women or men, he seeks your guidance. Which of the following is not an effective strategy?**
    (Competency 1.G, Rigorous)

    A. Use the generic "he" and explain that people will understand and accept the male pronoun as all-inclusive.

    B. Switch to plural nouns and use "they" as the gender-neutral pronoun.

    C. Use passive voice so that the subject is not required.

    D. Use male pronouns for one part of the speech and then use female pronouns for the other part of the speech.

8. **Which of the following bits of information best describes the structure of English?**
    (Competency 1.I, Rigorous)

    A. Syntax based on word order

    B. Inflected

    C. Romantic

    D. Orthography is phonetic

9. **All of the following are true about phonological awareness except**
(Competency 2.A, Rigorous)

A. it may involve print.

B. it is a prerequisite for spelling and phonics.

C. activities can be done by the children with their eyes closed.

D. it starts before letter recognition is taught.

10. **Middle school students bring little, if any, initial experience in**
(Competency 2.E Average)

A. phonics.

B. phonemics.

C. textbook reading assignments.

D. stories read by the teacher.

11. **Reading a piece of student writing to assess the overall impression of the product is**
(Competency 2.G, Easy)

A. holistic evaluation.

B. portfolio assessment.

C. analytical evaluation.

D. using a performance system.

12. **Regularly requiring students to practice reading short, instructional-level texts at least three times to a peer and to give and receive peer feedback about these readings mainly addresses which reading competency?**
(Competency 2.G, Rigorous)

A. Comprehension

B. Fluency

C. Evaluation

D. Word-solving

13. **Reading assessment should take place**
(Competency 2.I, Easy)

A. at the end of the semester.

B. at the end of a unit.

C. constantly.

D. All of the above.

14. **Effective assessment means that**
(Competency 2.I, Rigorous)

A. it ignores age and cultural considerations.

B. students' weaknesses are emphasized.

C. only reading competencies count.

D. it is integrated with instruction and is not intrusive.

15. Which of the following approaches is not useful in assessing slower or immature readers?
(Competency 2.J, Rigorous)

A. Repeated readings

B. Echo reading

C. Wide reading

D. Reading content that is more difficult than their competency levels in order to "stretch" their abilities

16. Computer-assisted instruction (CAI) accommodates all of the following factors in reading instruction except for
(Competency 2.K, Rigorous)

A. free-form responses to comprehension questions.

B. increased motivation.

C. the addition of speech with computer-presented text.

D. the use of computers for word processing and the integration of writing instruction with reading.

17. To enhance reading comprehension, experts recommend all of these techniques except for
(Competency 3.A, Rigorous)

A. reading material through only once, but reading slowly and carefully.

B. reading material through more than once according to a plan.

C. creating a map for the next reading.

D. highlighting or taking notes during reading.

18. Which vocabulary strategy does the table below exemplify?
(Competency 3.B, Rigorous)

	Math Usage	Usage
bi (two)	Bilinear	Bicycle
	Bimodal	Biplane
	Binomial	bifocals
cent (100)	Centimeter	century
	Centigram	centigrade
	Percent	centipede
circum (around)	circumference	circumnavigate
	circumradius	circumstance
	circumcenter	circumspect

A. Frayer method

B. Morphemic analysis

C. Semantic mapping

D. Word mapping

19. **Which item below is not a research-based strategy that supports reading?** *(Competency 3.F, Rigorous)*

    A. Reading more

    B. Reading along with a more proficient reader

    C. Reading a passage no more than twice

    D. Self-monitoring progress

20. **The term graphophonemic awareness refers to** *(Competency 3.M, Average)*

    A. handwriting competencies.

    B. letter to sound recognition.

    C. alphabetic principle.

    D. phonemic awareness

21. **The best way for a teacher to track a student's progress in demonstrating the alphabetic principal/ graphophonemic awareness is to** *(Competency 3.N, Rigorous)*

    A. provide group assessments.

    B. maintain individual records.

    C. assess with standardized tests.

    D. have the student assessed by a team of teachers.

22. **Making inferences from the text means that the reader** *(Competency 4.B, Rigorous)*

    A. is making informed judgments based on available evidence.

    B. is making a guess based on prior experiences.

    C. is making a guess based on what the reader would like to be true of the text.

    D. All of the above.

23. **Factors that affect the level of comprehension a student demonstrates when reading a story include all of the following except** *(Competency 4.C, Rigorous)*

    A. lack of background knowledge.

    B. inability to spell words correctly.

    C. lack of word recognition competencies.

    D. inability to determine the meanings of words through context clues.

24. **Four of Ms. Wolmark's students have lived in other countries. She is particularly pleased to be studying Sumerian proverbs with them as part of the sixth grade unit in analyzing the sayings of other cultures because** *(Competency 4.C, Rigorous)*

    A. this gives her a break from teaching and the children can share sayings from other cultures they and their families have experienced.

    B. this validates the experiences and expertise of ELL learners in her classroom.

    C. this provides her children from the US with a lens on other cultural values.

    D. All of the above.

25. **A teacher has taught his students to self-monitor their reading by locating where in the passage they are having difficulty, identifying the specific problem there, and restating the difficult sentence or passage in their own words. These strategies are examples of** *(Competency 4.H, Rigorous)*

    A. graphic and semantic organizers.

    B. metacognition.

    C. recognizing story structure.

    D. summarizing.

26. **Which of the following would be the most significant factor in teaching Homer's Iliad and Odyssey to any particular group of students?** *(Competency 4.I, Average)*

    A. Selecting a translation on the appropriate reading level

    B. Determining the student's interest level

    C. Selecting an appropriate evaluative technique

    D. Determining the scope and delivery methods of background study

27. The students in Mrs. Cline's seventh grade language arts class were invited to attend a performance of Romeo and Juliet presented by the drama class at the high school. To best prepare, they should *(Competency 4.J, Average)*

A. Read the play as a homework exercise.

B. Read a synopsis of the plot and a biographical sketch of the author.

C. Examine a few main selections from the play to become familiar with the language and style of the author.

D. Read a condensed version of the story and practice attentive listening competencies.

28. Written on the sixth grade reading level, most of S. E. Hinton's novels (for instance, The Outsiders) have the greatest reader appeal with *(Competency 4.K, Average)*

A. sixth graders.

B. ninth graders.

C. twelfth graders.

D. adults.

29. Which of the following responses to literature typically give middle school students the most problems? *(Competency 4.M, Rigorous)*

A. Interpretive

B. Evaluative

C. Critical

D. Emotional

30. What type of reasoning does Henry David Thoreau use in the following excerpt from "Civil Disobedience"? *(Competency 4.M, Rigorous)*

Unjust laws exist; shall we be content to obey them, or shall we endeavor to amend them, and obey them until we have succeeded, or shall we transgress them at once? Men generally, under such a government as this, think that they ought to wait until they have persuaded the majority to alter them. They think that, if they should resist, the remedy would be worse than the evil. But it is the fault of the government itself that the remedy *is* worse than the evil. Why does it always crucify Christ, excommunicate Copernicus and Luther, and pronounce Washington and Franklin rebels?
--"Civil Disobedience" by Henry David Thoreau

A. Ethical reasoning

B. Inductive reasoning

C. Deductive reasoning

D. Intellectual reasoning

31. **The English department is developing strategies to encourage all students to become a community of readers. From the list of suggestions below, which would be the least effective way for teachers to foster independent reading?** *(Competency 4.P, Average)*

   A. Each teacher will set aside a weekly 30-minute in-class reading session during which the teacher and students read a magazine or book for enjoyment.

   B. Teacher and students develop a list of favorite books to share with each other.

   C. The teacher assigns at least one book report each grading period to ensure that students are reading from the established class list.

   D. The students gather books for a classroom library so that books may be shared with each other.

32. **A paper written in first person and having characters, a setting, a plot, some dialogue, and events sequenced chronologically with some flashbacks exemplifies which genre?** *(Competency 5.A, Easy)*

   A. Exposition

   B. Narration

   C. Persuasion

   D. Speculation

33. **To explain or to inform belongs in the category of** *(Competency 5.A, Easy)*

   A. Exposition.

   B. Narration.

   C. Persuasion.

   D. Description.

34. **Oral debate is most closely associated with which form of discourse?** *(Competency 5.A, Average Rigor)*

   A. Description

   B. Exposition

   C. Narration

   D. Persuasion

35. **What is the main form of discourse in this passage?**
(Competency 5.A, Average)

It would have been hard to find a passer-by more wretched in appearance. He was a man of middle height, stout and hardy, in the strength of maturity; he might have been forty-six or seven. A slouched leather cap hid half his face, bronzed by the sun and wind, and dripping with sweat.

A. Description

B. Exposition

C. Narration

D. Persuasion

36. **A paper explaining the relationship between food and weight gain contains the signal words "because," "consequently," "this is how," and "due to." These words suggest that the paper has which text structure?**
(Competency 5.B, Average)

A. Cause and effect structure

B. Compare and contrast structure

C. Descriptive structure

D. Sequential structure

37. **Varying the complexity of a graphic organizer exemplifies differentiating which aspect of a lesson?**
(Competency 5.C, Rigorous)

A. Its content/topic

B. Its environment

C. Its process

D. Its product

38. **Before reading a passage, a teacher gives her students an anticipation guide with a list of statements related to the topic they are about to cover in the reading material. She asks the students to indicate their agreement or disagreement with each statement on the guide. This activity is intended to**
(Competency 5.C, Average)

A. Elicit students' prior knowledge of the topic and set a purpose for reading.

B. Help students to identify the main ideas and supporting details in the text.

C. Help students to synthesize information from the text.

D. Help students to visualize the concepts and terms in the text.

39. In Ms. Francine's class, dictionary use is a punishment. Her principal observes her class and is *(Competency 5.F, Average)*

A. Pleased with the way that Ms. Francine approaches dictionary use.

B. Unconcerned with this approach to the use of the dictionary.

C. Convinced that the teacher should model her own fascination and pleasure in using the dictionary for the children.

D. Delighted by the fact that children are being forced to use the dictionary.

40. Mr. Brown's students are having a tough time interpreting information in a story, so he uses an illustration to help them. What type of help is this? *(Competency 5.G, Average)*

A. Classification

B. Qualitive Descriptions

C. Indifference

D. Modeling

41. What game in lower-level classrooms helps students with abstract learning? *(Competency 5.H- Average)*

A. Monopoly

B. Checkers

C. Operation

D. Go Fish

42. The following lines from Robert Browning's poem "My Last Duchess" come from an example of what form of dramatic literature? *(Competency 5.I, Rigorous)*

That's my last Duchess
    painted on the wall,
Looking as if she were alive. I
    call
That piece a wonder, now:
    Frà Pandolf's hands
Worked busily a day, and
    there she stands.
Will 't please you sit and look
    at her?

A. Tragedy

B. Comic opera

C. Dramatis personae

D. Dramatic monologue

43. **Among junior-high school students of low-to-average readability levels, which work would most likely stir reading interest?**
(Competency 5.J, Average)

A. *Elmer Gantry*, Sinclair Lewis

B. *Smiley's People*, John Le Carre

C. *The Outsiders*, S.E. Hinton

D. *And Then There Were None*, Agatha Christie.

44. **The most significant drawback to applying learning theory research to classroom practice is that**
(Competency 5.K, Rigorous)

A. today's students do not acquire reading competencies with the same alacrity as when greater emphasis was placed on reading classical literature.

B. development rates are complicated by geographical and cultural differences that are difficult to overcome.

C. homogeneous grouping has contributed to faster development of some age groups.

D. social and environmental conditions have contributed to an escalated maturity level than research done twenty or more years ago would seem to indicate.

45. **Which is an untrue statement about a theme in literature?**
(Competency 5.L, Average)

A. The theme is always stated directly somewhere in the text.

B. The theme is the central idea in a literary work.

C. All parts of the work (plot, setting, mood) should contribute to the theme in some way.

D. By analyzing the various elements of the work, the reader should be able to arrive at an indirectly stated theme.

46. **The arrangement and relationship of words in sentences or sentence structures best describes**
(Competency 5.M, Easy)

A. Style

B. Discourse

C. Thesis

D. Syntax

47. **What type of comprehension do questions beginning with "who," "what," "where," or "how" assess?**
(Competency 5.O, Average)

A. Evaluative

B. Inferential

C. Literal

D. Narrative

48. **Environmental print is available in all of the following except**
(Competency 6.A, Average)

A. within a newspaper.

B. on the page of a library book.

C. on a supermarket circular.

D. in a commercial flyer.

49. **Which group of words is not a sentence?**
(Competency 6.B Easy)

A. In keeping with the graduation tradition, the students, in spite of the rain, standing in the cafeteria tossing their mortarboards.

B. Rosa Parks, who refused to give up her seat on the bus, will be forever remembered for her courage.

C. Taking advantage of the goalie's being out of the net, we scored our last and winning goal.

D. When it began to rain, we gathered our possessions and ran for the pavilion.

50. **Which of the following sentences is unambiguously properly punctuated?**
(Competency 6.B, Easy)

A. The more you eat; the more you want.

B. The authors—John Steinbeck, Ernest Hemingway, and William Faulkner—are staples of modern writing in American literature textbooks.

C. Handling a wild horse, takes a great deal of competency and patience

D. The man, who replaced our teacher, is a comedian.

51. **A punctuation mark indicating omission, interrupted thought, or an incomplete statement is a/an**
(Competency 6.B, Average)

   A. ellipsis

   B. anachronism

   C. colloquy

   D. idiom

52. **In the following sentence, which word group below best conveys the intended meaning of the underlined section?**
(Competency 6.E, Average)

   Joe *didn't hardly know his cousin Fred*, who'd had a rhinoplasty.

   A. Hardly did know his cousin Fred

   B. Didn't know his cousin Fred hardly

   C. Hardly knew his cousin Fred

   D. Didn't know his cousin Fred

53. **In the following sentence, which phrase below best represents the logical intent of the underlined phrase?**
(Competency 6.E, Average)

   Mr. Brown is a school volunteer with a reputation and twenty years service.

   A. With a reputation for twenty years' service

   B. With a reputation for twenty year's service

   C. Who has served twenty years

   D. With a service reputation of twenty years

54. **Which of the four underlined sections of the following sentence contains an error that a word processing spellchecker probably wouldn't catch?**
(Competency 6.G, Easy)

   He tuc the hors by the rains and pulled it back to the stabel.

   A. Tuc

   B. Hors

   C. Rains

   D. Stabel

55. **For students with poor vocabularies, the teacher should recommend first that**
(Competency 6.G, Average)

A. they enroll in a Latin class/

B. they read newspapers, magazines, and books on a regular basis.

C. they write the words repetitively after looking them up in the dictionary.

D. they use a thesaurus to locate and incorporate the synonyms found there into their vocabularies.

56. **Which of the following contains an error in possessive punctuation?**
(Competency 6.I, Average)

A. Doris's shawl

B. Mother's-in-law frown

C. Children's lunches

D. Ambassador's briefcase

57. **Writing ideas quickly without interruption of the flow of thoughts or attention to conventions is called**
(Competency 7.E, Easy)

A. brainstorming.

B. mapping.

C. listing.

D. free writing.

58. **A formative evaluation of student writing**
(Competency 7.F, Rigorous)

A. requires a thorough marking of mechanical errors with a pencil or pen.

B. makes comments on the appropriateness of the student's interpretation of the prompt and the degree to which the objective was met.

C. requires the student to hand in all the materials produced during the process of writing.

D. involves several careful readings of the text for content, mechanics, spelling, and usage.

59. In a timed essay test of an hour's duration, how much time should be devoted to prewriting?
(Competency 7.H, Easy)

A. Five minutes

B. Ten minutes

C. Fifteen minutes

D. Twenty minutes

60. A student informative composition should consist of a minimum of how many paragraphs?
(Competency 7.H, Easy)

A. Three

B. Four

C. Five

D. Six

61. Which of the following should not be included in the opening paragraph of an informative essay?
(Competency 7.H, Easy)

A. Thesis sentence

B. Details and examples supporting the main idea

C. Broad general introduction to the topic

D. A style and tone that grabs the reader's attention

62. Which of the following is not a technique of prewriting?
(Competency 7.H, Average)

A. Clustering

B. Listing

C. Brainstorming

D. Proofreading

63. Modeling is a practice that requires students to
(Competency 7.I, Average)

A. create a style unique to their own language capabilities.

B. emulate the writing of professionals.

C. paraphrase passages from good literature.

D. peer evaluate the writings of other students.

64. **Which of the following is the least effective procedure for promoting consciousness of audience?**
(Competency 7.K, Average)

A. Pairing students during the writing process

B. Reading all the rough drafts before the students write the final copies

C. Having students compose stories or articles for publication in school literary magazines or newspapers

D. Writing letters to friends or relatives

65. **If a student uses slang and expletives, what is the best course of action to take in order to improve the student's formal communication competencies?**
(Competency 7.I, Average)

A. Ask the student to rephrase their writing; that is, translate it into language appropriate for the school principal to read.

B. Refuse to read the student's papers until he conforms to a more literate style.

C. Ask the student to read his work aloud to the class for peer evaluation.

D. Rewrite the flagrant passages to show the student the right form of expression.

66. **The new teaching intern is developing a unit on creative writing and is trying to encourage her students to write poetry. Which of the following would not be an effective technique?**
(Competency 7.B, Rigorous)

A. In groups, students will draw pictures to illustrate "The Love Song of J. Alfred Prufrock" by T.S. Eliot.

B. Either individually or in groups, students will compose a song, writing lyrics that try to use poetic devices.

C. Students will bring to class the lyrics of a popular song and discuss the imagery and figurative language.

D. Students will read aloud their favorite poems and share their opinions of and responses to the poems.

67. **The following passage is written from which point of view?**
(Competency 7.C, Average)

As she mused the pitiful vision of her mother's life laid its spell on the very quick of her being—that life of commonplace sacrifices closing in final craziness. She trembled as she heard again her mother's voice saying constantly with foolish insistence: *Dearevaun Seraun! Dearevaun Seraun!**
* "The end of pleasure is pain!" (Gaelic)

A. First person, narrator

B. Second person, direct address

C. Third person, omniscient

D. First person, omniscient

68. **Mr. Ledbetter has instructed his students to prepare a slide presentation that illustrates an event in history. Students are to include pictures, graphics, media clips and links to resources. What competencies will students exhibit at the completion of this project?**
(Competency 8.A, Rigorous)

   A. Analyze the impact of society on media.

   B. Recognize the media's strategies to inform and persuade.

   C. Demonstrate strategies and creative techniques to prepare presentations using a variety of media.

   D. Identify the aesthetic effects of a media presentation.

69. **A sixth grade teacher has subscribed to an online version of a local newspaper. She can help the students examine this resource and how it compares to the print version by noting the following differences:**
(Competency 8.C, Rigorous)

   A. Use of video to document events

   B. Use of sound clips in addition to written text

   C. Links to other web resources

   D. All of the above

70. **For their research paper on the use of technology in the classroom, students have gathered data that shows a sharp increase in the number of online summer classes over the past five years. What would be the best way for them to depict this information visually?**
(Competency 8.G, Rigorous)

   A. A line chart

   B. A table

   C. A pie chart

   D. A flow chart

71. In presenting a report to peers about the effects of Hurricane Katrina on New Orleans, the students wanted to use various media in their argument to persuade their peers that more needed to be done. Which of these would be the most effective?
(Competency 8.I, Rigorous)

A. A PowerPoint presentation showing the blueprints of the levees before the flood and redesigned now for current construction.

B. A collection of music clips made by the street performers in the French Quarter before and after the flood.

C. A recent video showing the areas devastated by the floods and the current state of rebuilding.

D. A collection of recordings of interviews made by the various government officials and local citizens affected by the flooding.

72. Which of the following are secondary research materials?
(Competency 9.A, Average)

A. The conclusions and inferences of other historians.

B. Literature and nonverbal materials, novels, stories, poetry and essays from the period, as well as coins, archaeological artifacts, and art produced during the period.

C. Interviews and surveys conducted by the researcher.

D. Statistics gathered as the result of the research's experiments.

73. In preparing your students to write a research paper about a social problem, what recommendation can you make so they can determine the credibility of their information?
(Competency 9.A, Average)

A. Assure them that information on the Internet has been peer-reviewed and verified for accuracy.

B. Find one solid source and use that exclusively.

C. Use only primary sources.

D. Cross check your information with another credible source.

74. **Teaching students how to set goals, modeling how to take notes, and how to create an outline are all examples of**
(Competency 9.A, Average)

A. study competencies.

B. comprehension strategies.

C. read aloud strategies.

D. discussion competencies.

75. **To determine the credibility of information, researchers should do all of the following except**
(Competency 9.C, Rigorous)

A. establish the authority of the document.

B. disregard documents with bias.

C. evaluate the currency and reputation of the source.

D. use a variety of research sources and methods.

76. **Students have been asked to write a research paper on automobiles and have brainstormed a number of questions they will answer based on their research findings. Which of the following is not an interpretive question to guide research?**
(Competency 9.F, Rigorous)

A. Who were the first ten automotive manufacturers in the United States?

B. What types of vehicles will be used fifty years from now?

C. How do automobiles manufactured in the United States compare and contrast with each other?

D. What do you think is the best solution for the fuel shortage?

Use the information below to answer the following questions:

Mr. Anderson, an English teacher, creates an activity to promote discussion with students after reading a chapter of a novel that has been studied as a class. He places a list of question starters on the board that students can use to create questions for their classmates. Next, Mr. Anderson has them both ask and answer the questions in a small group setting.

Question Starters:

1. What must have happened when (use chapter and page number to describe a specific event)

2. What happens next (refer to person, conflict, or page number)

3. What were some similar thoughts, actions, or events that occurred in (specific chapter) and (specific chapter)?

4. What did the author mean when he said, "quote"? (use chapter and page number)

5. If you had to make suggestions for making the story better, what would they be? (use chapter and page number)

6. What sorts of problems does the main character face? (use chapter and page number)

77. Mr. Anderson's activity promotes students to use which of the following critical-reading skills? *(Competency 5.B, Rigorous)*

    A. Providing evidence from within the text to support conclusions

    B. Synthesizing information from more than one source

    C. Examining rhetorical devices for their effectiveness

    D. Comparing textural structures

78. When students respond to questions 1 and 4, which of the following skills are being practiced? *(Competency 5.C, Rigorous)*

    A. Visualization

    B. Summarization

    C. Inference

    D. Prediction

79. **Which of the listed question starters would facilitate a students' connection with the text?**
(Competency 4.D, Average)

A. Question 2

B. Question 3

C. Question 1

D. Question 5

80. **Why would this activity be especially good for students who are English-language learners?**
(Competency 1.G, Average)

A. Because the activity develops phonemic awareness

B. Gives the learner many opportunities to speak and use language.

C. The activity gives direct instruction on language use

D. The activity allows for word analysis

81. **A seventh-grade teacher has her class listen to recording of a well-known speech. She has them listen to it twice, first listening to respond to content, and the second time to evaluate the presentation, itself. The purpose of this module would be to do which of the following:**
(Competency 1.L, Rigorous)

A. Understand the types of skills that are needed to speak successfully in public.

B. Compare speech presentations

C. Prepare for their own informal speaking assignments

D. Collaborate with their classmates to improve the speech's effectiveness

82. In an effort to motivate her students in Language Arts class, a teacher creates learning clubs that students can become involved with. Students are assigned a small group to work with in order to research a given topic, and then reflect on the information gathered. The students are then instructed to create a blog based on their findings. What does this instructional design show the teacher understands the importance of?
(Competency 2.K, Rigorous)

A. That the teacher understands the need to provide explicit instruction for language building.

B. That the teacher understands the need for placing students in skills based small groups based on ability.

C. Allowing students to choose their own topics are a great motivating factor.

D. The need to provide literacy skills using multiple language-arts contexts.

83. What would assist a teacher in assessing the phonics skills of her lower quartile students?
(Competency 2.A, Average)

A. Assessing sight word recall by the student

B. Assessing a student's handwriting

C. Giving timed reading tests

D. Assessing student's spelling attempts

84. A reading teacher meets with a small group of struggling readers to read a short book. Over the course of the week she asks the students to read the book again, to themselves, and together as a group, several times. What is the purpose of this technique?
(Competency 3.N, Average)

A. To reinforce letter-sounding skills

B. To develop comprehension

C. To instill a love of reading

D. To promote recognition of high frequency words

85. **Ms. Ingram, a fourth-grade teacher, is employing a technique where she reads a line in the workbook, then has the students read the same lines aloud, imitating her inflection and tone. What does this activity develop in students?**
(Competency 3.O, Average)

A. Oral comprehension

B. Fluency

C. Word identification

D. Word meanings

86. **Ms. Atkins wants to assess her students' reading levels on several levels: independent, frustration, and instructional. What is the best strategy for doing that?**
(Competency 4.I, Average)

A. Recording each student's mistakes as they read aloud from a short text.

B. Giving a vocabulary test after reading a text.

C. Making notes about a student's responses after reading a text.

D. Observing facial cues while a student is reading a text.

87. **Mrs. Clemons has her 8ᵗʰ grade class read several different versions of the Cinderella story, then asks them to write a comparison and contrast essay. The purpose of this activity is to have students do which of the following?**
(Competency 4.Q, Rigorous)

A. Use multiple texts to synthesize information gained.

B. Evaluate a variety of text structures.

C. Develop appropriate prosody.

D. Develop metacognitive strategies for use later

88. **Of the following activities, which would develop a student's metacognitive skills?**
(Competency 4.H, Average)

A. Creating a graphic organizer that uses the concept of layers.

B. Using a graphic organizer to create a summary of a story.

C. Using a graphic organizer while reading or writing independently.

D. Allowing students to work with a partner to complete a graphic organizer.

89. Mr. Phelps comes to Ms. Eades with a dilemma. His science class can gather facts well enough from the text, but when asked to restate the larger concepts they are unable to do so. He's asked for Ms. Eades' help. Which of the following techniques or activities would be most helpful in addressing the issue? *(Competency 5.D, Average)*

A. Summarizing the main ideas (outlining).

B. Discussing a part of the chapter they found interesting.

C. Reading the chapters out loud.

D. Pulling out important vocabulary words in the chapter.

90. When utilizing reading journals with his class, Mr. Morales hopes to motivate them to read more. Which of the following activities with the journal would help to achieve this goal? *(Competency 5.C, Easy)*

A. Summarizing each passage in the text.

B. Writing down personal reflections about the text.

C. Taking notes about main ideas in the text.

D. Writing to a prompt revolving around the text.

Use the following information to answer the following questions:

Mr. Ambergy wants to prepare a genre study which includes classical literature. To do this he proposes to place the students in small groups and allow them to choose from a list of traditional literature. Students will analyze this selection for themes, cultural influences, and literary devices. *(Competency 5.L, Rigorous)*

91. **Which of the following activities would facilitate students' ability to discover cultural influences over a text?** *(Competency 5.K, Rigorous)*

A. Create and use a comparison chart while reading the moral lessons of two different folktales form dissimilar cultures.

B. Create a Venn diagram to compare and contrast the conflicts in the folktales.

C. Create a story map that represents the cultural elements of two stories by the same author.

D. Use a KWL chart when it comes to cultural features that have been learned after reading two myths from the same culture.

92. **To assist students in locating and identifying literary devices, Mr. Ambergy could have his students find evidence form the text that demonstrates which of the following?** *(Competency 5.L, Rigorous)*

A. Settings that offer specific times and details within the story.

B. Complex plots that develop slowly.

C. Details that explain the resolution of conflicts when they occur.

D. Characters that seem to have similar characteristics and familiar traits.

Utilize the following student writing example to answer the following questions:

Yesterday I went to the mall with Sophie and my sister. Sophie likes to go to the record store, and my sister likes records. There was a lot of people at the mall yesterday. We had fun.

93. **What does the writing sample above suggest the teacher focus on as far as additional instruction for the student?**
(Competency 6.E, Average)

    A. Using pronouns correctly.

    B. Working on creating compound sentences.

    C. Working on correct verb tenses.

    D. Recognizing and correcting sentence fragments.

94. **A teacher introduces transitional words and phrases such as 'therefore' and 'as a result' to her class. With the particular choice of transitions, the teacher is preparing her class to work on an essay that will use which of the following:**
(Competency 7.C, Average)

    A. A sequence of events

    B. Cause and effect patterns

    C. A list of steps

    D. Specific examples, or descriptions

95. **Mrs. Lyons, a seventh-grade English teacher, notices that her students are able to make word counts for assigned essays, but that the material added to make the essays longer are often vague. She wants to help students learn how to improve their revision process. To do this, she should teach the students how to do which of the following techniques:** *(Competency 7.G, Average)*

A. A checklist for revising.

B. A box and explode strategy to expand upon a main idea

C. An activity to work on varying sentence lengths

D. A list of upper level vocabulary (sparkle words) to utilize when writing

96. **An assignment has been made to a group of eighth-grade students in an English class involving the creation of a PowerPoint presentation, which they must present to the class. Before they begin their work, the teacher shows them examples of both good presentations and poorly designed presentations. This activity is designed to help students with their understanding of how to do which of the following:** *(Competency 7.M, Easy)*

A. Make sure that the presentations are not too long

B. Match what is said with what is presented in the slides.

C. Show the appropriate use of graphics which support the text shown.

D. Show how to design the slides correctly and appropriately.

97. **Mr. Stegnar wants his students to have the opportunity to write for an authentic audience and for an authentic purpose. Which of the assignments below best achieves this goal:**
(Competency 7.L, Average)

A. A newspaper style article about some event in their own lives.

B. A letter to the principal discussing a personal opinion about some issue at the school.

C. Review of a movie as written by a critic.

D. A letter to a character in a story about some event.

98. **In Mr. Spragins' fifth grade class they are discussing the high school football game from the night before. Mr. Spragins shows his students various video clips, newspaper stories, and newscasts in regards to the championship game. Students are placed in small groups to discuss the information and how it is presented by the various media groups. What is Mr. Spragins having his students practice with this activity?**
(Competency 8.B, Average)

A. Assessing the use of images by different media types

B. Interpreting propaganda techniques used by the media

C. Analyzing varying viewpoints on the same event

D. Analyzing the use of images in the media in regards to the event

Use the following information to answer the following questions.

Mr. Lamar teaches American History and wants his students to learn how to do research on the Internet. In order to facilitate their online search, he's prepared a list of questions for them to use.

1. **Is the author's name and contact information available?**
2. **Does the author provide a listing of sources he or she used?**
3. **Are there advertisements on the website (what are they if so)?**
4. **What is the title of the website and the date of publication?**
5. **How is the main idea of the website supported by the material on the website?**
(Competency 8.A, Average)

99. **Based on the student's answers to question three, how might Mr. Lamar extend the lesson and what additional evaluations might be made?**
(Competency 8.A, Average)

    A. Historical significance

    B. Figurative language used

    C. Targeted audience

    D. Themes

100. **What is the primary goal of Mr. Lamar's website exercise?**
(Competency 9.A, Average)

    A. To evaluate the information on the website as credible
    B. To identify the sources of information for the website
    C. To identify a source with complete information
    D. To gather information from a reliable source

Answer Key

1	A	34	D	67	C	100	A
2	A	35	A	68	B		
3	A	36	A	69	D		
4	B	37	C	70	A		
5	A	38	A	71	C		
6	D	39	C	72	A		
7	A	40	B	73	D		
8	A	41	D	74	A		
9	A	42	D	75	B		
10	C	43	C	76	A		
11	A	44	D	77	A		
12	B	45	A	78	C		
13	D	46	D	79	B		
14	D	47	C	80	B		
15	D	48	B	81	A		
16	A	49	A	82	D		
17	A	50	B	83	D		
18	B	51	A	84	D		
19	C	52	C	85	B		
20	C	53	D	86	A		
21	B	54	C	87	A		
22	A	55	B	88	C		
23	B	56	B	89	A		
24	D	57	D	90	B		
25	B	58	B	91	A		
26	A	59	B	92	D		
27	D	60	C	93	C		
28	B	61	B	94	B		
29	B	62	D	95	B		
30	C	63	B	96	D		
31	C	64	B	97	B		
32	B	65	A	98	C		
33	A	66	A	99	C		

Explanation of Rigor

Easy: The majority of test takers would get this question correct. It is a simple understanding of the facts and/or the subject matter is part of the basics of an education for teaching English.

Average Rigor: This question represents a test item that most people would pass. It requires a level of analysis or reasoning and/or the subject matter exceeds the basics of an education for teaching English.

Rigor: The majority of test takers would have difficulty answering this question. It involves critical thinking competencies such as a very high level of abstract thought, analysis or reasoning, and it would require a very deep and broad education for teaching English.

Rigor Table

	Easy 20%	Average Rigor 40%	Rigorous 40%
Question	1, 5, 11, 13, 32, 32, 40, 45, 48, 49, 53, 56, 58, 59, 60	2, 4, 6, 10, 20, 26, 27, 28, 31, 34, 35, 36, 39, 42, 44, 46, 47, 50, 51, 52, 54, 55, 61, 62, 63, 64, 66, 71, 72, 73	3, 7, 8, 9, 12, 14, 15, 16, 17, 18, 19, 21, 22, 23, 24, 25, 29, 30, 37, 38, 41, 43, 57, 65, 67, 68, 69, 70, 74, 75

Answers with Rationales

1. **Which of the following is not true about English?**
    (Competency 1.A, Easy)

    A. English is the easiest language to learn
    B. English is the least inflected language
    C. English has the most extensive vocabulary of any language
    D. English originated as a Germanic tongue

The correct answer is A.
English has its own inherent quirks which make it difficult to learn. Plus it has incorporated words and structures from many disparate language groups in its lexicon and syntax. Languages with lexicons limited to words governed by a consistent set of relatively simple rules exist, so English is certainly not the easiest language to learn.

2. **Students are fluent readers if they**
    (Competency 1.A, Average)

    A. read texts fast enough with appropriate expression or prosody.
    B. read word-to-word and haltingly.
    C. must intentionally decode a majority of the words.
    D. write disorganized sentences.

The correct answer is A.
A fluent reader reads words accurately, at target speeds, and with appropriate expression. It is a positive term. The other choices describe negative outcomes.

3. **Which aspect of language is innate?**
    (Competency 1.A, Rigorous)

    A. Biological capability to articulate sounds understood by other humans
    B. Cognitive ability to create syntactical structures
    C. Capacity for using semantics to convey meaning in a social environment
    D. Ability to vary inflections and accents

The correct answer is A.
The biological capability to articulate sounds understood by other humans is innate, and, later, children learn semantics and syntactical structures through trial and error. Linguists agree that language is first a vocal system of word symbols that enable a human to communicate his or her feelings, thoughts, and desires to other human beings.

4. **All of the following techniques are used to conduct ongoing informal assessment of student progress except for**
    (Competency 1.B, Average)

    A. analyzing the student work product at key stages
    B. collecting data from assessment tests
    C. posing strategic questions
    D. observing students as they work

The correct answer is B.
The key here hinges on the adjective "informal." Assessment tests employ standardized materials and formats to monitor student progress and to report it in statistical terms. The other choices are relatively informal, teacher-specific techniques addressing more current, lesson-specific products and dynamics.

5. **Which of the following sentences contains an error in agreement?**
    (Competency 1.C, Easy)

    A. Jennifer is one of the women who writes for the magazine.
    B. Each one of their sons plays a different sport.
    C. This band has performed at the Odeum many times.
    D. The data are available online at the listed website.

The correct answer is A.
"Women" is the plural antecedent of the relative pronoun "who," which is functioning as the subject in its clause; so "who" is plural and requires the 3rd person plural form for the verb "write."

6. **A teacher should refer all of the following concerns to the appropriate expert except for**
    (Competency 1.E, Average)

    A. auditory trauma.
    B. ear infection.
    C. vision problems.
    D. underdeveloped vocabulary.

The correct answer is D.
The teacher is the expert in vocabulary development. The other choices require a medical professional.

7.   In preparing a speech for a contest, your student has encountered problems with gender specific language. Not wishing to offend either women or men, he seeks your guidance. Which of the following is not an effective strategy?
     (Competency 1.G, Rigorous)

   A. Use the generic "he" and explain that people will understand and accept the male pronoun as all-inclusive.
   B. Switch to plural nouns and use "they" as the gender-neutral pronoun.
   C. Use passive voice so that the subject is not required.
   D. Use male pronouns for one part of the speech and then use female pronouns for the other part of the speech.

The correct answer is A.
No longer is the male pronoun considered the universal pronoun. Speakers and writers should choose gender-neutral words and avoid nouns and pronouns that inaccurately exclude one gender or another.

8.   Which of the following bits of information best describes the structure of English?
     (Competency 1.I, Rigorous)

   A. Syntax based on word order
   B. Inflected
   C. Romantic
   D. Orthography is phonetic

The correct answer is A.
The syntax of English, reflective of its Germanic origins, relies on word order rather than inflection. Because of this and the many influences of other languages (particularly with regard to vocabulary), the orthography is not phonetic which complicates the teaching of standardized spelling.

9.   All of the following are true about phonological awareness except
     (Competency 2.A, Rigorous)

   A. it may involve print.
   B. it is a prerequisite for spelling and phonics.
   C. activities can be done by the children with their eyes closed.
   D. it starts before letter recognition is taught.

The correct answer is A.
Phonological Awareness is the ability to recognize the sounds of spoken language and how they can be blended together, segmented, and switched/manipulated to form new combinations and words.

10. **Middle school students bring little, if any, initial experience in**
(Competency 2.E Average)

A. phonics.
B. phonemics.
C. textbook reading assignments.
D. stories read by the teacher.

The correct answer is C.
In middle school, probably for the first time, the students will be expected to read textbook assignments and come to class prepared to discuss the content. Students get phonics (the systematic study of decoding) in the early grades, and they normally get phonemics (familiarity with the syllable sounds of English) even earlier. They will have almost certainly had stories read to them by a teacher by the time they get to middle school.

11. **Reading a piece of student writing to assess the overall impression of the product is**
(Competency 2.G, Easy)

A. holistic evaluation.
B. portfolio assessment.
C. analytical evaluation.
D. using a performance system.

The correct answer is A.
In holistic scoring, the teacher reads quickly through a paper once to get a general impression and assigns a rating based on a rubric that includes the criteria for achievement in a few key dimensions of the assignment. Portfolio assessment involves tracking work over stages or over time. Analytical evaluation involves breaking down the assignment into discrete traits and determining achievement in each of those traits. A performance system refers to engaging students in writing assignments meant to generate products in a given time frame. Often, such products are scored holistically.

12. Regularly requiring students to practice reading short, instructional-level texts at least three times to a peer and to give and receive peer feedback about these readings mainly addresses which reading competency?
(Competency 2.G, Rigorous)

A. Comprehension
B. Fluency
C. Evaluation
D. Word-solving

The correct answer is B.
Fluency is the ability to read text quickly with accuracy, phrasing, and expression. Fluency develops over time and requires substantial reading practice. This activity provides just this sort of practice. The peer feedback portion does address comprehension, evaluation, and some word-solving, but the main thrust is on fluency development.

13. Reading assessment should take place
(Competency 2.I, Easy)

A. at the end of the semester.
B. at the end of a unit.
C. constantly.
D. All of the above.

The correct answer is D.
End-of-unit and end-of-semester measurements yield important information regarding achievement of course objectives and the evaluation of students' growth; however, assessment should be ongoing so that the teacher can adjust instruction to meet the day-to-day needs of the students.

14. Effective assessment means that
(Competency 2.I, Rigorous)

A. it ignores age and cultural considerations.
B. students' weaknesses are emphasized.
C. only reading competencies count.
D. it is integrated with instruction and is not intrusive.

The correct answer is D.
Effective assessment reinforces instruction and practice. It is one phase of an integrated instructional cycle. Choice A ignores reality and distorts rather than informs. Choice B discourages students. Choice C ignores other important ways of demonstrating growth in understanding.

15. **Which of the following approaches is not useful in assessing slower or immature readers?**
(Competency 2.J, Rigorous)

A. Repeated readings
B. Echo reading
C. Wide reading
D. Reading content that is more difficult than their competency levels in order to "stretch" their abilities

The correct answer is D.
Reading content for such students should be at a level where they can read and understand the word nuances, not at a level beyond such understanding and competence. Repeated readings of appropriate material build this foundation. So does echo reading or listening to a competent reader and then trying to imitate his or her delivery. Wide reading is an approach intended to motivate students to read for pleasure and information from a variety of sources and involving socially-motivating processing routines.

16. **Computer-assisted instruction (CAI) accommodates all of the following factors in reading instruction except for**
(Competency 2.K, Rigorous)

A. free-form responses to comprehension questions.
B. increased motivation.
C. the addition of speech with computer-presented text.
D. the use of computers for word processing and the integration of writing instruction with reading.

The correct answer is A.
CAI does not accommodate free-form responses to comprehension questions and relies heavily on drill-and-practice and multiple-choice formats. This is a limitation of CAI.

17. To enhance reading comprehension, experts recommend all of these techniques except for
(Competency 3.A, Rigorous)

A. reading material through only once, but reading slowly and carefully.
B. reading material through more than once according to a plan.
C. creating a map for the next reading.
D. highlighting or taking notes during reading.

The correct answer is A.
While reading at a rate that assures accuracy is desirable, there is no evidence to support a recommendation to avoid rereading something. Choice B is advisable because it proposes a purpose for the rereading. Choice C is advisable because it also addresses purpose. Choice D is advisable because it helps students maintain focus as they read.

18. Which vocabulary strategy does the table below exemplify?
(Competency 3.B, Rigorous)

	Math Usage	Usage
bi (two)	Bilinear	Bicycle
	Bimodal	Biplane
	Binomial	bifocals
cent	Centimeter	century
(100)	Centigram	centigrade
	Percent	centipede
circum	circumference	circumnavigate
(around)	circumradius	circumstance
	circumcenter	circumspect

A. Frayer method
B. Morphemic analysis
C. Semantic mapping
D. Word mapping

The correct answer is B.
Morphemes are the smallest units of language that have an associated meaning. The purpose of morphemic analysis is to apply morphemic awareness to the task of learning new words. The Frayer method involves having students use their own words to define new words and to link those definitions to personal experiences. Semantic mapping incorporates graphical clues to concepts and is a subset of graphic organizers. Word mapping is another subset of graphic organizers and consists of displaying such information as the various forms a word may take as it transforms through the parts of speech.

19. **Which item below is not a research-based strategy that supports reading?**
(Competency 3.F, Rigorous)

A. Reading more
B. Reading along with a more proficient reader
C. Reading a passage no more than twice
D. Self-monitoring progress

The correct answer is C.
Actually, research shows that reading a passage several times improves fluency and, depending on the complexity of the material, improves comprehension, too. The more complex the material, the more comprehension value comes from repeated readings.

20. **The term graphophonemic awareness refers to**
(Competency 3.M, Average)

A. handwriting competencies.
B. letter to sound recognition.
C. alphabetic principle.
D. phonemic awareness

The correct answer is C.
Graphophonemic involves:

- Match all consonant and short vowel sounds.
- Read one's own name.
- Read one syllable words and high frequency words.
- Demonstrate ability to read and understand that as letters in words change, so do the sounds.
- Generate the sounds from all letters including consonant blends and long vowel patterns. Blend those different sounds into recognizable words.
- Read common sight words.
- Read common word families.

21. **The best way for a teacher to track a student's progress in demonstrating the alphabetic principal/ graphophonemic awareness is to**
(Competency 3.N, Rigorous)

   A. provide group assessments.
   B. maintain individual records.
   C. assess with standardized tests.
   D. have the student assessed by a team of teachers.

The correct answer is B.
The teacher will want to maintain individual records of children's reading behaviors demonstrating alphabetic principle/graphophonemic awareness.

22. **Making inferences from the text means that the reader**
(Competency 4.B, Rigorous)

   A. is making informed judgments based on available evidence.
   B. is making a guess based on prior experiences.
   C. is making a guess based on what the reader would like to be true of the text.
   D. All of the above.

The correct answer is A.
Inferencing is a process that involves the reader making a reasonable judgment based on the information given and engages children to literally construct meaning.

23. **Factors that affect the level of comprehension a student demonstrates when reading a story include all of the following except**
(Competency 4.C, Rigorous)

   A. lack of background knowledge.
   B. inability to spell words correctly.
   C. lack of word recognition competencies.
   D. inability to determine the meanings of words through context clues.

The correct answer is B.
Although spelling is an important competency for students to learn, it does not affect a student's level of comprehension.

24. **Four of Ms. Wolmark's students have lived in other countries. She is particularly pleased to be studying Sumerian proverbs with them as part of the sixth grade unit in analyzing the sayings of other cultures because**
(*Competency 4.C, Rigorous*)

   A. this gives her a break from teaching and the children can share sayings from other cultures they and their families have experienced.
   B. this validates the experiences and expertise of ELL learners in her classroom.
   C. this provides her children from the US with a lens on other cultural values.
   D. All of the above.

The correct answer is D.
It is recommended that all teachers of reading and particularly those who are working with ELL students use meaningful, student centered, and culturally customized activities. These activities may include: language games, word walls, and poems. Some of these activities might, if possible, be initiated in the child's first language and then reiterated in English.

25. **A teacher has taught his students to self-monitor their reading by locating where in the passage they are having difficulty, identifying the specific problem there, and restating the difficult sentence or passage in their own words. These strategies are examples of**
(*Competency 4.H, Rigorous*)

   A. graphic and semantic organizers.
   B. metacognition.
   C. recognizing story structure.
   D. summarizing.

The correct answer is B.
Good readers use metacognitive strategies (various ways of thinking about thinking) to improve their reading. Before reading, they clarify their purpose for reading and preview the text. During reading, they monitor their understanding, adjusting their reading speed to fit the difficulty of the text and fixing any comprehension problems they have. After reading, they check their understanding of what they read.

26.   **Which of the following would be the most significant factor in teaching Homer's Iliad and Odyssey to any particular group of students?**
       (Competency 4.I, Average)

   A. Selecting a translation on the appropriate reading level
   B. Determining the student's interest level
   C. Selecting an appropriate evaluative technique
   D. Determining the scope and delivery methods of background study

The correct answer is A.
Students will appreciate these two works if the translation reflects both the vocabulary they know and their reading level. Choice B is moot because most students aren't initially interested in Homer. Choice C skips to later matters. Choice D is tempting and significant but not as crucial as having an accessible text.

27.   **The students in Mrs. Cline's seventh grade language arts class were invited to attend a performance of Romeo and Juliet presented by the drama class at the high school. To best prepare, they should**
       (Competency 4.J, Average)

   A. read the play as a homework exercise.
   B. read a synopsis of the plot and a biographical sketch of the author.
   C. examine a few main selections from the play to become familiar with the language and style of the author.
   D. read a condensed version of the story and practice attentive listening competencies.

The correct answer is D.
By reading a condensed version of the play, students will know the plot and, therefore, be better able to follow the play on stage. They will also practice being attentive. Choice A is far less dynamic and few will do it. Choice B is, likewise, dull. Choice C is not thorough enough.

28. **Written on the sixth grade reading level, most of S. E. Hinton's novels (for instance, The Outsiders) have the greatest reader appeal with**
(Competency 4.K, Average)

    A. sixth graders.
    B. ninth graders.
    C. twelfth graders.
    D. adults.

The correct answer is B.
Adolescents are concerned with their changing bodies, their relationships with each other and adults, and their place in society. Reading *The Outsiders* helps them confront different problems that they are only now beginning to experience as teenagers, such as gangs and social identity. The book is universal in its appeal to adolescents.

29. **Which of the following responses to literature typically give middle school students the most problems?**
(Competency 4.M, Rigorous)

    A. Interpretive
    B. Evaluative
    C. Critical
    D. Emotional

The correct answer is B.
Middle school readers will exhibit both emotional and interpretive responses. In middle/junior high school, organized study models enable students to identify main ideas and supporting details, recognize sequential order, distinguish fact from opinion, and determine cause/effect relationships. Middle school students can provide reasons to support their assertions that a particular book was boring or a particular poem made him or her feel sad, and this is to provide a critical reaction on a fundamental level. Evaluative responses, however, require students to address how the piece represents its genre, how well it reflects the social and ethical mores of a given society, or how well the author has employed a fresh approach to the subject. Evaluative responses are more sophisticated than critical responses, and they are more appropriate for advanced high school students.

30. What type of reasoning does Henry David Thoreau use in the following excerpt from "Civil Disobedience"?
(Competency 4.M, Rigorous)

Unjust laws exist; shall we be content to obey them, or shall we endeavor to amend them, and obey them until we have succeeded, or shall we transgress them at once? Men generally, under such a government as this, think that they ought to wait until they have persuaded the majority to alter them. They think that, if they should resist, the remedy would be worse than the evil. But it is the fault of the government itself that the remedy *is* worse than the evil. Why does it always crucify Christ, excommunicate Copernicus and Luther, and pronounce Washington and Franklin rebels?

--"Civil Disobedience" by Henry David Thoreau

    A. Ethical reasoning
    B. Inductive reasoning
    C. Deductive reasoning
    D. Intellectual reasoning

The correct answer is C.
Deductive reasoning begins with a general statement that leads to the particulars. In this essay, Thoreau begins with the general question about what should be done about unjust laws. His argument leads to the government's role in suppressing dissent.

31. **The English department is developing strategies to encourage all students to become a community of readers. From the list of suggestions below, which would be the least effective way for teachers to foster independent reading?**
(Competency 4.P, Average)

A. Each teacher will set aside a weekly 30-minute in-class reading session during which the teacher and students read a magazine or book for enjoyment.
B. Teacher and students develop a list of favorite books to share with each other.
C. The teacher assigns at least one book report each grading period to ensure that students are reading from the established class list.
D. The students gather books for a classroom library so that books may be shared with each other.

The correct answer is C.
Teacher-directed assignments such as book reports appear routine and unexciting. Students will be more excited about reading when they can actively participate. In Choice A, the teacher is modeling reading behavior and providing students with a dedicated time during which time they can read independently and still be surrounded by a community of readers. In Choices B and D, students share and make available their reading choices.

32. **A paper written in first person and having characters, a setting, a plot, some dialogue, and events sequenced chronologically with some flashbacks exemplifies which genre?**
(Competency 5.A, Easy)

A. Exposition
B. Narration
C. Persuasion
D. Speculation

The correct answer is B.
Narrative writing tells a story, and all the listed elements pertain to stories. Expository writing explains or informs. Persuasive writing states an opinion and attempts to persuade an audience to accept the opinion or to take some specified action. Speculative writing explores possible developments from given circumstances.

33. **To explain or to inform belongs in the category of**
(Competency 5.A, Easy)

   A. exposition.
   B. narration.
   C. persuasion.
   D. description.

The correct answer is A.
Exposition sets forth a systematic explanation of any subject and informs the audience about various topics. It can also introduce the characters of a story and their situations as the story begins. Narration tells a story. Persuasion seeks to influence an audience so that they will adopt some new point of view or take some action. Description provides sensory details and addresses spatial relationships of objects.

34. **Oral debate is most closely associated with which form of discourse?**
(Competency 5.A, Average)

   A. Description
   B. Exposition
   C. Narration
   D. Persuasion

The correct answer is D.
The purpose of a debate is to convince an audience or set of judges about something which is very much the same as persuading some audience or set of judges about something.

35. **What is the main form of discourse in this passage?**
   (Competency 5.A, Average)

It would have been hard to find a passer-by more wretched in appearance. He was a man of middle height, stout and hardy, in the strength of maturity; he might have been forty-six or seven. A slouched leather cap hid half his face, bronzed by the sun and wind, and dripping with sweat.

   A. Description
   B. Exposition
   C. Narration
   D. Persuasion

The correct answer is A.
The passage describes the appearance of a person in detail. Narration tells a story. Exposition explains or informs. Persuasion promotes a point of view or course of action.

36. **A paper explaining the relationship between food and weight gain contains the signal words "because," "consequently," "this is how," and "due to." These words suggest that the paper has which text structure?**
   (Competency 5.B, Average)

   A. Cause and effect structure
   B. Compare and contrast structure
   C. Descriptive structure
   D. Sequential structure

The correct answer is A.
These signal words connect events in a causal chain, creating an explanation of some process or event. Compare and contrast structure presents similarities and differences. Descriptive structure presents a sensory impression of something or someone. Sequential structure references what comes first, next, last, and so on.

37.	Varying the complexity of a graphic organizer exemplifies differentiating which aspect of a lesson?
	(Competency 5.C, Rigorous)

	A. Its content/topic
	B. Its environment
	C. Its process
	D. Its product

The correct answer is C.
Differentiating the process means offering a variety of learning activities or strategies to students as they manipulate the ideas embedded within the lesson concept. For example, students may use graphic organizers, maps, diagrams, or charts to display their comprehension of concepts covered. Varying the complexity of a graphic organizer can very effectively accommodate differing levels of cognitive processing so that students of differing ability are appropriately engaged. Lesson topic and content remain the same, the lesson is still taking place in the same environment and, in most lessons, the graphic organizer is not the product of the lesson.

38.	Before reading a passage, a teacher gives her students an anticipation guide with a list of statements related to the topic they are about to cover in the reading material. She asks the students to indicate their agreement or disagreement with each statement on the guide. This activity is intended to
	(Competency 5.C, Rigorous)

	A. elicit students' prior knowledge of the topic and set a purpose for reading.
	B. help students to identify the main ideas and supporting details in the text.
	C. help students to synthesize information from the text.
	D. help students to visualize the concepts and terms in the text.

The correct answer is A.
Establishing a purpose for reading, the foundation for a reading unit or activity, is intimately connected to activating the students' prior knowledge in strategic ways. When the reason for reading is developed in the context of the students' experiences, they are far better prepared to succeed because they can make connections from a base they thoroughly understand. This influences motivation and, with proper motivation, students are more enthused and put forward more effort to understand the text. The other choices are only indirectly supported by this activity and are more specific in focus.

39. **In Ms. Francine's class, dictionary use is a punishment. Her principal observes her class and is**
(Competency 5.F, Average)

A. pleased with the way that Ms. Francine approaches dictionary use.
B. unconcerned with this approach to the use of the dictionary.
C. convinced that the teacher should model her own fascination and pleasure in using the dictionary for the children.
D. delighted by the fact that children are being forced to use the dictionary.

The correct answer is C.
Competencies such as using a dictionary or reading should never be used as punishment. This can inhibit student progress. A good teacher should model the use of all tools so that children may come to learn to use and enjoy using various tools.

40. **Mr. Brown's students are having a tough time interpreting information in a story, so he uses an illustration to help them. What type of help is this?**
(Competency 5.G, Average)

A. Classification
B. Qualitive Descriptions
C. Indifference
D. Modeling

The correct answer is B.
A qualitive Description is an illustration, therefore helping the students. A classification wouldn't help the students if they don't understand the original information. Indifference may be what they are feeling, and modeling is what the teacher would be doing, not the students.

41. **What game in lower-level classrooms helps students with abstract learning?**
(Competency 5.H, Average)

A. Monopoly
B. Checkers
C. Operation
D. Go Fish

The correct answer is D.
Go Fish helps lower level students pair lower numbers, therefore helping them group and identify. The teacher could move from numbers to pictures and then to ideas. Choice A- Monopoly, is too high- level of a game. Checkers is also a high level game and would be a higher skill build. Operation does not apply to this skill.

42. **The following lines from Robert Browning's poem "My Last Duchess" come from an example of what form of dramatic literature? (Competency 5.I, Rigorous)**

That's my last Duchess painted on the wall,
Looking as if she were alive. I call
That piece a wonder, now: Frà Pandolf's hands
Worked busily a day, and there she stands.
Will 't please you sit and look at her?

A. Tragedy
B. Comic opera
C. Dramatis personae
D. Dramatic monologue

The correct answer is D.
A dramatic monologue is a speech given by a character or narrator that reveals characteristics of the character or narrator. This form was first made popular by Robert Browning, a Victorian poet. Tragedy is a form of literature in which the protagonist is overwhelmed by opposing forces. Comic opera is a form of sung music based on a light or happy plot. "Dramatis personae" is the Latin phrase for the cast of a play.

43. **Among junior-high school students of low-to-average readability levels, which work would most likely stir reading interest? (Competency 5.J, Average)**

A. *Elmer Gantry*, Sinclair Lewis
B. *Smiley's People*, John Le Carre
C. *The Outsiders*, S.E. Hinton
D. *And Then There Were None*, Agatha Christie.

The correct answer is C.
The students can easily identify with the characters, the social issues, the vocabulary, and the themes in the book. The book deals with teenage concerns such as fitting-in, cliques, and appearance in ways that have proven very engaging for young readers.

44. **The most significant drawback to applying learning theory research to classroom practice is that**
   (Competency 5.K, Rigorous)

   A. today's students do not acquire reading competencies with the same alacrity as when greater emphasis was placed on reading classical literature.
   B. development rates are complicated by geographical and cultural differences that are difficult to overcome.
   C. homogeneous grouping has contributed to faster development of some age groups.
   D. social and environmental conditions have contributed to an escalated maturity level than research done twenty or more years ago would seem to indicate.

The correct answer is D.
A mismatch exists between what interests today's students and the learning materials presented to them. Choice A is a significant problem only if the school insists on using classical literature exclusively. Choice B does describe a drawback, but students are more alike in their disengagement from anachronistic learning materials than they are different due to their culture and geographical location. Choice C describes a situation that is not widespread.

45. **Which is an untrue statement about a theme in literature?**
   (Competency 5.L, Average)

   A. The theme is always stated directly somewhere in the text.
   B. The theme is the central idea in a literary work.
   C. All parts of the work (plot, setting, mood) should contribute to the theme in some way.
   D. By analyzing the various elements of the work, the reader should be able to arrive at an indirectly stated theme.

The correct answer is A.
The theme may be stated directly, but it can also be implicit in various aspects of the work, such as the interaction between characters, symbolism, or description.

46. **The arrangement and relationship of words in sentences or sentence structures best describes**
(Competency 5.M, Easy)

    A. style
    B. discourse
    C. thesis
    D. syntax

The correct answer is D.
Syntax is the grammatical structure of sentences. Style is not limited to considerations of syntax only, but it includes vocabulary, voice, genre, and other language features. Discourse refers to investigating some idea. A thesis is a statement of opinion.

47. **What type of comprehension do questions beginning with "who," "what," "where," or "how" assess?**
(Competency 5.O, Average)

    A. Evaluative
    B. Inferential
    C. Literal
    D. Narrative

The correct answer is C.
Literal questions ask for facts from the reading. The student can put his finger right on the answer and prove that he is correct. These questions are sometimes referred to as "right there" questions. Evaluative questions require a judgment of some sort. Inferential questions ask students to make an educated guess. Narrative questions involve aspects of a story beyond literal considerations.

48. **Environmental print is available in all of the following except**
    (Competency 6.A, Average)

    A. within a newspaper.
    B. on the page of a library book.
    C. on a supermarket circular.
    D. in a commercial flyer.

The correct answer is B.
Environmental print involves print from items such as signs, boxes, etc. Magazines and catalogues are another source of environmental print that is accessible with ads for child centered products. Supermarket circulars and coupons from the newspaper are also excellent for engaging children in using environmental print as reading, especially when combined with dramatic play centers or prop boxes.

49. **Which group of words is not a sentence?**
    (Competency 6.B, Easy)

    A. In keeping with the graduation tradition, the students, in spite of the rain, standing in the cafeteria tossing their mortarboards.
    B. Rosa Parks, who refused to give up her seat on the bus, will be forever remembered for her courage.
    C. Taking advantage of the goalie's being out of the net, we scored our last and winning goal.
    D. When it began to rain, we gathered our possessions and ran for the pavilion.

The correct answer is A.
This is a sentence fragment because sentences require a subject and a verb and there is no verb. Changing "the students, in spite of the rain, standing" to "the students, in spite of the rain, were standing" corrects the problem.

50. **Which of the following sentences is unambiguously properly punctuated?**
(Competency 6.B, Easy)

   A. The more you eat; the more you want.
   B. The authors—John Steinbeck, Ernest Hemingway, and William Faulkner—are staples of modern writing in American literature textbooks.
   C. Handling a wild horse, takes a great deal of competency and patience
   D. The man, who replaced our teacher, is a comedian.

The correct answer is B.
Dashes should be used instead of commas when commas are used elsewhere in the sentence for amplification or explanation as seen here within the dashes. Choice A has a semicolon where there should be a comma. Choice C has a comma that shouldn't be there at all. Choice D could be correct in a non-restrictive context; so, whether or not it is correct, it is ambiguous.

51. **A punctuation mark indicating omission, interrupted thought, or an incomplete statement is a/an**
(Competency 6.B, Average)

   A. ellipsis
   B. anachronism
   C. colloquy
   D. idiom

The correct answer is A.
Ellipses represent words that are omitted that would clarify the sentence's message, yet it is still possible to understand the sentence from the context. An anachronism is something out of its proper time frame. A colloquy is a formal conversation or dialogue. An idiom is a saying peculiar to some language group.

52. **In the following sentence, which word group below best conveys the intended meaning of the underlined section?**
(Competency 6.E, Average)

Joe *didn't hardly know his cousin Fred*, who'd had a rhinoplasty.

A. Hardly did know his cousin Fred
B. Didn't know his cousin Fred hardly
C. Hardly knew his cousin Fred
D. Didn't know his cousin Fred

The correct answer is C.
It contains a correctly-phrased negative expressed in the appropriate tense. Choice A has tense and awkwardness problems. Choice B has tense and double negative problems. Choice D ignores the fact that he knew Fred a little.

53. **In the following sentence, which phrase below best represents the logical intent of the underlined phrase?**
(Competency 6.E, Average)

Mr. Brown is a school volunteer *with a reputation and twenty years service*.

A. With a reputation for twenty years' service
B. With a reputation for twenty year's service
C. Who has served twenty years
D. With a service reputation of twenty years

The correct answer is D.
His reputation pertains to his service performance, not its duration. Choice A implies that it was for its duration. Choice B has Choice A's problem plus an incorrectly punctuated possessive. Choice C ignores his service reputation.

54. **Which of the four underlined sections of the following sentence contains an error that a word processing spellchecker probably wouldn't catch?**
(Competency 6.G, Easy)

He <u>tuc</u> the <u>hors</u> by the <u>rains</u> and pulled it back to the <u>stabel</u>.

    A. Tuc
    B. Hors
    C. Rains
    D. Stabel

The correct answer is C.
Spellcheckers only catch errors in conventional modern English spelling. They cannot catch errors involving incorrect homophone usage. "Rains" is the only one of the four words to conform to conventional English spelling, but it clearly is not the word called for by the context.

55. **For students with poor vocabularies, the teacher should recommend first that**
(Competency 6.G, Average)

    A. they enroll in a Latin class/
    B. they read newspapers, magazines, and books on a regular basis.
    C. they write the words repetitively after looking them up in the dictionary.
    D. they use a thesaurus to locate and incorporate the synonyms found there into their vocabularies.

The correct answer is B.
Regularly reading a wide variety of materials for pleasure and information is the best way to develop a stronger vocabulary. The other suggestions have limited application and do not serve to reinforce an enthusiasm for reading.

56. **Which of the following contains an error in possessive punctuation?**
(Competency 6.I Average)

    A. Doris's shawl
    B. Mother's-in-law frown
    C. Children's lunches
    D. Ambassador's briefcase

The correct answer is B.
Mother-in-law is a compound, common noun, and the apostrophe should come at the end of the word according to convention. The other choices are correctly punctuated.

57. **Writing ideas quickly without interruption of the flow of thoughts or attention to conventions is called**
(Competency 7.E, Easy)

   A. brainstorming.
   B. mapping.
   C. listing.
   D. free writing.

The correct answer is D.
Free writing is a particular type of brainstorming (techniques used to generate ideas). Mapping is another type of brainstorming which results in products resembling flow charts. Listing is another brainstorming technique that differs from free writing in that free writing is more open-ended and looks more like sentences.

58. **A formative evaluation of student writing**
(Competency 7.F, Rigorous)

   A. requires a thorough marking of mechanical errors with a pencil or pen.
   B. makes comments on the appropriateness of the student's interpretation of the prompt and the degree to which the objective was met.
   C. requires the student to hand in all the materials produced during the process of writing.
   D. involves several careful readings of the text for content, mechanics, spelling, and usage.

The correct answer is B.
Formative evaluations should support the students' writing process through strategic feedback at key points. Teacher comments and feedback should encourage recursive revision and metacognition. Choice A applies, if anywhere, to a summative evaluation of student writing. Choice C is a neutral management strategy. A teacher can make formative evaluations without collecting all the materials. Choice D, again, is more suited for summative evaluation or for the very last issue in the composition process, namely proofreading.

59. **In a timed essay test of an hour's duration, how much time should be devoted to prewriting?**
(Competency 7.H, Easy)

    A. Five minutes
    B. Ten minutes
    C. Fifteen minutes
    D. Twenty minutes

The correct answer is B.
Ten minutes of careful planning allows sufficient time for the other stages of the writing process. Five minutes would result in dead-ends and backtracking during the writing. Fifteen and twenty minutes would result in rushing during the drafting, revising, and editing stages.

60. **A student informative composition should consist of a minimum of how many paragraphs?**
(Competency 7.H, Easy)

    A. Three
    B. Four
    C. Five
    D. Six

The correct answer is C.
This composition would consist of an introductory paragraph, three body paragraphs, and a concluding paragraph. A three or four paragraph composition could include all three types of paragraphs but would be less likely to provide the student with enough paragraphs to include adequate information to address the topic properly.

61. **Which of the following should not be included in the opening paragraph of an informative essay?**
(Competency 7.H, Easy)

    A. Thesis sentence
    B. Details and examples supporting the main idea
    C. Broad general introduction to the topic
    D. A style and tone that grabs the reader's attention

The correct answer is B.
The introductory paragraph should introduce the topic, capture the reader's interest, state the thesis, and prepare the reader for the main points in the essay. Details and examples, however, belong in the second part of the essay, the body paragraphs.

62. **Which of the following is not a technique of prewriting?**
   (Competency 7.H, Average)

   A. Clustering
   B. Listing
   C. Brainstorming
   D. Proofreading

The correct answer is D.
You cannot proofread something that you have not yet written. While it is true that prewriting involves written techniques, prewriting is not concerned with punctuation, capitalization, and spelling (proofreading). Brainstorming is a general term denoting generating ideas, and clustering and listing are specific methods of brainstorming.

63. **Modeling is a practice that requires students to**
   (Competency 7.I, Average)

   A. create a style unique to their own language capabilities.
   B. emulate the writing of professionals.
   C. paraphrase passages from good literature.
   D. peer evaluate the writings of other students.

The correct answer is B.
Modeling engages students in analyzing the writing of professional writers and in imitating the syntactical, grammatical, and stylistic mastery of that writer. Choice A is an issue of voice. Choice C is a less rigorous form of the correct answer. Choice D is only very indirectly related to modeling.

64. **Which of the following is the least effective procedure for promoting consciousness of audience?**
    (Competency 7.K, Average)

    A. Pairing students during the writing process
    B. Reading all the rough drafts before the students write the final copies
    C. Having students compose stories or articles for publication in school literary magazines or newspapers
    D. Writing letters to friends or relatives

The correct answer is B.
Reading all rough drafts will do the least to promote consciousness of audience. Students are very used to turning papers into the teacher, and most don't think much about impressing the teacher. Pairing students will ensure a small, constant audience about whom they care, and having them compose stories for literary magazines will encourage them to put their best efforts forward because their work will be read by an actual audience in an impressive format. Writing letters also engages students in thinking about how best to communicate with a particular audience.

65. **If a student uses slang and expletives, what is the best course of action to take in order to improve the student's formal communication competencies?**
    (Competency 7.I, Average)

    A. Ask the student to rephrase their writing; that is, translate it into language appropriate for the school principal to read.
    B. Refuse to read the student's papers until he conforms to a more literate style.
    C. Ask the student to read his work aloud to the class for peer evaluation.
    D. Rewrite the flagrant passages to show the student the right form of expression.

The correct answer is A.
Asking the student to write to the principal, a respected authority figure, will alert the student to the need to use formal language. Simply refusing to read the paper is not only negative, but it also sets up a power struggle. Asking the student to read slang and expletives aloud to the class for peer evaluation is to risk unproductive classroom chaos and to support the class clowns. Rewriting the flagrant passages for the student to model formal expression does not immerse the student in the writing process.

66. The new teaching intern is developing a unit on creative writing and is trying to encourage her students to write poetry. Which of the following would not be an effective technique?
(Competency 7.B, Rigorous)

   A. In groups, students will draw pictures to illustrate "The Love Song of J. Alfred Prufrock" by T.S. Eliot.
   B. Either individually or in groups, students will compose a song, writing lyrics that try to use poetic devices.
   C. Students will bring to class the lyrics of a popular song and discuss the imagery and figurative language.
   D. Students will read aloud their favorite poems and share their opinions of and responses to the poems.

The correct answer is A.
While drawing is creative, it will not accomplish as much as the other activities to encourage students to write their own poetry. Furthermore, "The Love Song of J. Alfred Prufrock" is not an at-level poem. The other activities involve students in music and their own favorites, which will be more appealing.

67. The following passage is written from which point of view?
(Competency 7.C, Average)

   As she mused the pitiful vision of her mother's life laid its spell on the very quick of her being —that life of commonplace sacrifices closing in final craziness. She trembled as she heard again her mother's voice saying constantly with foolish insistence: *Dearevaun Seraun! Dearevaun Seraun!**
   * "The end of pleasure is pain!" (Gaelic)

   A. First person, narrator
   B. Second person, direct address
   C. Third person, omniscient
   D. First person, omniscient

The correct answer is C.
The passage is clearly in the third person (the subject is "she"), and it is omniscient since it gives the characters' inner thoughts.

68. **Mr. Ledbetter has instructed his students to prepare a slide presentation that illustrates an event in history. Students are to include pictures, graphics, media clips and links to resources. What competencies will students exhibit at the completion of this project?**
(Competency 8.A, Rigorous)

    A. Analyze the impact of society on media.
    B. Recognize the media's strategies to inform and persuade.
    C. Demonstrate strategies and creative techniques to prepare presentations using a variety of media.
    D. Identify the aesthetic effects of a media presentation.

The correct answer is B.
Students will have learned how to use various media to convey a unified message. By employing multimedia in their presentations, students will be telling a story with more than words.

69. **A sixth-grade teacher has subscribed to an online version of a local newspaper. She can help the students examine this resource and how it compares to the print version by noting the following differences:**
(Competency 8.C, Rigorous)

    A. Use of video to document events
    B. Use of sound clips in addition to written text
    C. Links to other web resources
    D. All of the above

The correct answer is D.
Online resources contain other forms of media that go beyond the printed word. Audio and video clips can be used to enhance the experience of the learner.

70. For their research paper on the use of technology in the classroom, students have gathered data that shows a sharp increase in the number of online summer classes over the past five years. What would be the best way for them to depict this information visually? *(Competency 8.G, Rigorous)*

    A. A line chart
    B. A table
    C. A pie chart
    D. A flow chart

The correct answer is A.
A line chart is used to show trends over time and will emphasize the sharp increase. A table is appropriate to show the exact numbers but does not have the same impact as a line chart. Not appropriate is a pie chart which shows the parts of a whole or a flow chart which details processes or procedures.

71. In presenting a report to peers about the effects of Hurricane Katrina on New Orleans, the students wanted to use various media in their argument to persuade their peers that more needed to be done. Which of these would be the most effective? *(Competency 8.I, Rigorous)*

    A. A PowerPoint presentation showing the blueprints of the levees before the flood and redesigned now for current construction.
    B. A collection of music clips made by the street performers in the French Quarter before and after the flood.
    C. A recent video showing the areas devastated by the floods and the current state of rebuilding.
    D. A collection of recordings of interviews made by the various government officials and local citizens affected by the flooding.

The correct answer is C.
For maximum impact, a video would offer dramatic scenes of the devastated areas. A video by its very nature is more dynamic than a static PowerPoint presentation. Further, the condition of the levees would not provide as much impetus for change as seeing the devastated areas. Oral messages such as music clips and interviews provide another way of supplementing the message but, again, they are not as dynamic as video.

72. **Which of the following are secondary research materials?**
    (Competency 9.A, Average)

    A. The conclusions and inferences of other historians.
    B. Literature and nonverbal materials, novels, stories, poetry and essays from the period, as well as coins, archaeological artifacts, and art produced during the period.
    C. Interviews and surveys conducted by the researcher.
    D. Statistics gathered as the result of the research's experiments.

The correct answer is A.
Secondary sources are works written significantly after the period being studied and based upon primary sources. In this case, historians have studied artifacts of the time and drawn their conclusion and inferences. Primary sources are the basic materials that provide raw data and information. Students or researchers may use literature and other data they have collected to draw their own conclusions or inferences.

73. **In preparing your students to write a research paper about a social problem, what recommendation can you make so they can determine the credibility of their information?**
    (Competency 9.A, Average)

    A. Assure them that information on the Internet has been peer-reviewed and verified for accuracy.
    B. Find one solid source and use that exclusively.
    C. Use only primary sources.
    D. Cross check your information with another credible source.

The correct answer is D.
When researchers find the same information in multiple reputable sources, the information is considered credible. Using the Internet for research requires strong critical evaluation of the source. Nothing from the Internet should be taken without careful scrutiny of the source. To rely on only one source is dangerous and shortsighted. Most high school freshmen would have limited competencies to conduct primary research for a paper about a social problem.

74. **Teaching students how to set goals, modeling how to take notes, and how to create an outline are all examples of**
(Competency 9.A, Average)

    A. study skills.
    B. comprehension strategies.
    C. read aloud strategies.
    D. discussion competencies.

The correct answer is A.
One of the most important ways of helping students experience success in school, especially with reading and studying in the content areas, is to teach them how to study. This involves such competencies as how to take notes, summarize, find information in reference materials, and use maps and graphics. A fundamental part of teaching study competencies also involves teaching students to set goals, organize their material, and manage their time.

75. **To determine the credibility of information, researchers should do all of the following except**
(Competency 9.C, Rigorous)

    A. establish the authority of the document.
    B. disregard documents with bias.
    C. evaluate the currency and reputation of the source.
    D. use a variety of research sources and methods.

The correct answer is B.
Keep an open mind. Researchers should examine the assertions, facts and reliability of the information. Bias does not automatically invalidate information invalid. Being completely objective is an ideal not often realized. The researcher should analyze this information with more scrutiny to determine its reliability.

76. **Students have been asked to write a research paper on automobiles and have brainstormed a number of questions they will answer based on their research findings. Which of the following is not an interpretive question to guide research?**
(Competency 9.F, Rigorous)

   A. Who were the first ten automotive manufacturers in the United States?
   B. What types of vehicles will be used fifty years from now?
   C. How do automobiles manufactured in the United States compare and contrast with each other?
   D. What do you think is the best solution for the fuel shortage?

The correct answer is A.

The question asks for objective facts. Choice B is a prediction that asks how something will look or be in the future, based on the way it is now. Choice C asks for similarities and differences, which is a higher-level research activity that requires analysis. Choice D is a judgment question that requires informed opinion.

Use the information below to answer the following questions:

Mr. Anderson, an English teacher, creates an activity to promote discussion with students after reading a chapter of a novel that has been studied as a class. He places a list of question starters on the board that students can use to create questions for their classmates. Next, Mr. Anderson has them both ask and answer the questions in a small group setting.

Question Starters:

1. What must have happened when (use chapter and page number to describe a specific event)
2. What happens next (refer to person, conflict, or page number)
3. What were some similar thoughts, actions, or events that occurred in (specific chapter) and (specific chapter)?
4. What did the author mean when he said, "quote"? (Use chapter and page number)
5. If you had to make suggestions for making the story better, what would they be? (use chapter and page number)
6. What sorts of problems does the main character face? (use chapter and page number)

77. Mr. Anderson's activity promotes students to use which of the following critical-reading skills?
    (Competency 5.B, Rigorous)

    A. Providing evidence from within the text to support conclusions
    B. Synthesizing information from more than one source
    C. Examining rhetorical devices for their effectiveness
    D. Comparing textural structures

The correct answer is A.
Choice A is the correct answer because each of the question starters asks students to cite the chapter and page number in their answer. B doesn't work because the questions don't require students to actually synthesize or interact with multiple sources of information. C is also incorrect because the questions don't require any sort of analyzation, and D is not a good choice because the questions don't ask the students to compare structures within the text.

78. **When students respond to questions 1 and 4, which of the following skills are being practiced?**
    (Competency 5.C, Rigorous)

    A. Visualization
    B. Summarization
    C. Inference
    D. Prediction

The correct answer is C.
Choice C is the correct answer because questions 1 and 4 ask students to make inferences or to interpret the text. Choice A is incorrect because there is little visualization taking place. Likewise, B is not a good choice because the questions do not ask students to summarize what they have read. Choice D is not the best answer either because while prediction is part of the grouping, it is NOT in question 1 or 4.

79. **Which of the listed question starters would facilitate a students' connection with the text?**
    (Competency 4.D, Average)

    A. Question 2
    B. Question 3
    C. Question 1
    D. Question 5

The correct answer is B.
Choice B is the correct answer because question 3 directly asks students to use their current text and to compare it with other texts that they may have already read. The rest of the answer options are incorrect because they only refer to the one text that the students are currently studying.

80. **Why would this activity be especially good for students who are English-language learners?**
    (Competency 1.G, Average)

    A. Because the activity develops phonemic awareness
    B. Gives the learner many opportunities to speak and use language.
    C. The activity gives direct instruction on language use
    D. The activity allows for word analysis

The correct answer is B.
The best answer for this question is Choice B because the small group interaction, as well as the construction of questions and answers, allows the English language learners a chance to utilize the language in several different ways.

81. A seventh-grade teacher has her class listen to recording of a well-known speech. She has them listen to it twice, first listening to respond to content, and the second time to evaluate the presentation, itself. The purpose of this module would be to do which of the following:
(Competency 1.L, Rigorous)

A. Understand the types of skills that are needed to speak successfully in public.
B. Compare speech presentations
C. Prepare for their own informal speaking assignments
D. Collaborate with their classmates to improve the speech's effectiveness

The correct answer is A.
A is the correct answer because it asks the students to evaluate the speech when given two specific criteria, each designed to help students understand the skills needed when speaking publicly. B is incorrect because there is only one speech being given. As the students are not presenting their own speeches, C is a poor choice as well. D is incorrect because students have not been asked to collaborate on making the speech better.

82. In an effort to motivate her students in Language Arts class, a teacher creates learning clubs that students can become involved with. Students are assigned a small group to work with in order to research a given topic, and then reflect on the information gathered. The students are then instructed to create a blog based on their findings. What does this instructional design show the teacher understands the importance of?
(Competency 2.K, Rigorous)

A. That the teacher understands the need to provide explicit instruction for language building.
B. That the teacher understands the need for placing students in skills based small groups based on ability.
C. Allowing students to choose their own topics are a great motivating factor.
D. The need to provide literacy skills using multiple language-arts contexts.

The correct answer is D.
D is the answer because the learning clubs give students a chance to meet in smaller groups, to facilitate reflection, and then collaboration on a blog which builds students' literacy skills. While it is true that C is a great motivator, students were not given the option to research topics they had chosen. A is incorrect because explicit instruction is not being given. B is incorrect because we aren't given that information, so it is not clear if the teacher grouped by ability or not.

83. **What would assist a teacher in assessing the phonics skills of her lower quartile students?**
(Competency 2.A, Average)

A. Assessing sight word recall by the student
B. Assessing a student's handwriting
C. Giving timed reading tests
D. Assessing student's spelling attempts

The correct answer is D.
The answer is D, because spelling attempts give the instructor a glimpse into the thought process of the student and how they are viewing the words phonetically.

84. **A reading teacher meets with a small group of struggling readers to read a short book. Over the course of the week she asks the students to read the book again, to themselves, and together as a group, several times. What is the purpose of this technique?**
(Competency 3.N, Average)

A. To reinforce letter-sounding skills
B. To develop comprehension
C. To instill a love of reading
D. To promote recognition of high frequency words

The correct answer is D.
The answer is D, because research indicates that struggling students who are exposed to high frequency words gain confidence and, in time, will be able to include words that do not occur at high frequency.

85. **Ms. Ingram, a fourth-grade teacher, is employing a technique where she reads a line in the workbook, then has the students read the same lines aloud, imitating her inflection and tone. What does this activity develop in students?**
(Competency 3.O, Average)

A. Oral comprehension
B. Fluency
C. Word identification
D. Word meanings

The correct answer is B.
The answer is B. Fluency is impacted by tone and accuracy, which the teacher is giving the students a chance to practice. The other answers focus on comprehension on some level, which is not the goal of the exercise.

86. **Ms. Atkins wants to assess her students' reading levels on several levels: independent, frustration, and instructional. What is the best strategy for doing that?**
(Competency 4.I, Average)

   A. Recording each student's mistakes as they read aloud from a short text.
   B. Giving a vocabulary test after reading a text.
   C. Making notes about a student's responses after reading a text.
   D. Observing facial cues while a student is reading a text.

The correct answer is A.
A is the answer because it is a very good way to identify a student's reading readiness level. The number of errors will indicate a student's readiness to move on to another level, or may be an indication that they need further and more inclusive instruction.

87. **Mrs. Clemons has her 8th grade class read several different versions of the Cinderella story, then asks them to write a comparison and contrast essay. The purpose of this activity is to have students do which of the following?**
(Competency 4.Q, Rigorous)

   A. Use multiple texts to synthesize information gained.
   B. Evaluate a variety of text structures.
   C. Develop appropriate prosody.
   D. Develop metacognitive strategies for use later

The correct answer is A.
Asking students to compare and contrast texts is a higher-level cognitive skill that requires a student to synthesize information and thus develop a deeper understanding of the text and the topic. The other answers ask the student to focus on the form and presentation of the text, and not on the actual understanding of it.

88. **Of the following activities, which would develop a student's metacognitive skills?**
(Competency 4.H, Average)

   A. Creating a graphic organizer that uses the concept of layers.
   B. Using a graphic organizer to create a summary of a story.
   C. Using a graphic organizer while reading or writing independently.
   D. Allowing students to work with a partner to complete a graphic organizer.

The correct answer is C.
The answer is C because it allows students the opportunity for self-reflection as well as uses it as a reference when evaluating or analyzing a text.

89. **Mr. Phelps comes to Ms. Eades with a dilemma. His science class can gather facts well enough from the text, but when asked to restate the larger concepts they are unable to do so. He's asked for Ms. Eades' help. Which of the following techniques or activities would be most helpful in addressing the issue?**
(Competency 5.D, Average)

    A. Summarizing the main ideas (outlining).
    B. Discussing a part of the chapter they found interesting.
    C. Reading the chapters out loud.
    D. Pulling out important vocabulary words in the chapter.

The correct answer is A.
The answer is A, because while the students are gathering the main ideas from the chapter, they can later put them together for a cohesive understanding of the larger concepts. Discussing interesting information, reading the chapters out loud, or working on vocabulary will not achieve the goal.

90. **When utilizing reading journals with his class, Mr. Morales hopes to motivate them to read more. Which of the following activities with the journal would help to achieve this goal?**
(Competency 5.C, Easy)

    A. Summarizing each passage in the text.
    B. Writing down personal reflections about the text.
    C. Taking notes about main ideas in the text.
    D. Writing to a prompt revolving around the text.

The correct answer is B.
If Mr. Morales' goal is to promote motivation for reading, then making personal connections about what they think about what they have read is a way for them to connect with the work on a deeper level.

Use the following information to answer the following questions:

Mr. Ambergy wants to prepare a genre study, which includes classical literature. To do this he proposes to place the students in small groups and allow them to choose from a list of traditional literature. Students will analyze this selection for themes, cultural influences, and literary devices. *(Competency 5.L, Rigorous)*

91. **Which of the following activities would facilitate students' ability to discover cultural influences over a text? (Competency 5.K, Rigorous)**

    A. Create and use a comparison chart while reading the moral lessons of two different folktales form dissimilar cultures.
    B. Create a Venn diagram to compare and contrast the conflicts in the folktales.
    C. Create a story map that represents the cultural elements of two stories by the same author.
    D. Use a KWL chart when it comes to cultural features that have been learned after reading two myths from the same culture.

The correct answer is A.
A is the correct answer because comparing two dissimilar folktales is a very effective way to develop comprehension of cross-cultural themes. The other answer choices focus too narrowly on only one culture.

92. **To assist students in locating and identifying literary devices, Mr. Ambergy could have his students find evidence form the text that demonstrates which of the following? (Competency 5.L, Rigorous)**

    A. Settings that offer specific times and details within the story.
    B. Complex plots that develop slowly.
    C. Details that explain the resolution of conflicts when they occur.
    D. Characters that seem to have similar characteristics and familiar traits.

The correct answer is D.
The answer is D, because in cultural stories (myths, fables, and folktales) archetypes are generally present. This allows students to see into the culture's notions and values, as well as see commonality of themes between cultures.

Utilize the following student writing example to answer the following questions:

Yesterday I went to the mall with Sophie and my sister. Sophie likes to go to the record store, and my sister likes records. There was a lot of people at the mall yesterday. We had fun.

93.   What does the writing sample above suggest the teacher focus on as far as additional instruction for the student?
       (Competency 6.E, Average)

       A. Using pronouns correctly.
       B. Working on creating compound sentences.
       C. Working on correct verb tenses.
       D. Recognizing and correcting sentence fragments.

The correct answer is C.
The answer is C, because in the third sentence the student uses 'there was' instead of 'there were'. The sentences, while not particularly complex, are complete, so focusing on sentence fragments (D) is not helpful. The pronouns are also all used correctly, so (A) is incorrect. Lastly, parallel construction is done correctly in sentence two, so (B) is incorrect.

94.   A teacher introduces transitional words and phrases such as 'therefore' and 'as a result' to her class. With the particular choice of transitions, the teacher is preparing her class to work on an essay that will use which of the following:
       (Competency 7.C, Average)

       A. A sequence of events
       B. Cause and effect patterns
       C. A list of steps
       D. Specific examples, or descriptions

The correct answer is B.
The answer is B, cause and effect patterns, because of the selection of the transitional phrases 'as a result' and 'therefore'. These lend themselves to the cause and effect essay, whereas a sequence of events or listing of steps would utilize the transitional phrases 'first, next, then'. Specific examples and their accompanying transitional phrases would be used when writing a narrative, or even for a persuasive paper.

95. Mrs. Lyons, a seventh-grade English teacher, notices that her students are able to make word counts for assigned essays, but that the material added to make the essays longer are often vague. She wants to help students learn how to improve their revision process. To do this, she should teach the students how to do which of the following techniques:
(Competency 7.G, Average)

   A. A checklist for revising.
   B. A box and explode strategy to expand upon a main idea
   C. An activity to work on varying sentence lengths
   D. A list of upper level vocabulary (sparkle words) to utilize when writing

The correct answer is B.
The answer is B because of all the selected activities, this is the only one that will assist students in expanding the details around a main idea, as well as remove the vagueness from the writing.

96. An assignment has been made to a group of eighth-grade students in an English class involving the creation of a PowerPoint presentation, which they must present to the class. Before they begin their work, the teacher shows them examples of both good presentations and poorly designed presentations. This activity is designed to help students with their understanding of how to do which of the following:
(Competency 7.M, Easy)

   A. Make sure that the presentations are not too long
   B. Match what is said with what is presented in the slides.
   C. Show the appropriate use of graphics which support the text shown.
   D. Show how to design the slides correctly and appropriately.

The correct answer is D.
The answer is D because the teacher's goal is to make sure that the presentations are designed correctly, not how they were presented, or what was presented within the context of the presentation slides.

97. **Mr. Stegnar wants his students to have the opportunity to write for an authentic audience and for an authentic purpose. Which of the assignments below best achieves this goal:**
(Competency 7.L, Average)

    A. A newspaper style article about some event in their own lives.
    B. A letter to the principal discussing a personal opinion about some issue at the school.
    C. Review of a movie as written by a critic.
    D. A letter to a character in a story about some event.

The correct answer is B.
The answer is B because it is the writer's personal opinion about something they have direct knowledge of. The students will be writing in their own voice, which promotes authenticity, and the school related topic creates the authentic audience and purpose.

98. **In Mr. Spragins' fifth grade class they are discussing the high school football game from the night before. Mr. Spragins shows his students various video clips, newspaper stories, and newscasts in regards to the championship game. Students are placed in small groups to discuss the information and how it is presented by the various media groups. What is Mr. Spragins having his students practice with this activity?**
(Competency 8.B, Average)

    A. Assessing the use of images by different media types
    B. Interpreting propaganda techniques used by the media
    C. Analyzing varying viewpoints on the same event
    D. Analyzing the use of images in the media in regards to the event

The correct answer is C.
The answer is C because the students are being asked to discuss how the same event was reported by different news agencies. This is a type of comparison and contrast exercise as opposed to discussing propaganda, use of images, or the differences between media types.

Use the following information to answer the following questions.

Mr. Lamar teaches American History and wants his students to learn how to do research on the Internet. In order to facilitate their online search, he's prepared a list of questions for them to use.

1. Is the author's name and contact information available?
2. Does the author provide a listing of sources he or she used?
3. Are there advertisements on the website (what are they if so)?
4. What is the title of the website and the date of publication?
5. How is the main idea of the website supported by the material on the website?

99.   Based on the student's answers to question three, how might Mr. Lamar extend the lesson and what additional evaluations might be made?
      (Competency 8.A, Average)

      A. Historical significance
      B. Figurative language used
      C. Targeted audience
      D. Themes

The correct answer is C.
The answer is C, targeted audiences. Being able to determine an author's audience can give a student valuable information about the author's purpose in writing the text presented. The rest of the answers are not germane to the intended goal and would not be helpful in determining themes, figurative language, or historical context.

100. What is the primary goal of Mr. Lamar's website exercise?
      (Competency 9.A, Average)

      A. To evaluate the information on the website as credible
      B. To identify the sources of information for the website
      C. To identify a source with complete information
      D. To gather information from a reliable source

The correct answer is A.
The answer is A because the skill that Mr. Lamar is attempting to develop is for students to have a way of evaluating websites for use in their future essays and writing assignments. He does not ask them to evaluate any one particular type of source cited on the website, nor is he asking the students to record information from the source.

CPSIA information can be obtained
at www.ICGtesting.com
Printed in the USA
BVHW05s1954280718
522828BV00018B/455/P

9 781607 876700